IMAGES
of America

MOKENA

I0806328

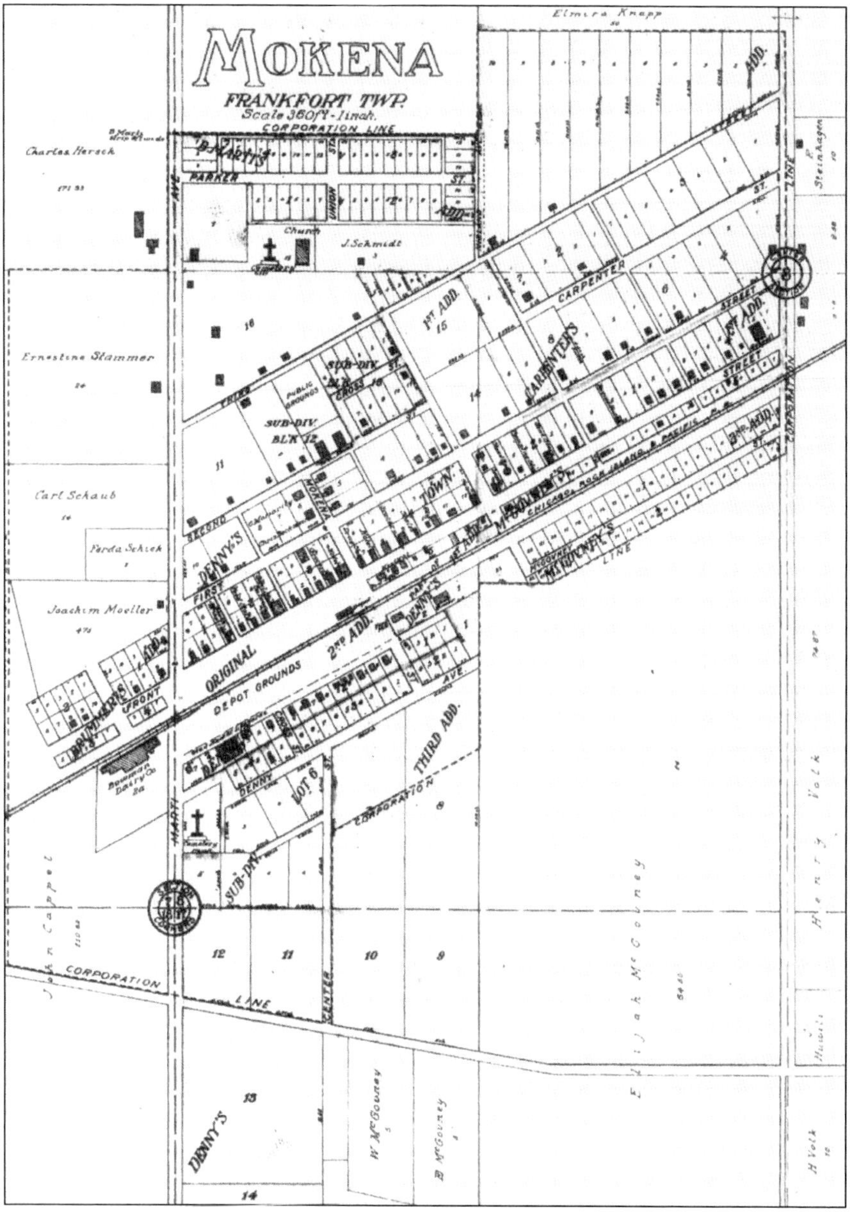

This 1907 plat map of Mokena clearly depicts how truly small the village was at the turn of the 20th century. The map's black squares and rectangles represent businesses, houses, and churches, with crosses indicating cemeteries. The clear regions on the edges of the map were agricultural areas, such as the large farm at lower right that belonged to Elijah McGovney. (Photograph courtesy of Robert Horras.)

ON THE COVER: Having stood at today's location of 19200 Wolf Road for over 125 years, the Henry Schiek farm was a familiar landmark for generations. After inheriting the farm from his father, Schiek began delivering milk locally in a horse-drawn wagon around 1902. Pictured here around 1910 are, from left to right, Henry Schiek, Dewey the dog, Lester Schiek, and Alma Schiek. (Photograph courtesy of Robert Horras.)

IMAGES
of America

MOKENA

Matthew T. Galik

ARCADIA
PUBLISHING

ISBN 978-0-7385-8272-6

Published by Arcadia Publishing
Charleston, South Carolina

Printed in the United States of America

Library of Congress Control Number: 2011937400

For all general information, please contact Arcadia Publishing:
Telephone 843-853-2070
Fax 843-853-0044
E-mail sales@arcadiapublishing.com
For customer service and orders:
Toll-Free 1-888-313-2665

Visit us on the Internet at www.arcadiapublishing.com

"I still consider myself a Mokena boy."

—John H. Cappel, 1926

This book is for Bill Semmler. Although our paths never crossed, his life's work as the editor of the Mokena News-Bulletin *has in no small part inspired me to become the person I am today. His passion for* Mokena *kindles mine. Here's to you, Bill.*

Contents

Acknowledgments		6
Introduction		7
1.	Thy Great Commercial Tree	9
2.	The Fountain of Knowledge	41
3.	A Symbol of Spiritual Fact	53
4.	Home Is Where the Heart Is	63
5.	Thy Whistle Blowing	79
6.	One Well Traveled	85
7.	Amber Waves of Grain	93
8.	For the Fun of It	103
9.	Not Without Thy Wondrous Story	113

ACKNOWLEDGMENTS

This book would not have been possible without the help and advice of Rob Horras, who has spent well over 20 years putting together an extensive collection of Mokena memorabilia. The community will now see but a few of the most impressive photographs that he has dedicated so many years to organizing. This book presents but a tiny portion of his labor. His assistance has helped shape this long overdue book; my sincerest thanks to him.

A tip of my hat to Val Horras, who not only offered her suggestions for this book, but made sure I never went hungry at her home.

My heartiest thanks to Dick Quinn, the first of us who actively researched the history of Mokena. Not only is he a fine historian, it was he who first encouraged and motivated the young boy who grew up to become me.

My deepest appreciation to Dave Kropp, not only for reminiscing with me, but for being a wonderful friend; to Carol Norton, for keeping my workdays exciting with talks of Hatches and McGovneys; and to Chuck Hostert, Chuck and Juanita Manhart, Helen Sippel, and Doris Yunker, for sharing their memories with me.

I cannot forget Carmen Smallwood and Joe Srsnick, whose work restoring Pioneer Cemetery first gave me the chance to come face-to-face with history.

Kudos to the Mokena Area Historical Society for documenting our village's story, along with the staff of Mokena Community Public Library, who are my coworkers as well as friends.

I also think of the Mokenians who have gone before me and blazed the trail upon which I now find myself. On another plane, I would like to nod to Julia Atkins, Charles Jones, and the Semmler family, all extremely beloved and insightful individuals who never forgot to write anything down. To Rev. Carl Schaub, *herzlichen Dank*; your meticulous record keeping has made my life as a historian much easier. Jennie Stellwagen, you were an excellent scrapbooker.

Thanks to my parents, who thought a Mokena book was a great idea and who also have a collective artist's eye. My thoughts also go to my late great-grandmother Ethel Iddings, who first made history fun, and to my grandfather Ray Galik, the best muse an author could ask for.

Unless otherwise noted, all images in this book come from the collection of Robert Horras.

INTRODUCTION

For over a century and half, Mokena has stood for solid and peaceful living. Highly regarded throughout Chicagoland for its churches, schools, and superior location, Mokena remains one of eastern Will County's most respected communities. Mokena is a place steeped in a long, interesting, and exciting history. Over time, our community has continually changed and developed, often in a way that conceals the past. Within the pages of this book, the longtime Mokenian will recognize the faces of beloved friends and recall places forever cherished. For the newcomers, there is no better way to become acquainted with a place than to know its history.

The region upon which Mokena was built was initially inhabited by Potawatomi tribesmen as early as 1760, although the Winnebago, Chippewa, Sauk, and Ottawa had also called this area home in previous times. The first white man to permanently settle the rugged prairie terrain where Mokena now stands was John McGovney, who arrived in the summer of 1831. After migrating with his family by wagon from Adams County, Ohio, McGovney found an untamed wilderness at his new homesite, devoid of neighbors and all comforts of civilization. Living in a region teaming with Potawatomis, the young family fled eastward at the outbreak of the Black Hawk War to the perceived safety of more densely settled areas.

With the cessation of hostilities and the eventual return of the McGovneys in 1834, more pioneers made the unforgiving prairie their home. Among those to arrive in this period were Eliphalet and John Atkins of Vermont, brothers Allen and Lysander Denny of New York, and Tilford Duncan of Kentucky. The majority of Potawatomi natives left the region during this same era due to the influx of white settlers. The early residents of Mokena's future location were attracted by wide, open space upon which to lay claim to parcels of government-owned land; many of the first settlers later became the full owners of their farms after having purchased them at auction. Dense forests afforded wood to construct primitive homes and to warm the hearths, abundant wildlife provided for food, and Hickory Creek had the might to power a sawmill built on its northern bank in 1834 by Lysander Denny.

The 1840s marked the coming of the first of the region's Germanic settlers, who fled their homeland due to economic difficulties and revolution in Europe. Among the German settlers were the families of Diederich Brumund, Friedrich Cappel, Martin Heim, and Heinrich Schiek, whose descendants live in and around Mokena to this day, as do those of early Swiss immigrants such as the Baumgartners, the Junkers (later anglicized as Yunker), and the Martis.

With the completion in 1852 of the Chicago, Rock Island & Pacific Railroad (CRI&P) through the northern half of the newly named Frankfort Township, local farmers no longer had to make the arduous journey to Chicago to sell their crops and visit trading posts. A railroad depot was completed in 1852 on the prairie expanse, and Allen Denny subdivided a cluster of lots parallel to the tracks that would be named Mokena, an early Algonquin word for "turtle."

Denny's original subdivision was composed of lots fronting on what is today the western section of Front Street, between Wolf Road and Division Street, along with several parcels facing First

Street. John McGovney laid out an addition to the east in 1853, with his lots being located on Front Street, between Division Street and Schoolhouse Road. A post office was formed in 1853, as were some of Mokena's first businesses—a general store owned by James Ducker, a hotel owned by Carl Gall, and a blacksmith shop owned by William McCoy. Mokena's first schoolhouse was constructed in 1855, as was a steam-powered sawmill near the railroad right-of-way.

The newly formed town would become a center of agricultural production for well over 100 years. The rich soil of eastern Will County proved fruitful for generations of Mokena farmers. The CRI&P Railroad provided excellent shipping facilities to Chicago markets. Around 1860, the first shipment of milk from Mokena was brought to the railroad by a large Newfoundland dog, and grain also became a valuable commodity. Eventually, livestock was shipped by rail to Chicago from a stockyard later built on the southern edge of town.

With the outbreak of the Civil War in 1861, Mokena proved her loyalty to the Union by furnishing at least 46 men to the armies of Abraham Lincoln. Before the war's end in 1865, no fewer than 16 of this group had died from disease, in Confederate prisons, or on the battlefield. The Battle of Chickamauga, Georgia, waged in September 1863, forever remains a tainted spot on Mokena's history—four Mokenians were killed in the conflict. In the period leading up to the war, Allen Denny ran a station on the Underground Railroad from his home, helping escaped slaves on their way to freedom in Canada.

Possibly as a direct result of this turbulent era, two of Mokena's first churches were founded around the time of the Civil War. In March 1862, the German United Evangelical St. John's Church passed their constitution under the guidance of Rev. William Meyer, and in the summer of the same year, the congregation erected a church building at the corner of Second and Union Streets. Shortly thereafter, in 1864, St. Mary's German Catholic Church was built north of town. In 1867, a Methodist Episcopal Church was constructed on Second Street, with the building being used on alternating Sundays by the Baptist congregation.

The immediate post–Civil War era in Mokena was a time of prosperity. By 1878, the population had reached 500, and, among other businesses, there were seven saloons, five general stores, three hotels, and two wagon shops in town. The *Joliet Republican* stated that Mokena's "streets are being filled from morning to night" and that "growth . . . is rapid, buildings are going up in all parts of town too numerous to mention." In May 1880, residents voted in favor of incorporation. A village board was elected, which in turn voted in Ozias McGovney as Mokena's first mayor.

With the 1917 entry of the United States into World War I, many Mokena men became soldiers, and all returned home with their lives. A significant amount of village revenue in the postwar period came from saloon license monies, and with the 1919 passage of the Volstead Act and the Eighteenth Amendment banning the sale and production of liquor, the village fathers found themselves in a unique predicament, and in 1920, the village declared itself broke. This dire situation was eventually remedied with the taxing of tobacco, ice cream, candy, and auto garages within village limits. With the repeal of Prohibition in 1933, the country found itself in the midst of the Great Depression, although Mokena was spared the worst of it.

After World War II, a new boom arrived in Mokena that was also experienced across the United States. Two new subdivisions were built; Sunny Acres, located a short distance northwest of the village on Wolf Road, was begun in 1946. A year later, the Mineral Springs subdivision, located between Denny Avenue and LaPorte Road, with the Yunker Farm to the east and Center Street to the west, was annexed to Mokena. By 1960, Mokena was home to 1,332 people.

The 1968 completion of Interstate 80 along Mokena's northern boundary ushered in a new era of mobility still enjoyed by local residents. Increased municipal services, the establishment of Mokena Junior High School, the building of a library, and the installation of Mokena's first stoplight in the 1970s further reflected the rising prominence of the village. In what has been Mokena's most prosperous decade to date, the 1990s saw the transition of the community from rural town to bustling suburb. In the 10 years from 1990 to 2000, Mokena gained roughly 8,000 new residents, boasting a staggering population of 14,583 in the first year of the new millennium.

One

Thy Great Commercial Tree

In the Mokena of the early 21st century, nearly any good or service can be had in or near the village. With Internet shopping becoming mainstream and the automobile having closed formerly long distances, any desired item is now within easy reach. Modern comforts have made it easy to forget the toil of our forefathers.

In the early days, before the establishment of Mokena, settlers likely did their shopping at the combination general store and post office of the Clayes brothers, which was located at Chelsea, near the site of today's Frankfort. With the construction of the Chicago, Rock Island & Pacific Railroad (CRI&P) in 1852, German farmer Diederich Brumund set up a small store in conjunction with a rooming house on his LaPorte Road farm, although this venture was quickly bested by a cluster of businesses that sprung up closer to the railroad.

Knapp and Smith built a store in 1852, distinguishing themselves as the first firm in Mokena proper. Although no details have survived on this partnership, Carl Gall built a hotel at the current corner of Front Street and Wolf Road in 1853, and William McCoy began a blacksmith shop shortly thereafter. By the end of the 1870s, around seven saloons were open in Mokena, enduring no shortage of weekend business from local farm workers.

Many enterprises have come and gone without leaving a deep impression on Mokena. A flour mill burned in 1860; a cigar manufacturer worked around 1900; and in the early 20th century, a mink farm was in business on Schoolhouse Road. Other operations, such as the Bowman Dairy Bottling Plant and Mitchel Brewery, were massive employers in their times.

During the post–World War II boom in America, Front Street was a bustling area; one consequence was that many visages of Mokena's illustrious past were lost to new development. By the end of the 20th century, the village's main commercial corridor had shifted to LaGrange Road. Although she rose from humble beginnings, Mokena's business prowess would make her founders proud.

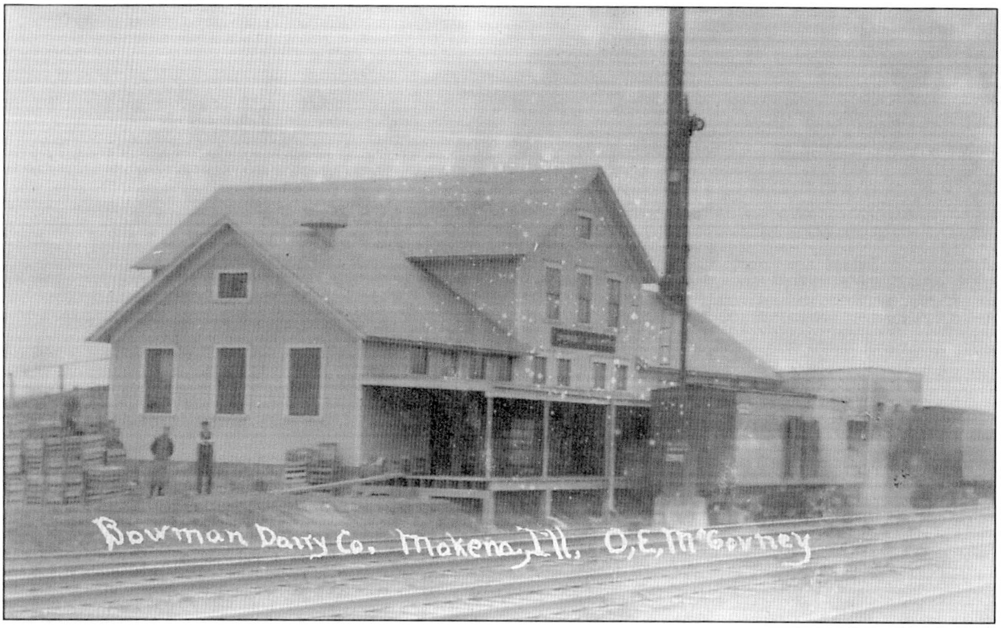

Tracing its beginnings to 1891, the Bowman Dairy Company achieved much success in Chicago before opening a Mokena milk-bottling plant, located on the south side of the Rock Island tracks on Wolf Road, in 1907. Preston Hird served as the first superintendent and chemist in charge. In this image, dated around 1910, railroad loading docks are plainly visible.

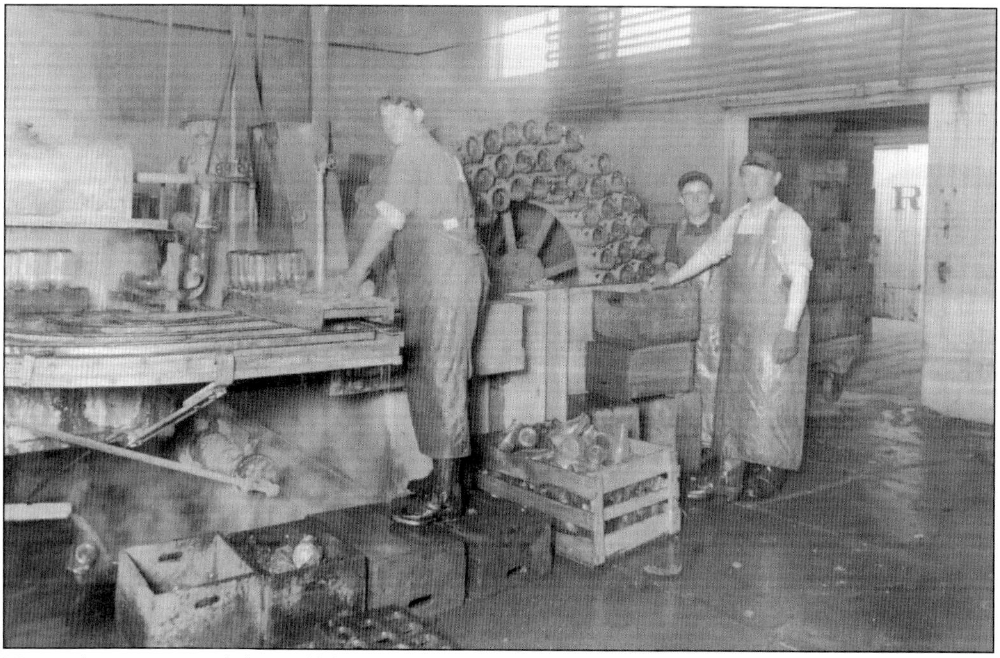

Upon the opening of the milk-bottling plant in November 1907, the first bottle of milk was presented to Julia Blaeser, Mokena's oldest resident. This c. 1910 interior view of the Bowman Dairy plant shows, from left to right, two unidentified men, worker John Schenkel, and manager Herman Schweser. The men pose with a machine called a Ferris wheel, which was used for washing milk bottles.

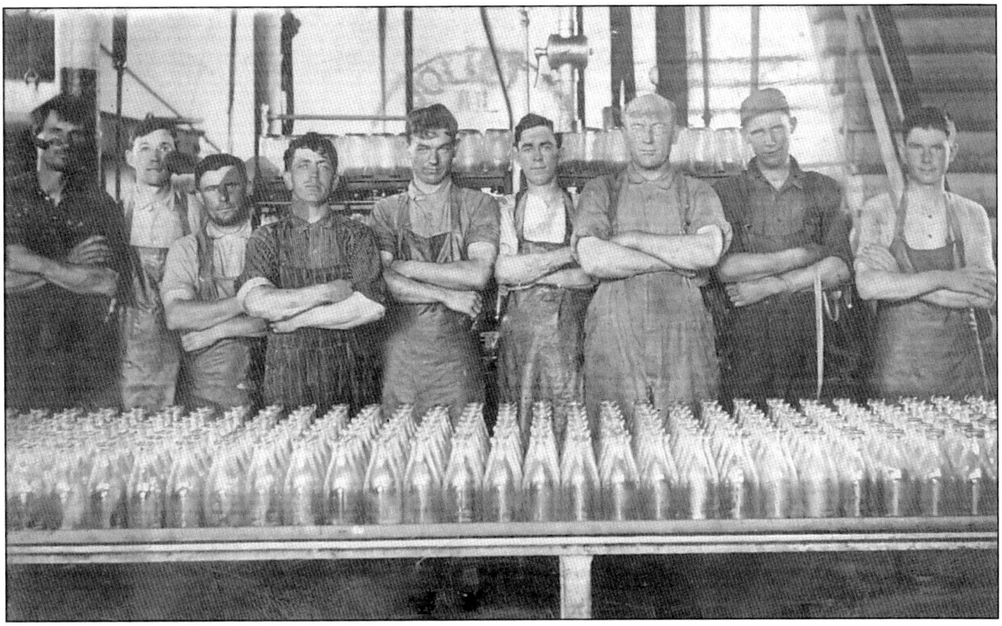

A routine workday at the Bowman Dairy was interrupted to take this photograph in 1911. Area farmers would sell their milk to the dairy, where it was bottled and shipped by railroad to Chicago markets. By the time of this photograph, roughly two carloads of milk and cream were being sent to the city every day.

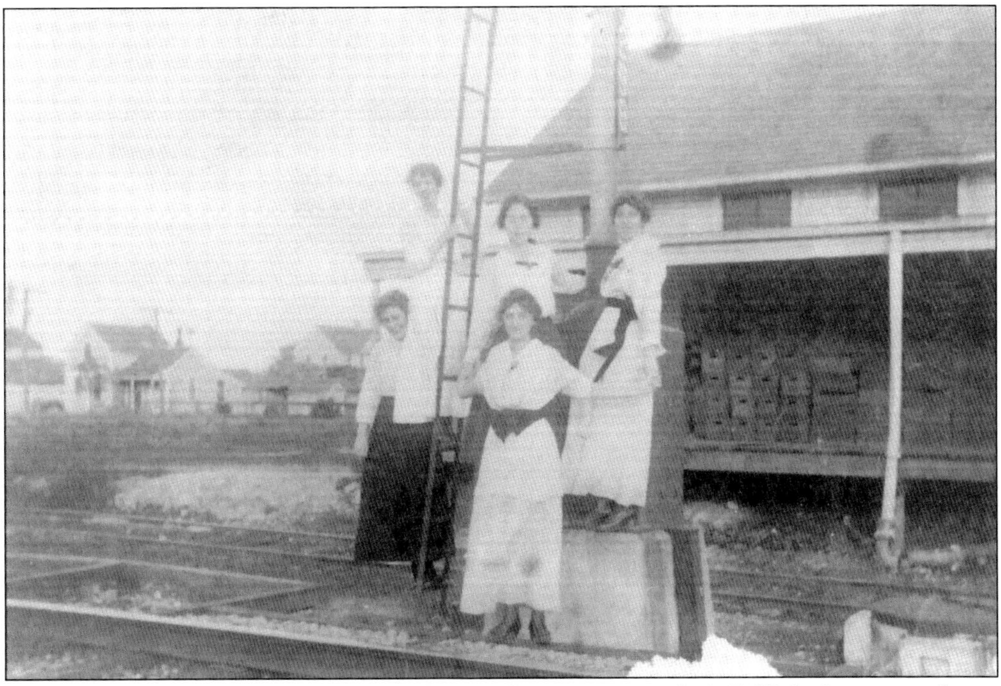

Women workers at the Bowman Dairy plant strike a pose around 1915. With the camera facing southeast from the Rock Island tracks, wooden milk crates are visible on the loading dock, as are several homes along McGovney Street. The plant also manufactured ice that was sold to village residents during the hot summer months.

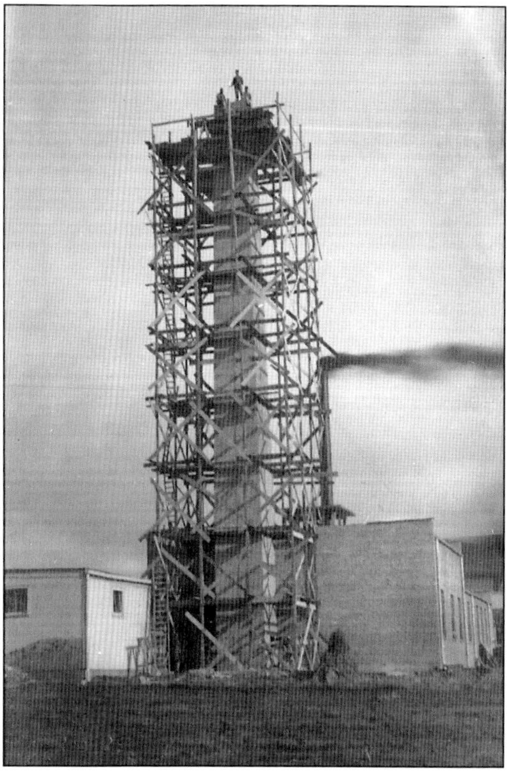

Reaching a high amount of success after its opening in 1907, many advances were quickly begun at the Bowman Dairy plant, such as the construction of this roughly 100-foot smokestack in 1911. For scale, note the workers atop the high scaffolding. Even after its removal around 1973, traces of this smokestack's foundation were still visible when the plant was demolished in 2004.

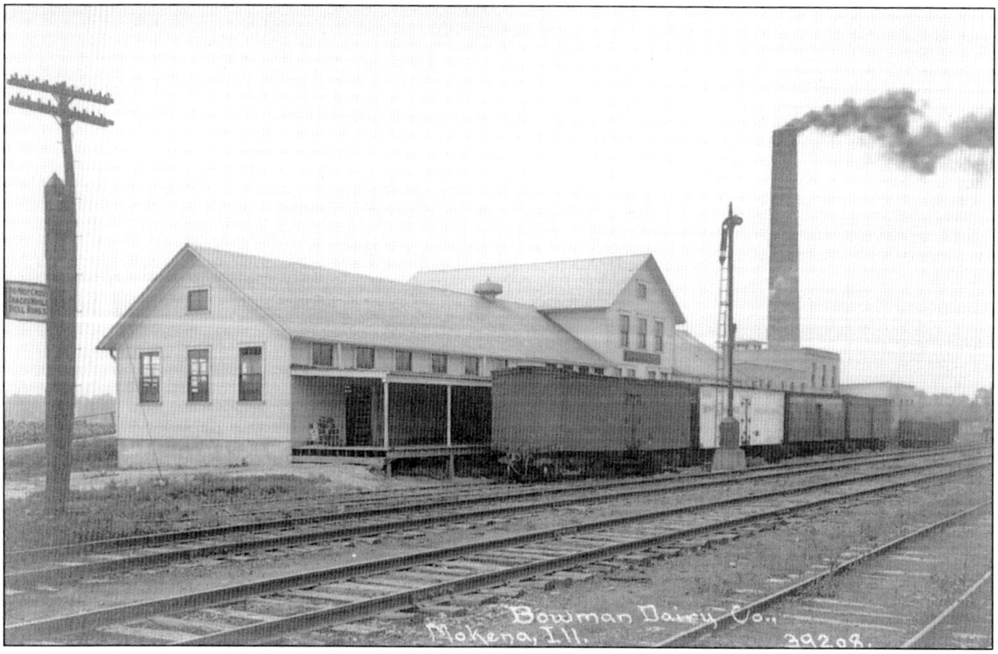

Another upgrade at the Bowman Dairy plant was a small addition erected on the eastern face of the building. In the middle of the train shown here, a light-colored refrigerated boxcar can be seen awaiting its load of bottled milk to be shipped to Chicago. Looking southwest from the Wolf Road railroad crossing, this postcard image dates from around 1910.

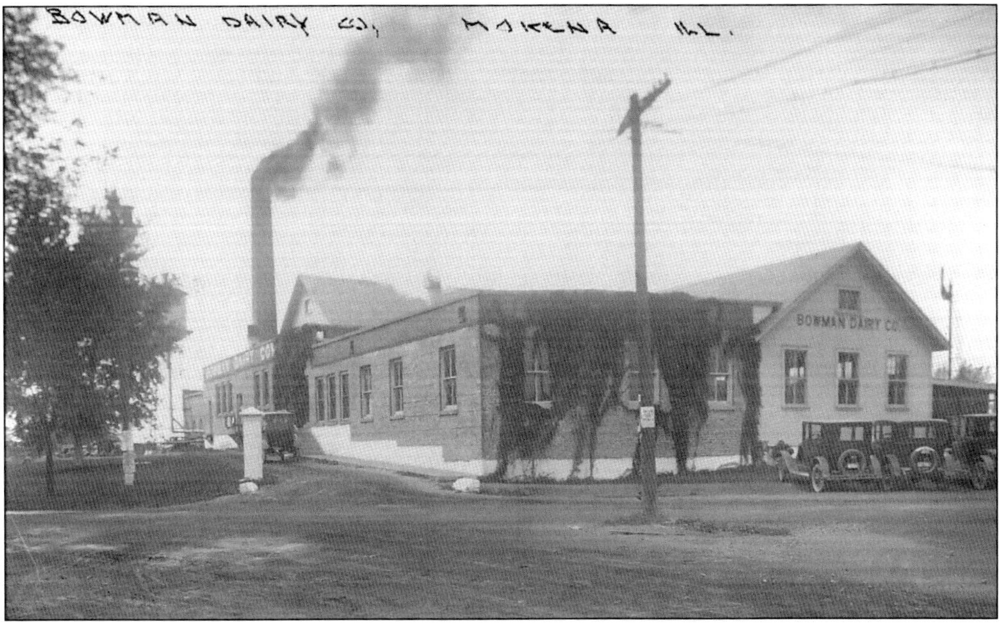

With Wolf Road in the foreground, the Bowman Dairy plant is seen here with its brick addition, built in 1916 by Mokena contractor George Hacker. Facing west, this image was taken around 1920. Within the decade, the City of Chicago passed a strict sanitation ordinance pertaining to milk sales, and in 1926, this productive plant was shuttered after local farmers refused to have their cattle tested for tuberculosis.

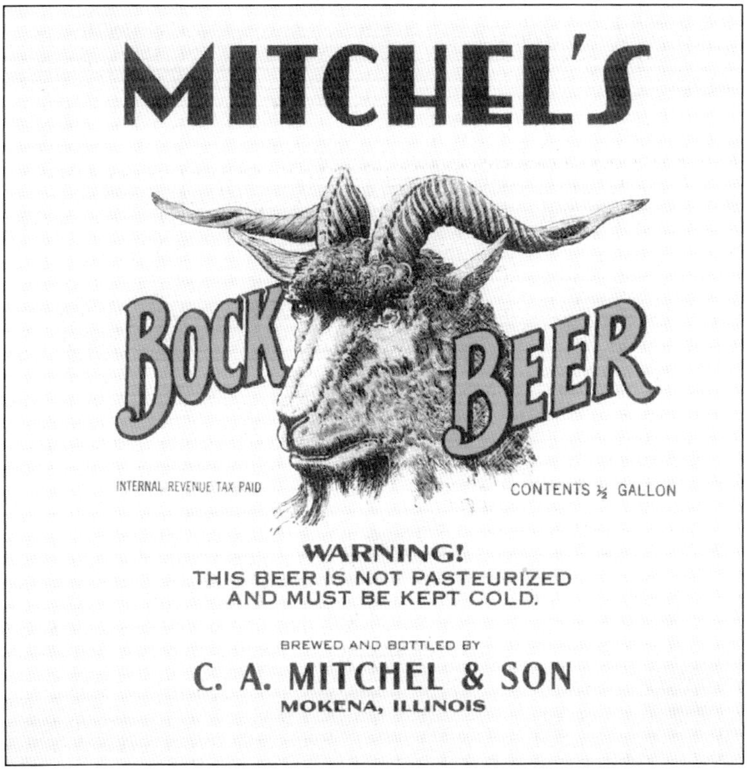

In 1933, when Prohibition ended, C.A. Mitchel & Son purchased the former bottling plant and opened a brewery at this location. After the death of Charles Mitchel Sr. in 1941, Joliet businessman John Scarth opened the Mokena Wallpaper Mill in the large building; wallpaper was produced there until the late 1990s. The historic structure was razed in 2004, and the site is now home to the four-story, mixed-use building at 19806 Wolf Road.

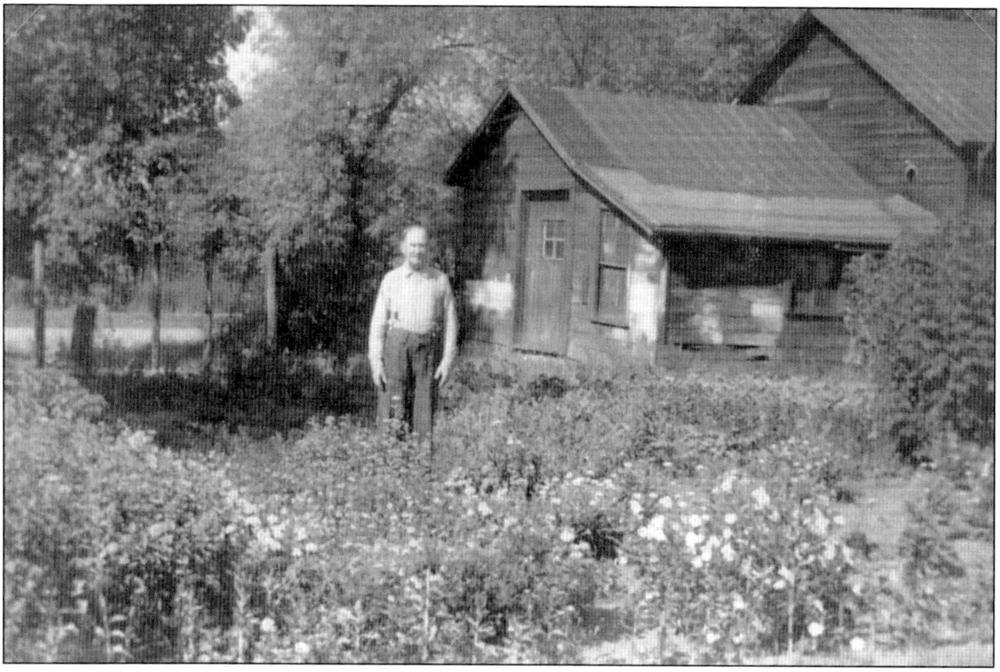

Bill Helenhouse, of Orland Park, opened a blacksmith shop on the southwest corner of Front Street and Wolf Road at the end of the 1920s. Prior to Helenhouse's possession of the structure, it was used as an outbuilding of the Bowman Dairy Company. In addition to shoeing horses, Helenhouse also set wagon wheels and sharpened implements, such as plows and shovels.

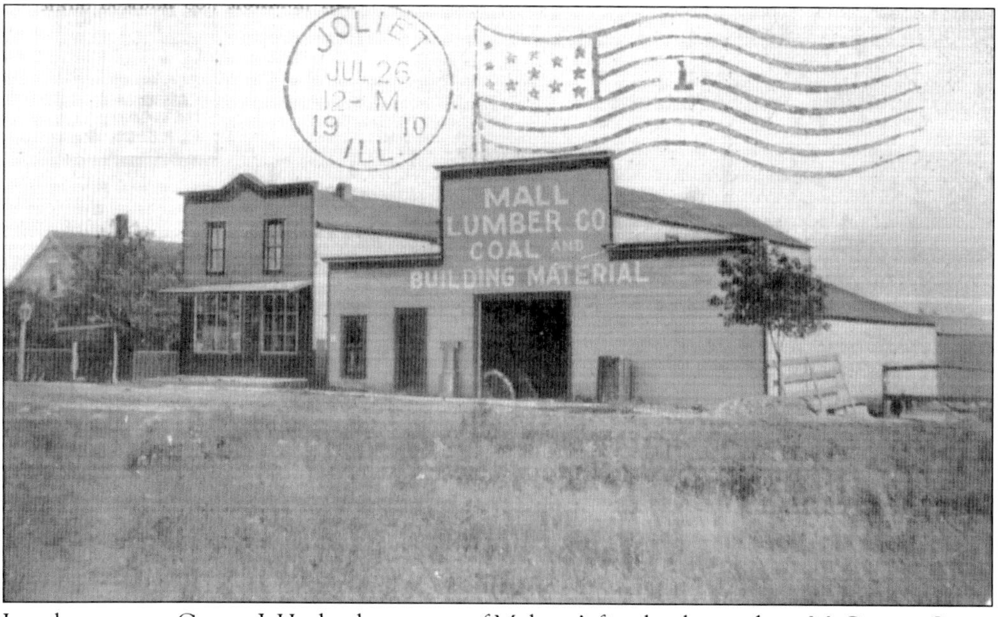

Local contractor George J. Hacker began one of Mokena's first lumberyards on McGovney Street around 1900. Being very successful at this location, he sold the business to the Frank Mall Lumber Company of Aurora in 1909. Harry Mall, son of the company's founder, managed the Mokena yard for years, dealing in farm implements, coal, and building supplies.

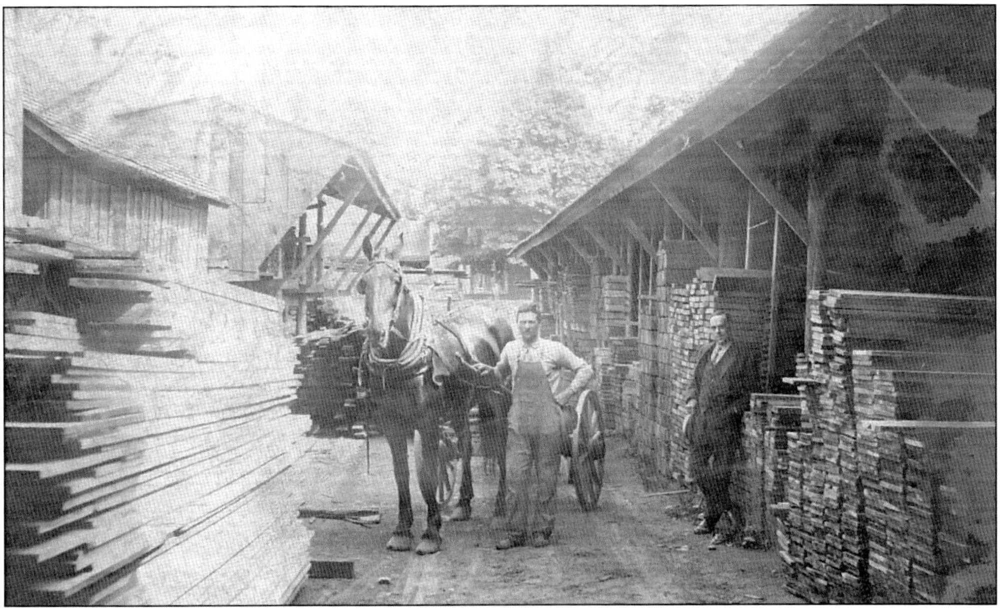

Oscar Klose (left) and Harry Mall are shown here around 1910, working at the Mall lumberyard. Klose was a lifelong Mokena resident and served a stint as village constable in the early part of the 20th century. The old lumberyard was demolished in the early 1970s; the present-day site contains the homes at 11125 and 11131 McGovney Street.

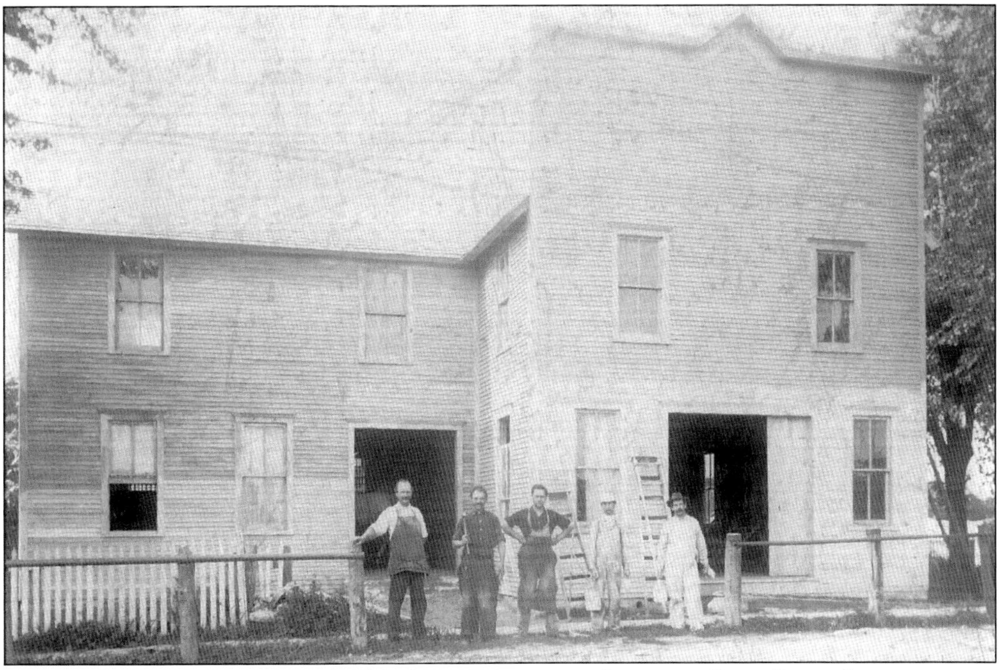

Built in 1903 for Henry Braun, this blacksmith shop was a fixture on Front Street for generations. Following his death a year later, Braun's son Albert took over the shop and ran it until his retirement in the 1950s. During the dreadful winter of 1908, Braun shod an impressive 340 horses in 10 days. In one section of the shop stood a potbelly stove, around which visitors discussed issues of the day.

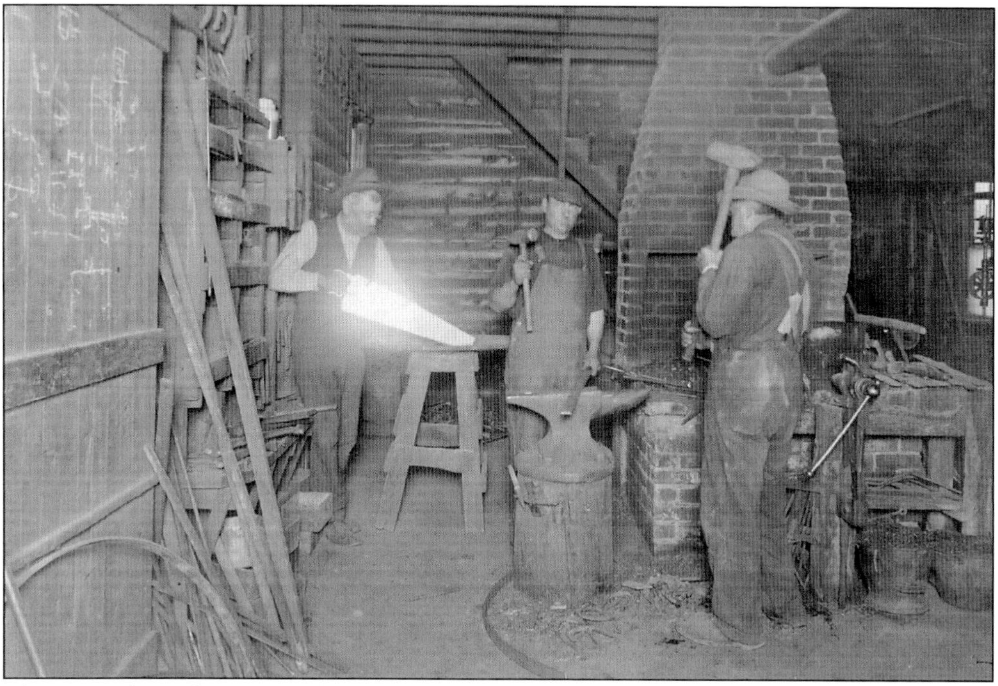

This image shows the interior of Al Braun's blacksmith shop in Mokena as it appeared around 1910. Pictured here are, from left to right, local farmer Henry Schiek, Al Braun, and village resident Christ Schenkel. Aside from blacksmithing, Braun was also known to repair wagon wheels that had been warped by summer heat. After Braun's retirement, the old building was torn down in 1960. Now standing at this location is 11134 Front Street.

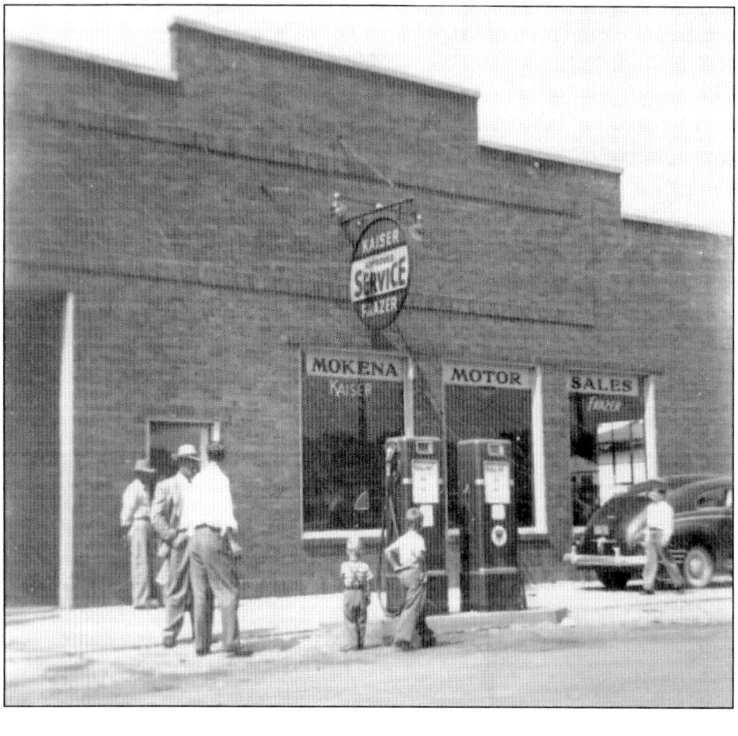

The garage at 11120 Front Street, a structure typical of the era in which it was built, remains a Mokena fixture. Built in 1945 by Walter Yunker for his trucking business, Yunker had branched into excavating by 1948. Beginning his work in 1927 as a truck driver for his father, Yunker began his own concern in 1939 before serving for years as Frankfort Township road commissioner.

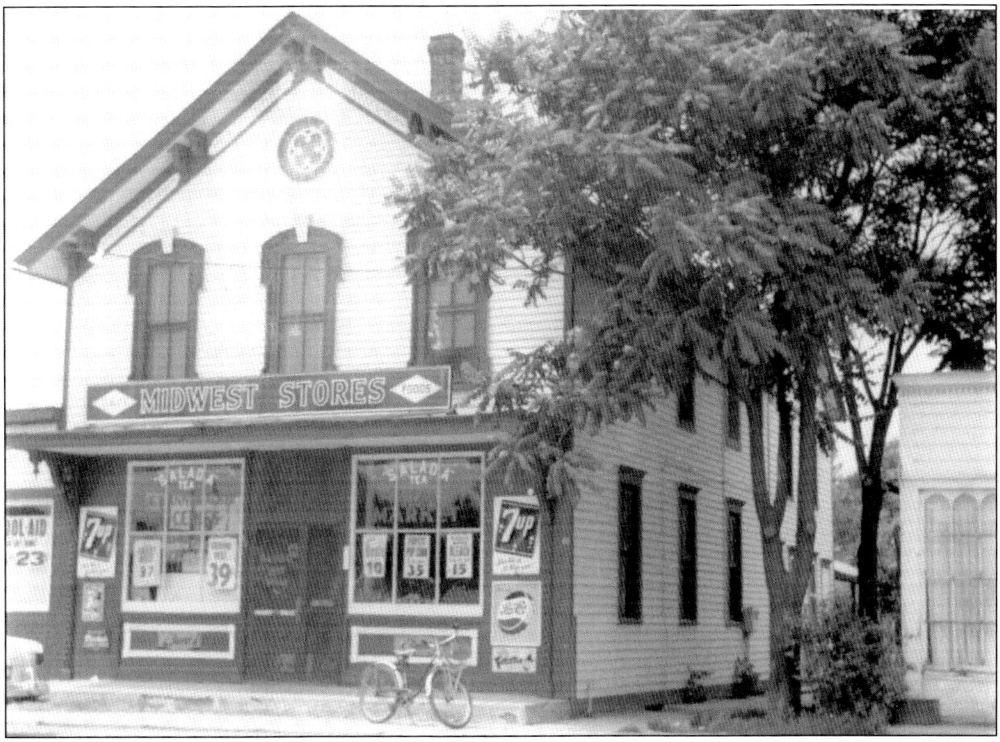

A saloon operated by Charles Moriarty existed here as early as 1892, from whence it was taken over by John Wannemacher. During the building's use by Wannemacher's son George in 1925, a raid by law enforcement officials netted illegal gambling devices and moonshine. After the raid, Wannemacher opened a grocery store in the location. Shown here about 1960 and still standing at 11116 Front Street, this building is a true Mokena landmark.

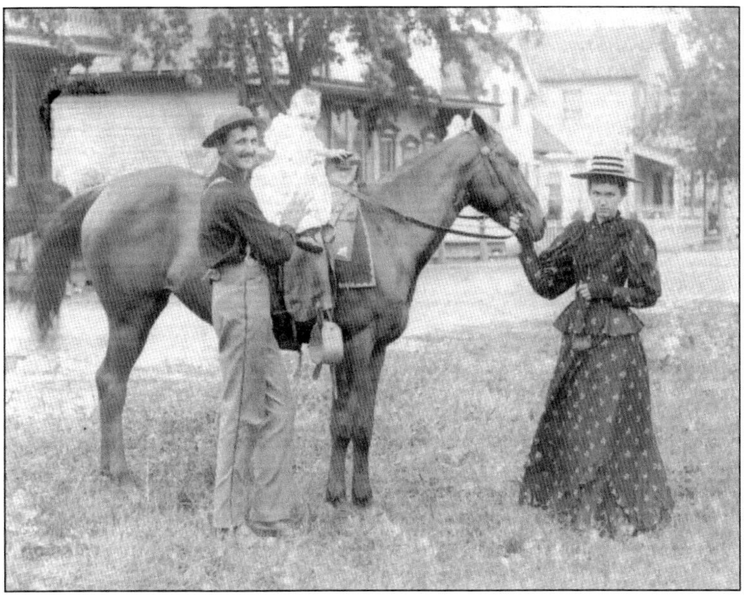

This image of an unidentified couple with a baby perched atop a horse is one of the oldest known photographs depicting Front Street. Likely taken around 1890, this view is of a way of life completely foreign to 21st-century Mokenians. At this point, no automobile had ever been seen in Mokena and none of the village's buildings had electricity or indoor plumbing.

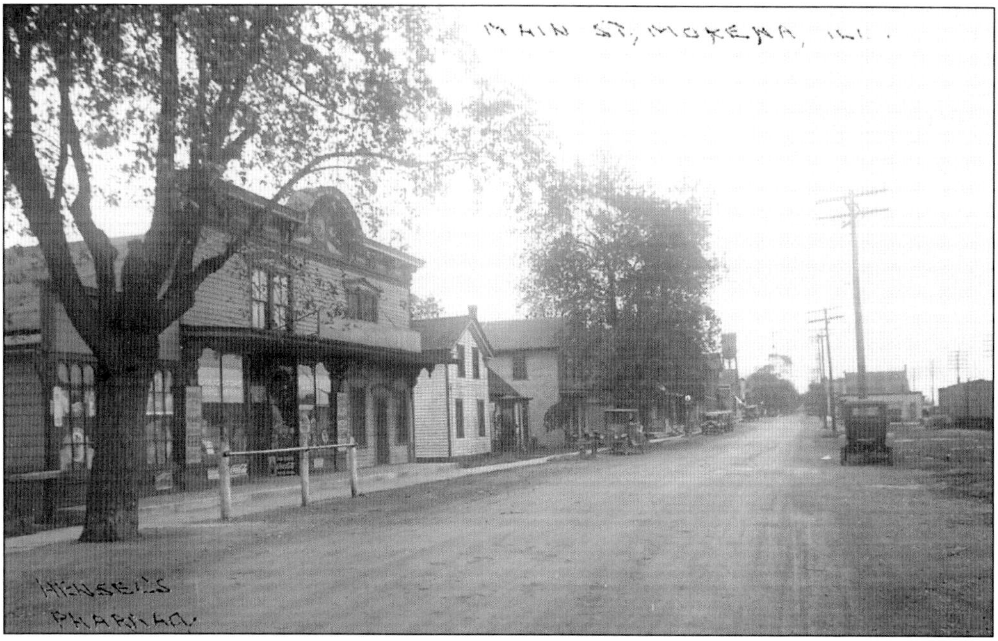

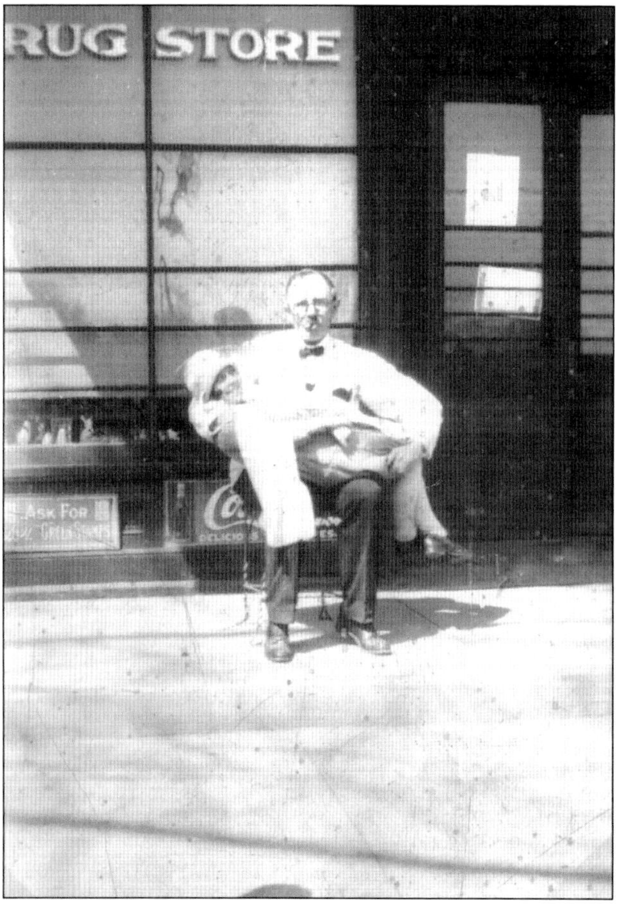

This scenic postcard of Front Street, dating from about 1925, prominently depicts the pharmacy of Richard Hensel. A native son of Mokena, Hensel acquired the former general store of Louis Zumstein in 1925. Likely dating to the Civil War era, this historic structure boasted a beautiful, artisan-crafted motif in its eaves of a large setting sun. On the same lot today is 11112 Front Street.

Pharmacist Richard Hensel is shown here in a lighthearted moment with Mokenian Genevieve Pfleger. Born in Mokena in 1868, Hensel attended the village public school and later worked at the Baumgartner Creamery in Frankfort before ultimately learning the druggist's trade in Chicago. Hensel served Mokena in various capacities as village trustee, school director, and justice of the peace.

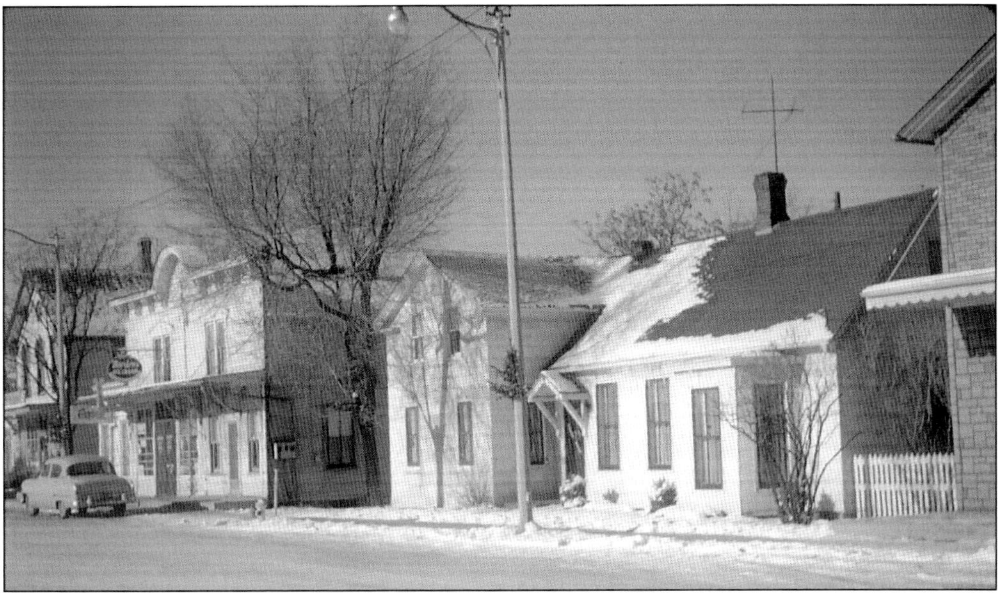

This photograph depicts a Front Street scene in December 1953. Behind the streetlight stands one of Mokena's most historic homes, having been inhabited in the 19th century by the family of Hessian carpenter Wilhelm Stermer. By the 1920s, the switchboard office of the Bell Telephone had moved into the home, with Clida Deadmore serving as chief operator. The old home was demolished about 1965; today, the parking lot of 11112 Front Street is on this site.

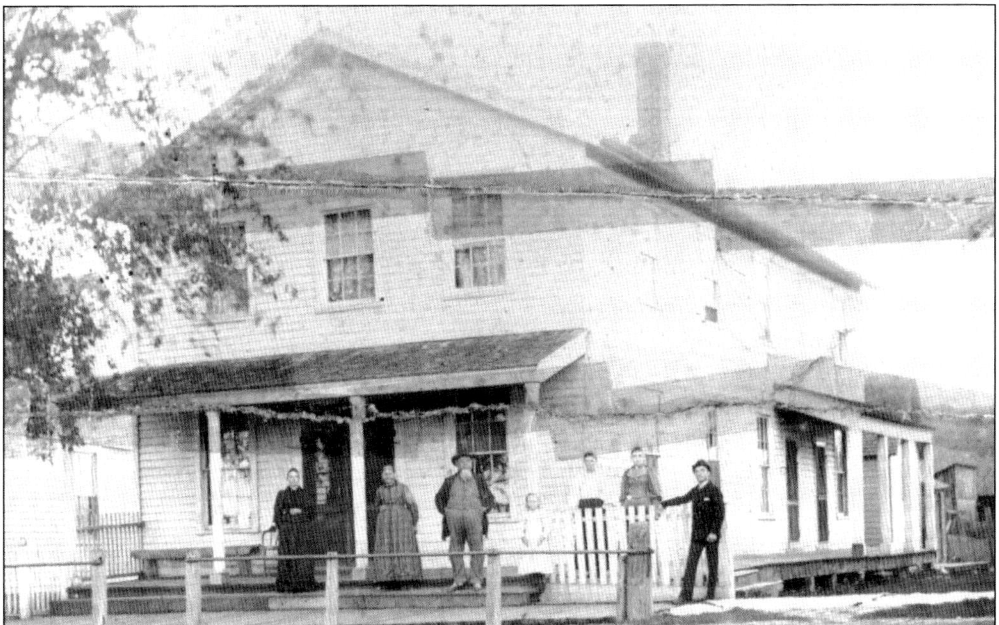

One of the oldest buildings in Mokena is the former store at 11106 Front Street. Visible here around 1895 is a business owned by the Bechstein family. John Baumgartner is standing at far right, and fourth from right is Lizzie Wishover. In the early 20th century, Dr. Elizabeth Ireland practiced dentistry here, and in 1917, August Pfleger acquired the building and opened a small grocery store.

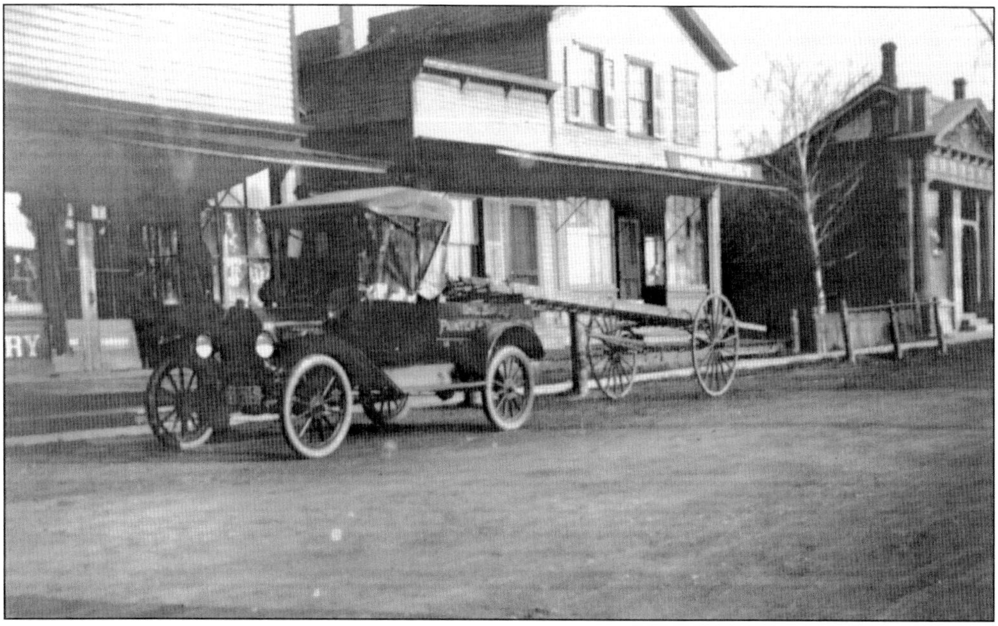

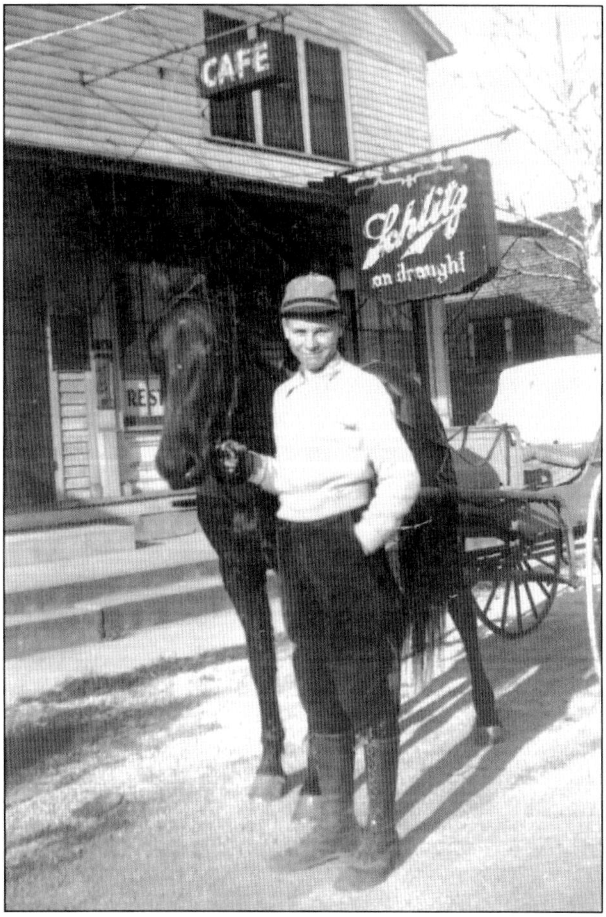

This quaint image of Front Street, dating from 1910, depicts an era when automobiles first became adapted to suit the livelihoods of their owners. The vehicle of local painter Emil Borges, modified to tow his ladder, is prominently visible. In the background are, from left to right, Stellwagen's Livery, the millinery of Mrs. Borges, and the Mokena State Bank. A sign of the progression of time, none of the depicted structures still stand.

Outfitted for a day of riding, Les Oakley poses with an equine companion in front of Morry's Tavern around 1940. Morris Larson of Joliet opened his tavern here, just east of today's 11104 Front Street, in 1934, then greatly remodeled and expanded the old building in 1939. Decades before, former cheese manufacturer John Sutter ran a general store at this location.

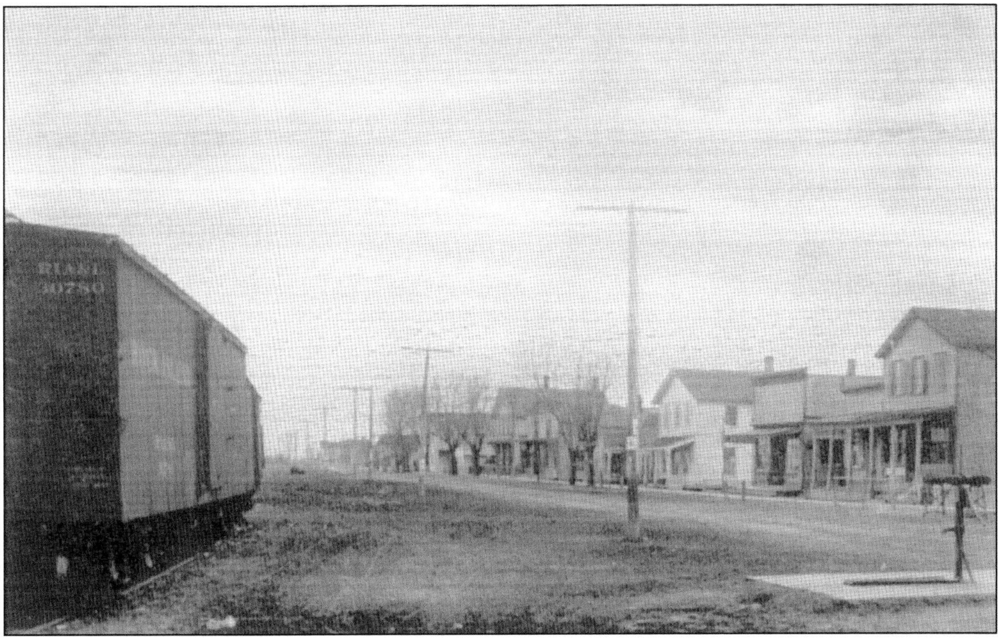

This early-20th-century image is a window to a different world, one that would be completely unrecognizable to modern residents of Mokena. Looking west down Front Street from a point just west of Mokena Street, all the trappings of an antiquated rural village can be seen here: a water pump, a horse trough, a dirt road, and hitching posts.

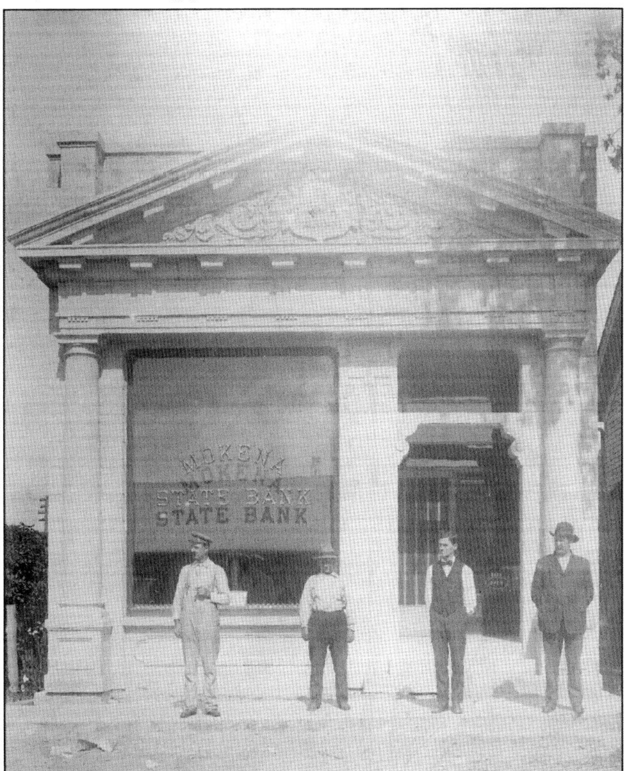

Founded by enterprising local businessmen in August 1909, the Mokena State Bank is seen here shortly after its opening. Pictured here are, from left to right, bank secretary W.H. Bechstein, John Cappel, cashier Frank Liess, and president Christian Bechstein. Neighbor David Kolber thwarted the first attempted robbery of the bank in 1911, although five masked robbers absconded with over $4,000 in October 1924; the thieves were never apprehended.

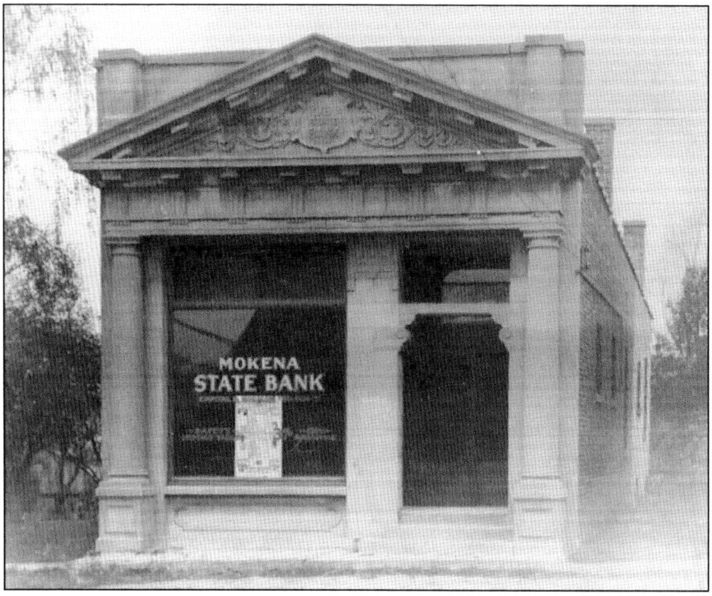

Built by Chicago architect John Aschlager in 1909, the Mokena State Bank was constructed of white Bedford stone and red brick. Originally heated by a coal stove, an addition, constructed on the north side of the building in 1922, housed a new fireproof vault. Depicted here around 1925 and having once stood at the present-day 11100 Front Street, the structure was razed around 1969, when a larger, more modern bank was erected.

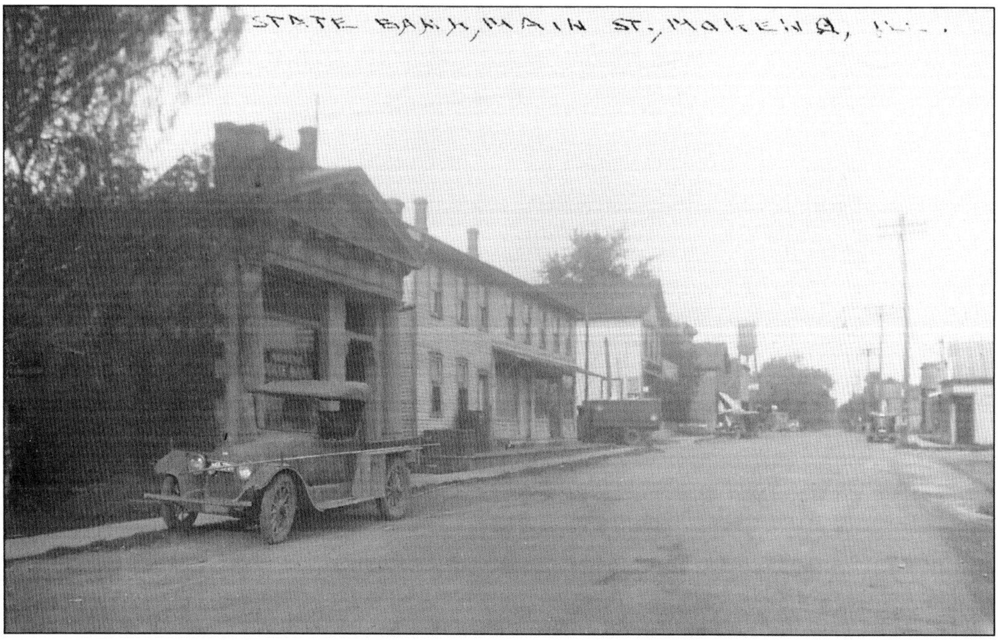

This c. 1920 view of Front Street is looking eastward. The Mokena State Bank is recognizable at left, as is the hardware store of David Kolber, to the right of the bank. A respected citizen of Mokena, originally hailing from Austria-Hungary, Kolber first came to the village in 1902 and moved his business into the building seen here around 1910. Third from left is the house that still stands at 11042 Front Street.

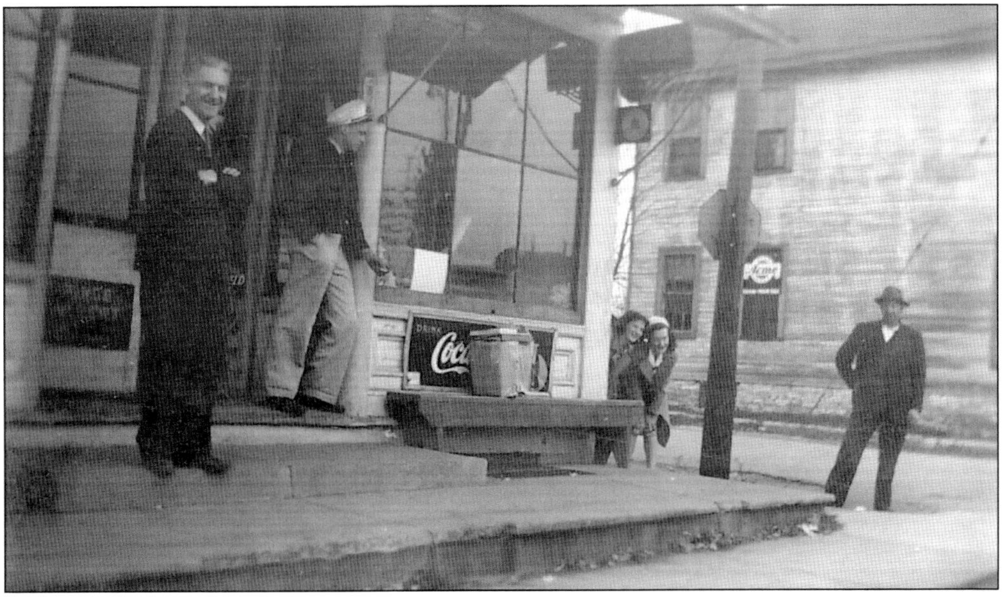

Gus Braun is shown here about 1940, smiling with arms crossed in front of his ice cream parlor and billiard hall. Having bought out the business interest of employer Willard Martie, Braun opened this popular Mokena gathering spot in the mid-1930s. Milton Geuther later converted the building, located at the northeast corner of Front and Mokena Streets, into an apartment house. This location is now the southern parking lot of Mokena State Bank.

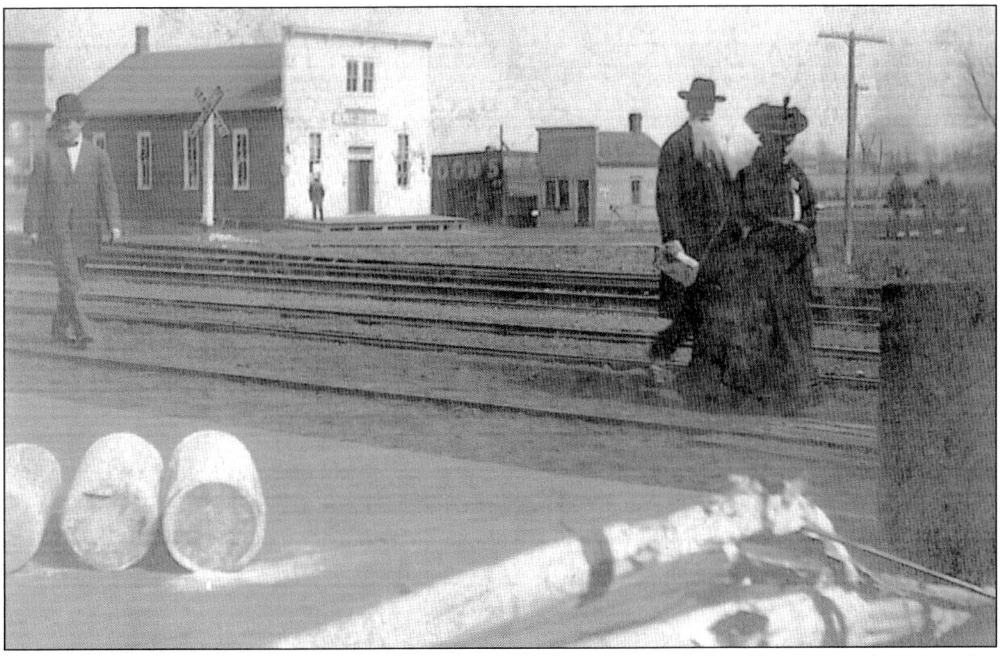

This c. 1900 image depicts a forgotten scene of yesteryear's Mokena. Facing southeast at the Mokena Street railroad crossing, the general store of John A. Hatch is easily recognized as the second building from left. Aside from offering a wide array of goods, Hatch was known to treat young customers to large clumps of maple sugar. The former Hatch store still stands at 19711 Mokena Street.

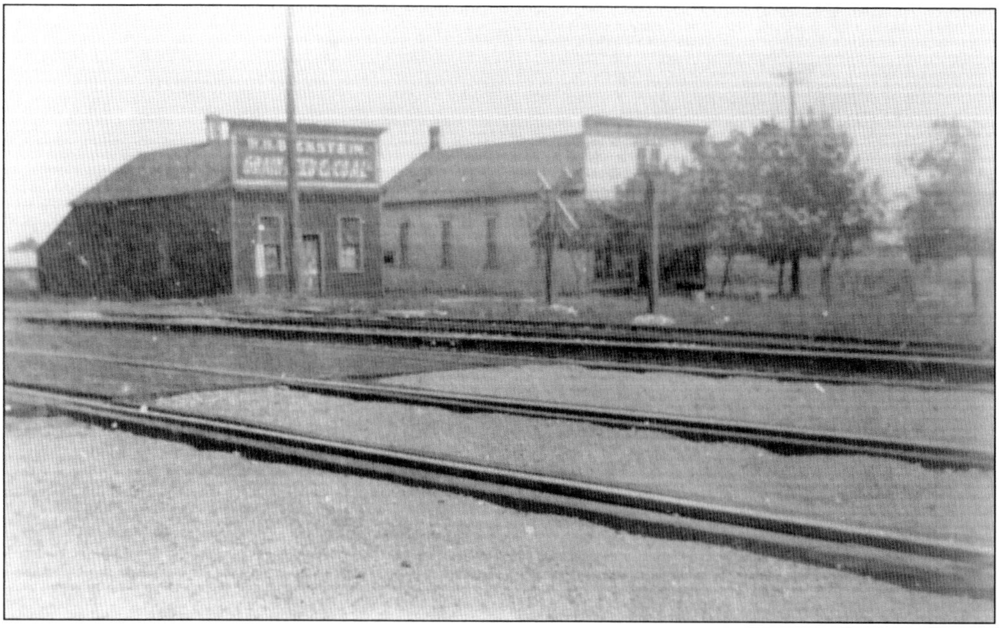

This image shows Mokena Street, south of the Rock Island tracks, around 1910. At left is the grain, feed, and coal dealership of W.H. Bechstein, a business that Bechstein sold to Mokena brothers Albert and Fred Cappel in 1926. Visible at right is the store of John A. Hatch. After Hatch's death in 1920, the building was converted into a hall where many Mokena social events were held.

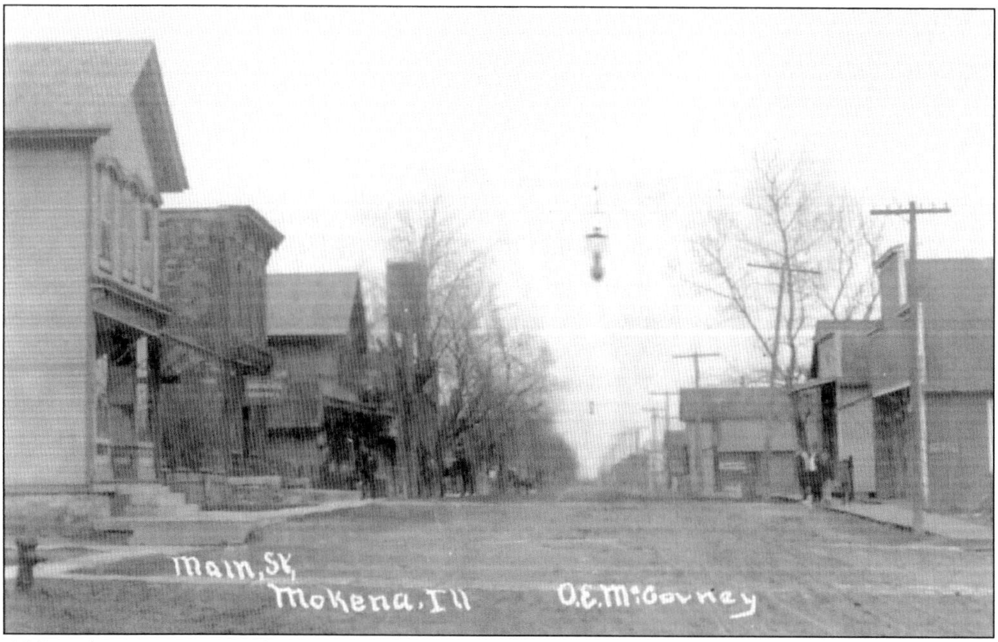

Although over 100 years have passed since this postcard view was made around 1910, this Front Street scene remains relatively unchanged. Looking east from the intersection of Mokena Street, most of the primary buildings in this photograph still stand as silent reminders of the town's illustrious past. Note the early streetlamp suspended over the street crossing. (Photograph courtesy of Richard Quinn.)

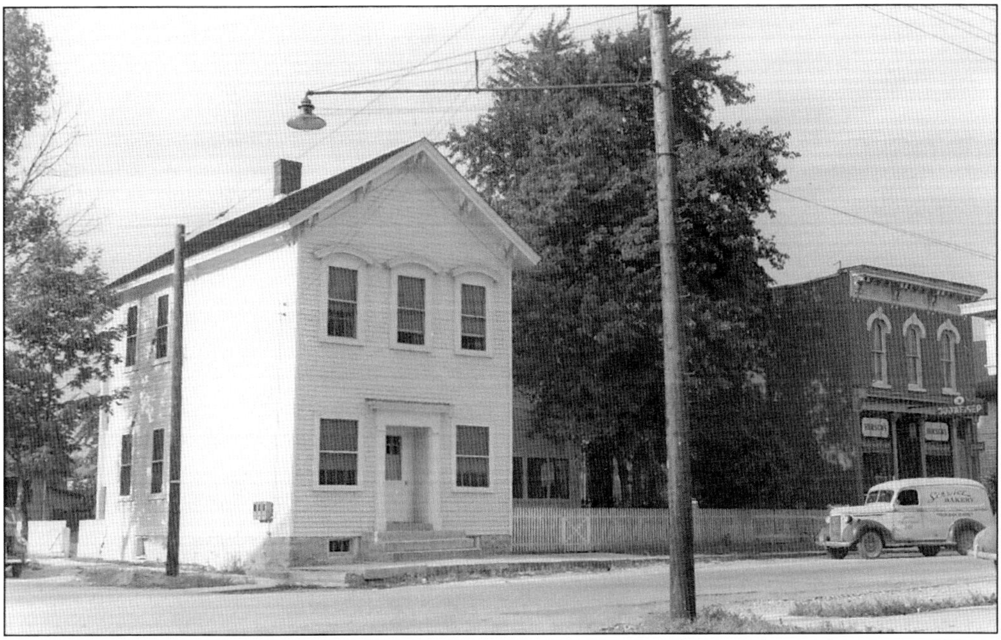

Standing at 11042 Front Street, this historic building was erected around 1869 by Moritz Weiss, who ran a pharmacy here. By the World War II years, the building was regarded by some in the village as a dilapidated eyesore and was remodeled and converted to an apartment house by Mr. Janes of Lincoln Estates.

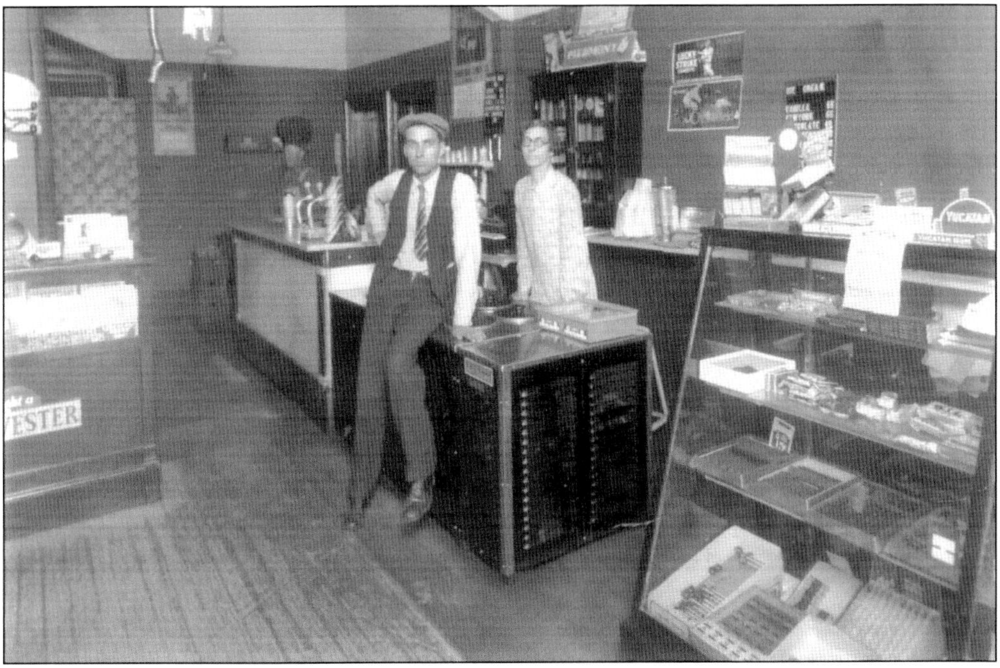

Willard Martie and his mother, Clara, pose in his ice cream parlor and candy store around 1927 at what is today 11042 Front Street. Martie eventually relocated his business to the former Kolber building one door west across Mokena Street. Examining Martie's goods for sale, one notices Hershey chocolate bars, Yucatan gum, Lucky Strike cigarettes, and vanilla ice cream for 55¢ per scoop.

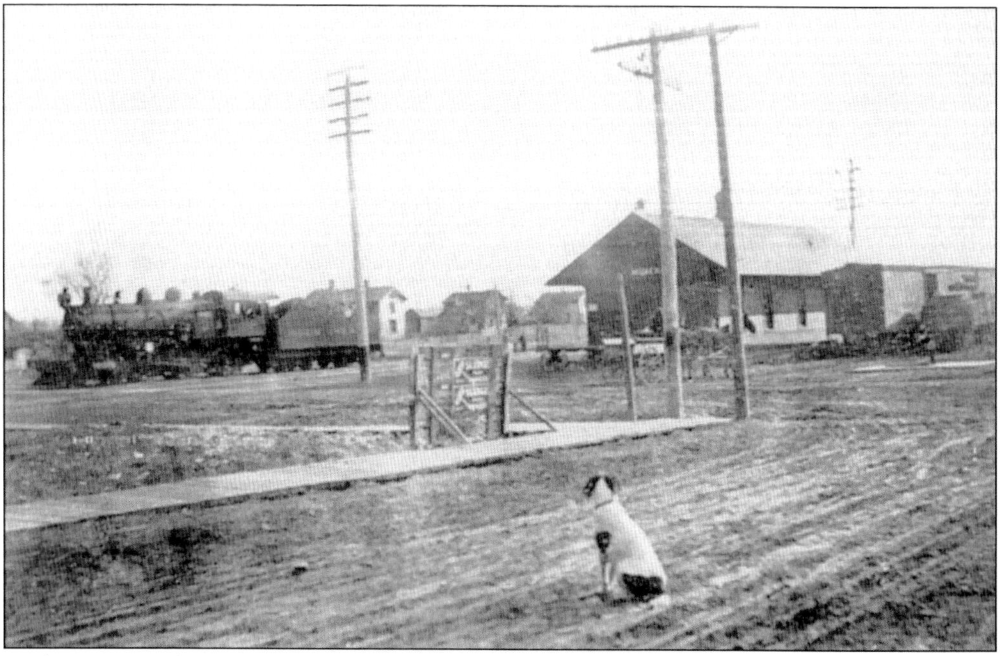

Looking quite solemn in this image from around 1909, a dog peers toward the southeast corner of Front and Mokena Streets and the original Rock Island depot. Although the lot is vacant in this image, it had previously been the location for the butcher shop of a Mr. Kennedy. This business, as well as the neighboring building to the east, fell victim to a horrific fire in 1892.

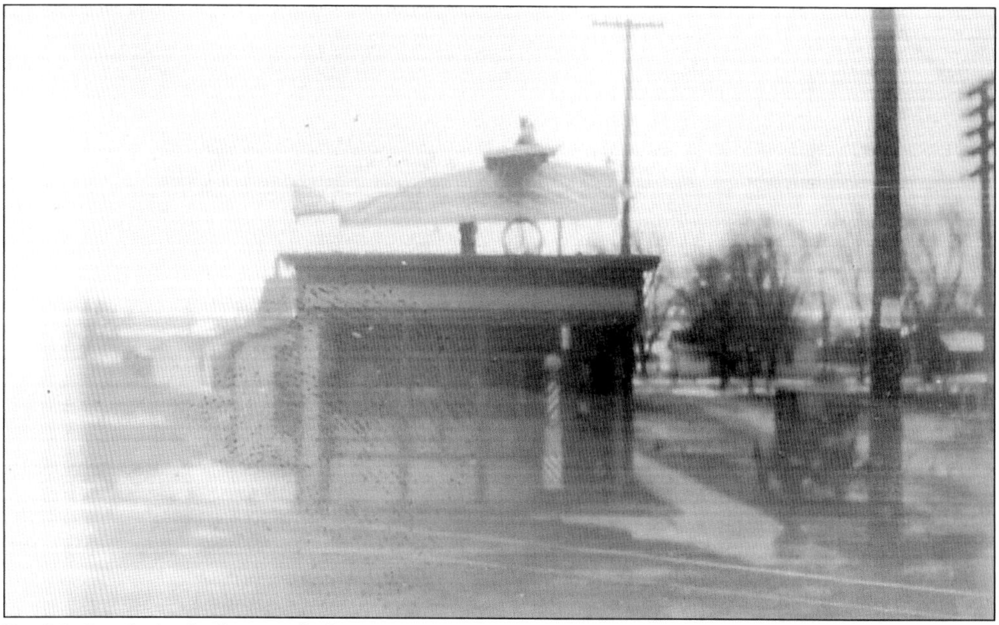

Dr. J.J. Coady built this small drugstore on the southeast corner of Front and Mokena Streets in 1911. With a room for his medical practice in the back, the drugstore was a popular hangout for Mokena baseball players in the era before World War I. Pictured here on December 30, 1931, with a large model airplane named *The Spirit of Mokena*, the building was known at the time as Frank's Barbershop.

Facing southeast from the intersection of Front and Mokena Streets, this May 1938 photograph shows William Evitt's grocery store to the right. Known as the Stop and Shop, this small building had been expanded on its eastern side in 1936. To the left of the grocery store is the George Kraus barbershop, still standing today at 11037 Front Street.

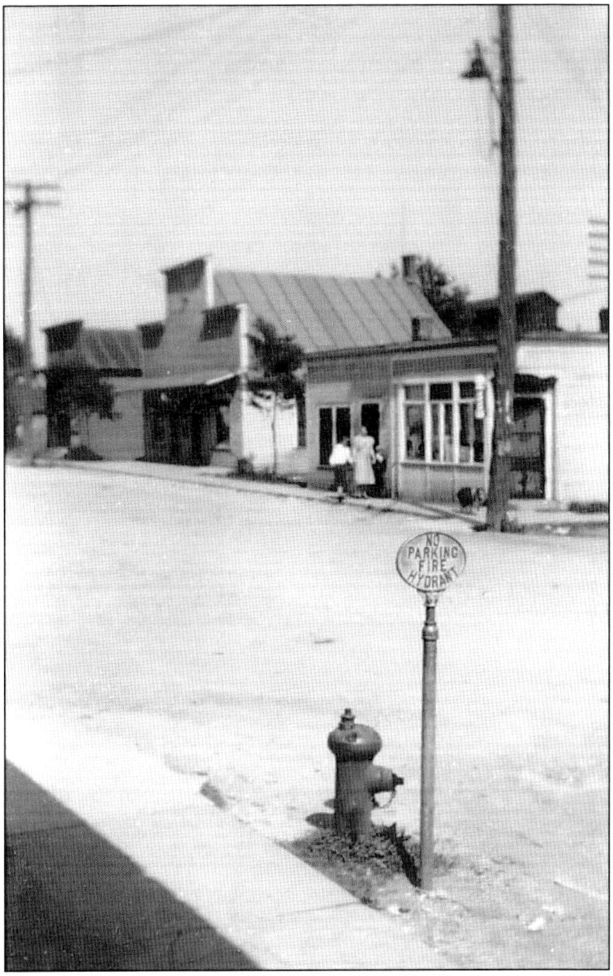

Situated at today's 11041 Front Street, Henry Boleman's drugstore is pictured here c. 1950. Standing in the doorway at left is Jean Boleman; the other two girls remain unidentified. Originally a Chicago pharmacist, Boleman relocated to Mokena in 1947, having purchased the business from Alan Cavett. Note the Cavett signage in the window at right.

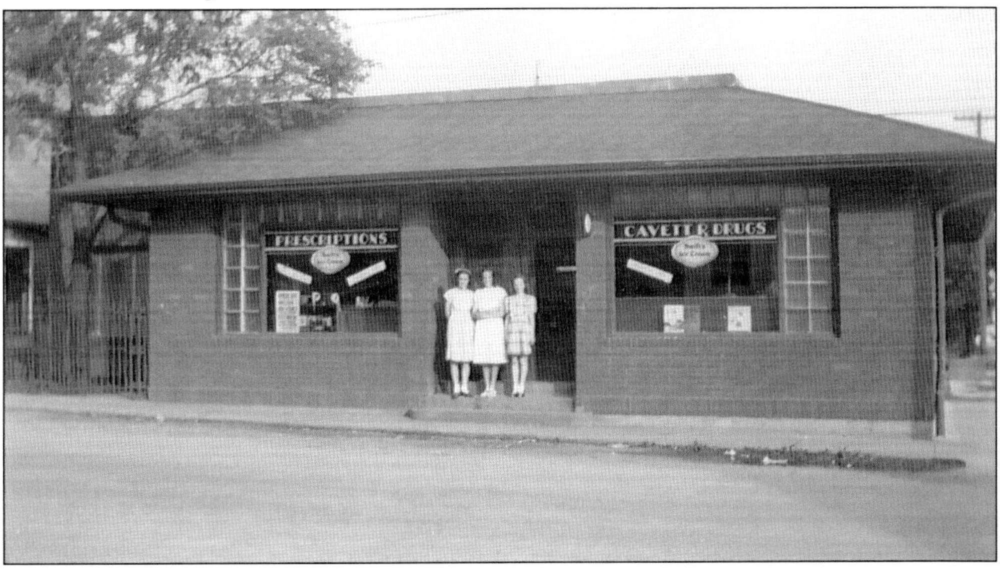

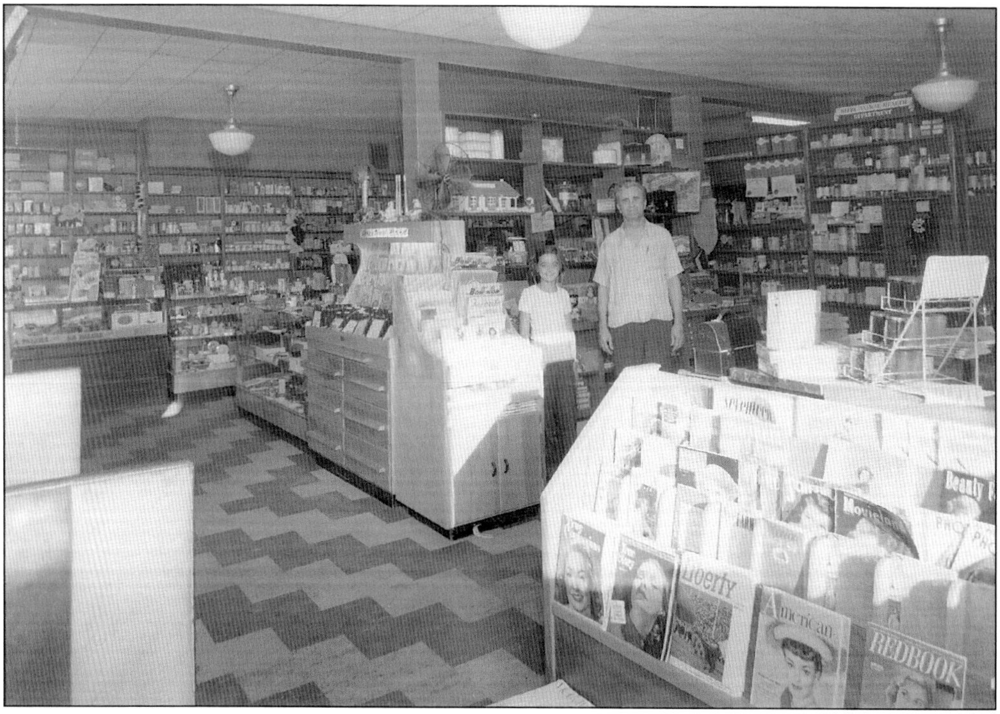

This c. 1950 interior image of the Boleman Drugstore shows Henry Boleman at right with an unidentified girl. During busy hours, Boleman's daughters also helped in the store. The brick building, located at the present-day site of 11041 Front Street, also housed a small apartment in which the Boleman family resided. In a uniquely American concept, drugstores became places to not only receive pharmaceuticals, but also to purchase such items as refreshments, candy, and magazines.

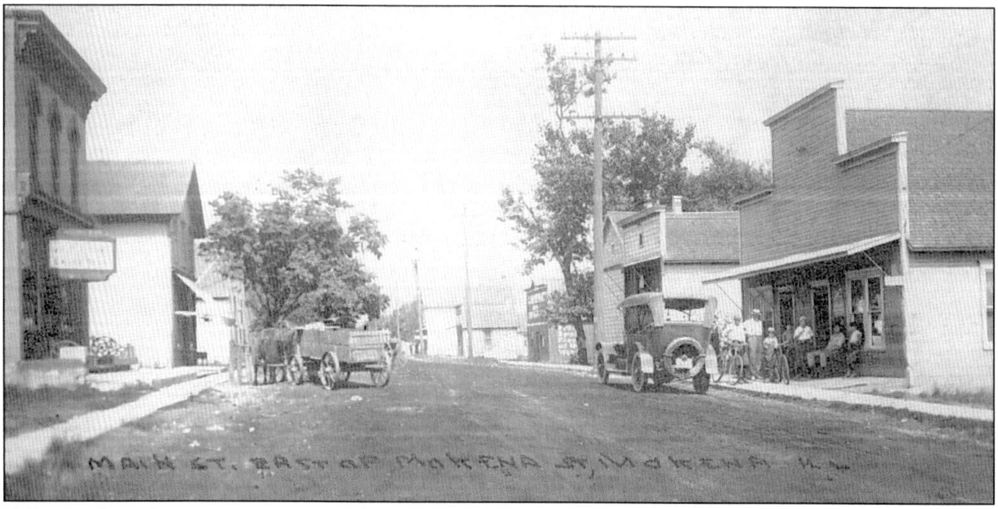

Often referred to as Main Street by locals, Front Street, facing east from Mokena Street, is depicted in this postcard dating from around 1910. The building at 11037 Front Street, seen in the right foreground, remains a prominent Mokena landmark. Built in 1902 as the Mokena Post Office, Paul Rinke Jr. was the rural deliveryman in this era. Occasionally hampered by bad road conditions, Rinke often delivered mail to country farms on foot.

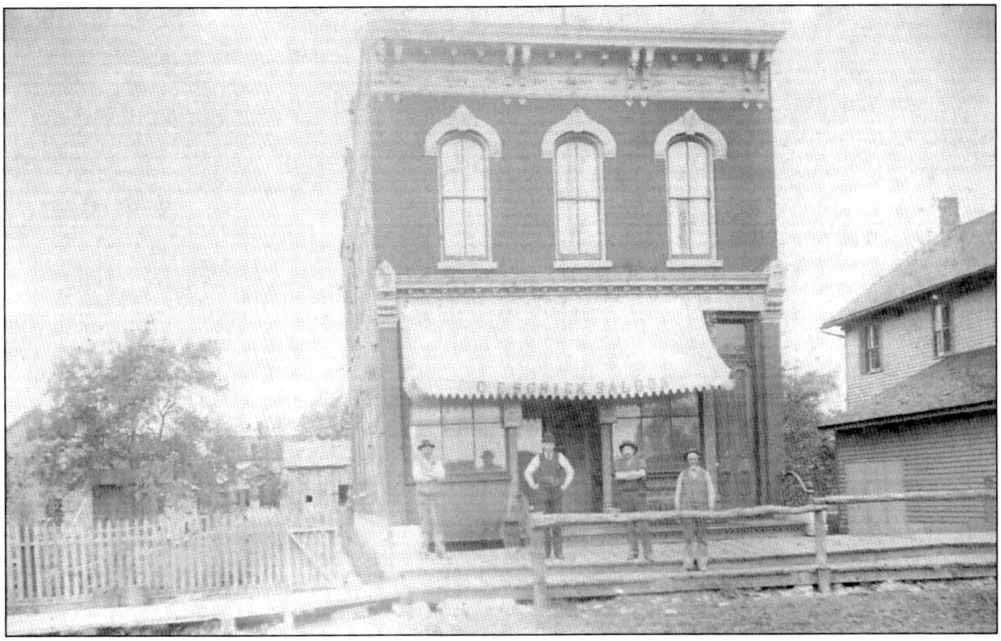

The oldest brick structure in Mokena stands at 11034 Front Street. The earliest traceable history of this location dates back to around 1875, in its iteration as a saloon run by Johann Schiek. By around 1885, the saloon was being operated by Schiek's son, Charles. Standing in front of the building around 1890 are, from left to right, John Cappel, Charles Schiek, Bob Turner, and Civil War veteran Elijah McGovney.

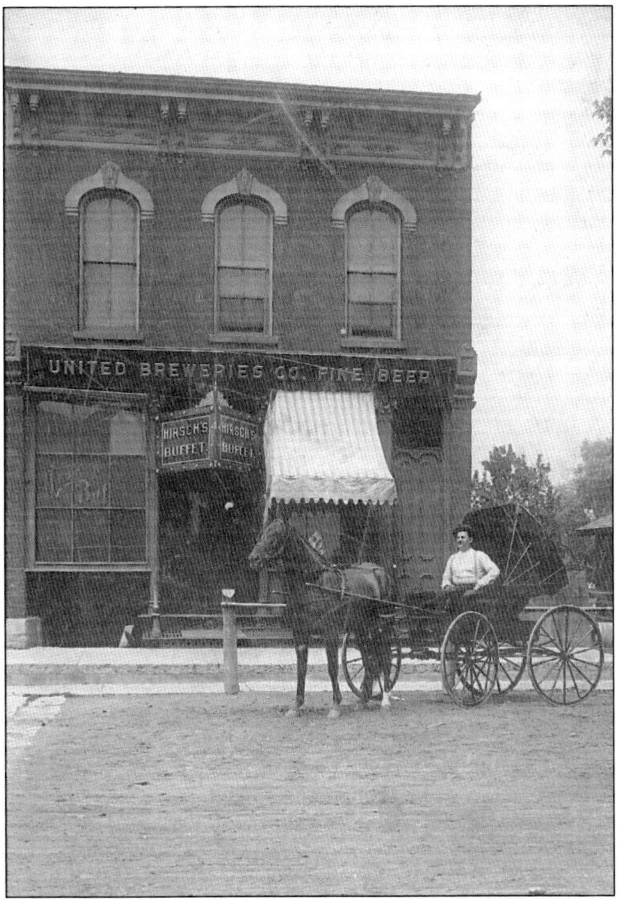

In 1902, local man Frank Hirsch opened his own tavern at this historic location. This image from around the same time period shows Charles Hirsch in a horse-drawn carriage. According to legend, the bricks used in this structure were baked from local clay at a kiln near Francis Road. Noticeable at lower left and right are the entrances to the building's basement and second floor, respectively, where rooms for travelers were available for rent.

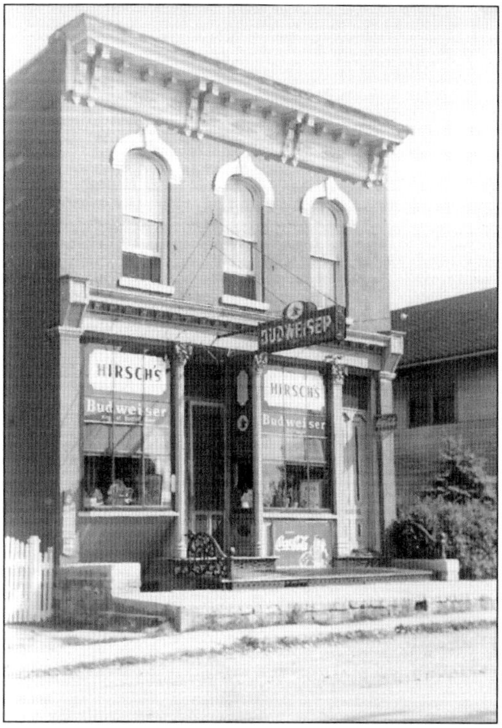

This photograph depicts Hirsch's Tavern on Front Street around 1930. Largely unchanged in appearance through the years, this location has had many interesting uses during its long existence. Under the ownership of Charles Schiek during the 1880s, village board meetings were held in the basement. Around the turn of the 20th century, the Mokena Baptist congregation used this building as a hall and Sunday school.

Displaying an ornate, old-fashioned back bar, Frank Hirsch Jr. (left) and Frank Hirsch Sr. enjoy a toast on the occasion of the senior Hirsch's 55th wedding anniversary. Pictured here on December 13, 1939, a large celebration was held in honor of this event at the Hirsch Tavern, located at the present-day 11034 Front Street.

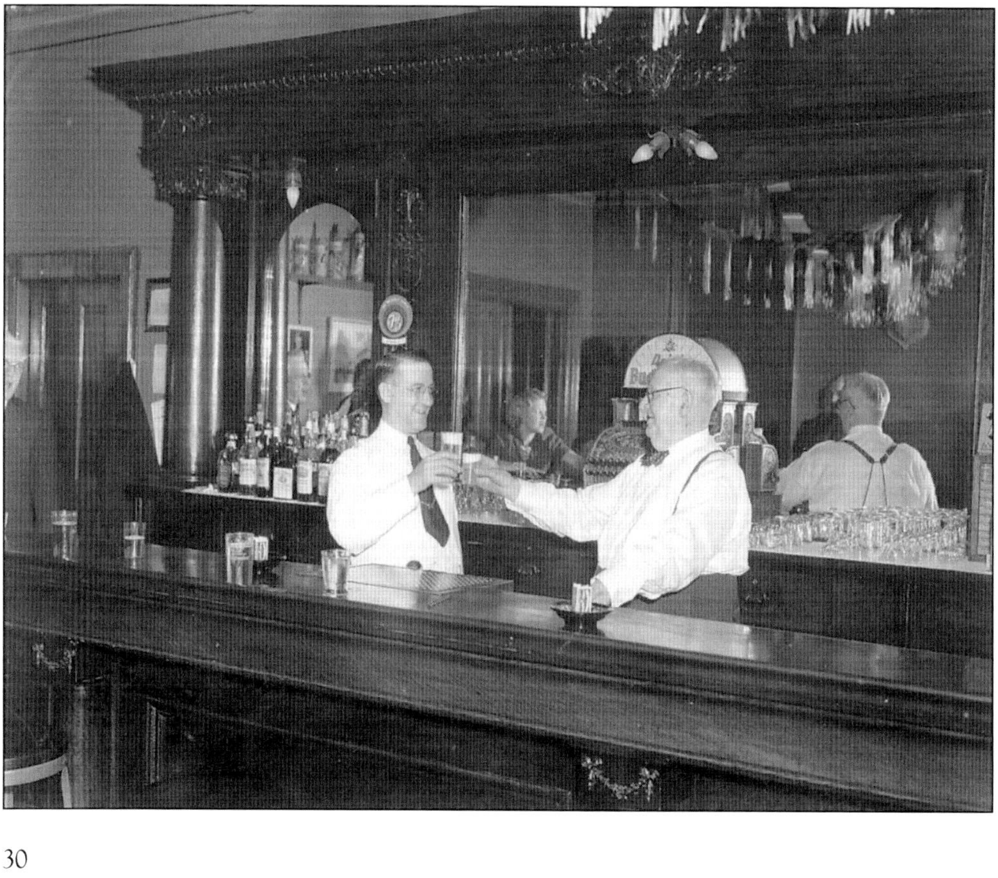

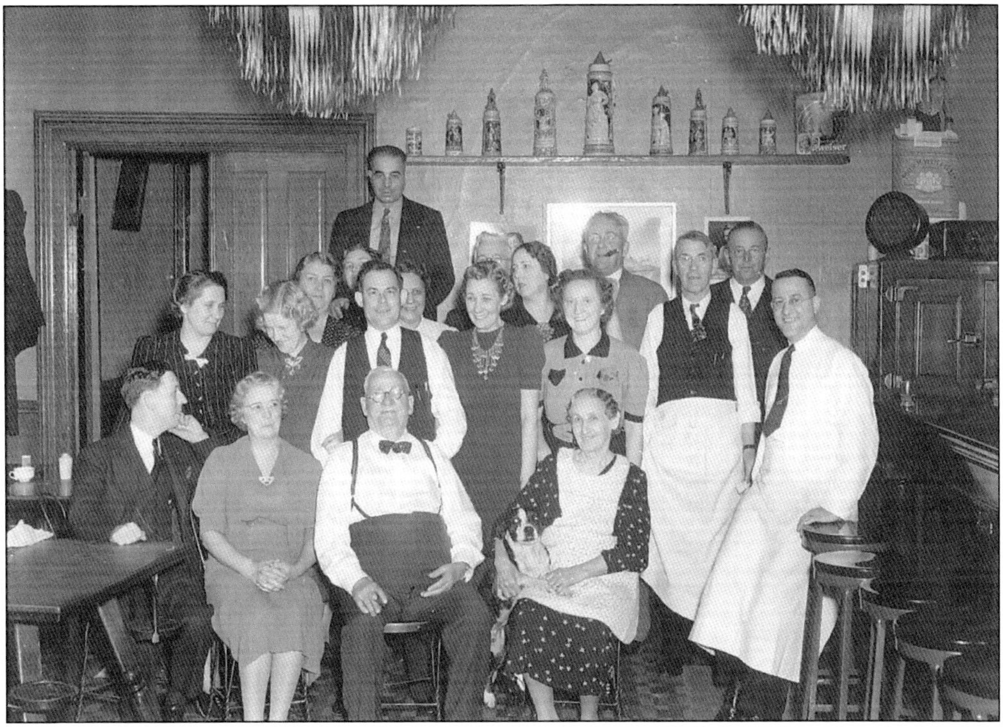

Friends and family gather at the Hirsch Tavern on Front Street in celebration of Frank and Philippine Hirsch's 55th wedding anniversary on December 13, 1939. Prominent residents of the village and members of pioneer families, Frank E. Hirsch married Philippine Zahn in a Mokena cottage on December 13, 1884. Rev. Carl Schaub performed the dual marriage ceremony, during which Philippine's brother Charles Zahn was united in matrimony to Louisa Groeger of Chicago.

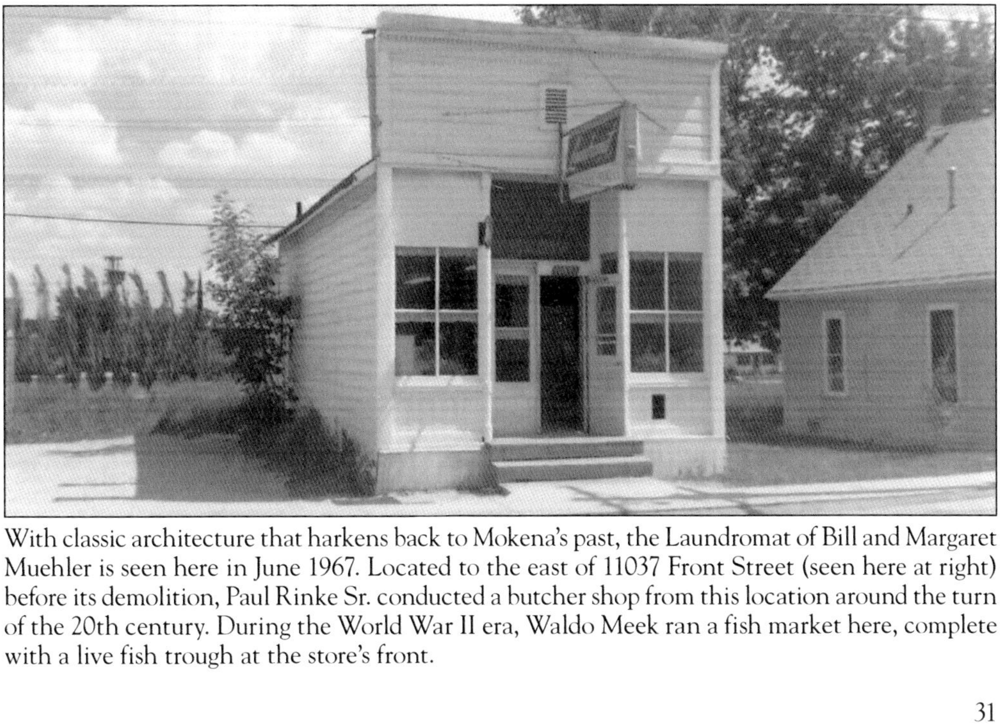

With classic architecture that harkens back to Mokena's past, the Laundromat of Bill and Margaret Muehler is seen here in June 1967. Located to the east of 11037 Front Street (seen here at right) before its demolition, Paul Rinke Sr. conducted a butcher shop from this location around the turn of the 20th century. During the World War II era, Waldo Meek ran a fish market here, complete with a live fish trough at the store's front.

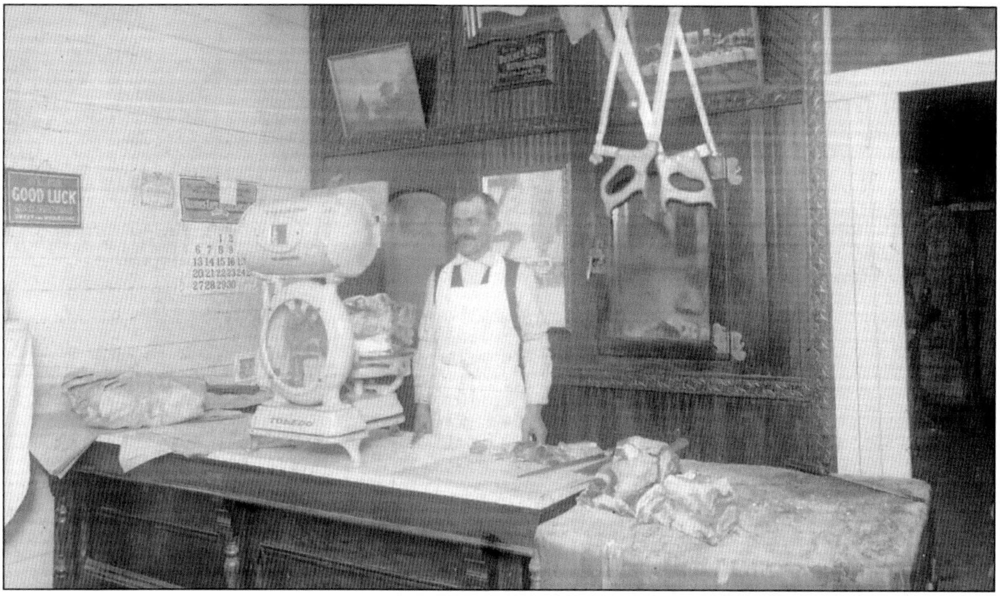

Paul Rinke Sr. is shown here in his Front Street meat market around 1914. Born in Germany in 1859, Rinke and his wife, Anna, immigrated to the United States in 1884, first settling in Chicago. After a brief sojourn there, the Rinkes were induced to Mokena by farm work, although Paul Rinke eventually grew tired of that vocation and later established a butcher shop.

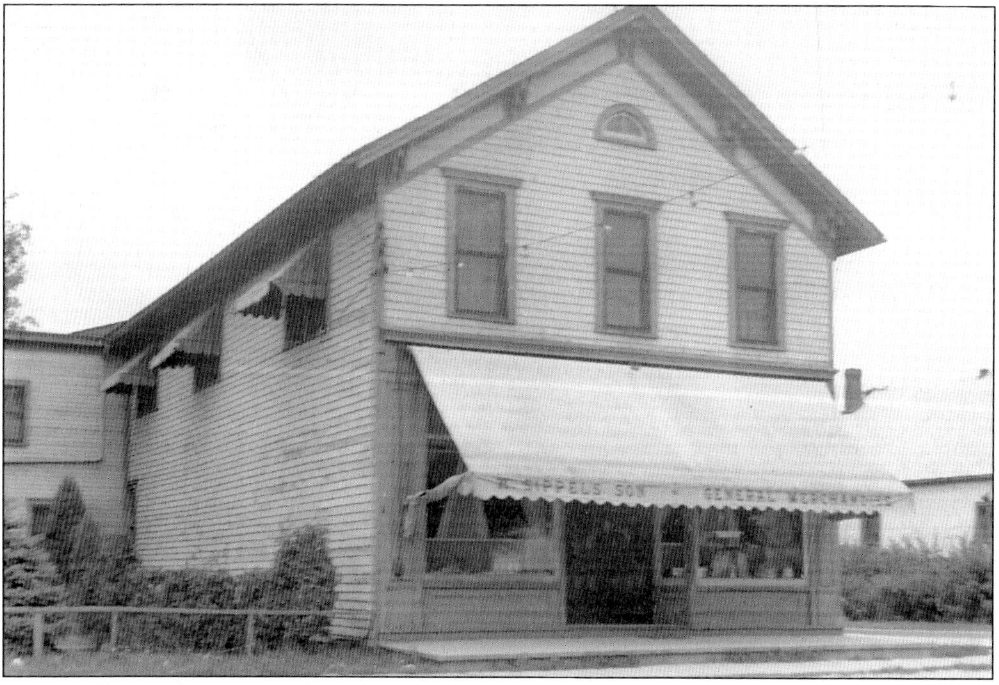

Depicted here about 1938, the general store of the Sippel family was a Mokena fixture for generations. Originally known as the Weber building, Kate Sippel and sons Elmer and Christian Sippel relocated their business from east Front Street to this location around 1911. After their mother's death in 1922, the Sippel brothers took over the family business. This landmark still stands at 11028 Front Street.

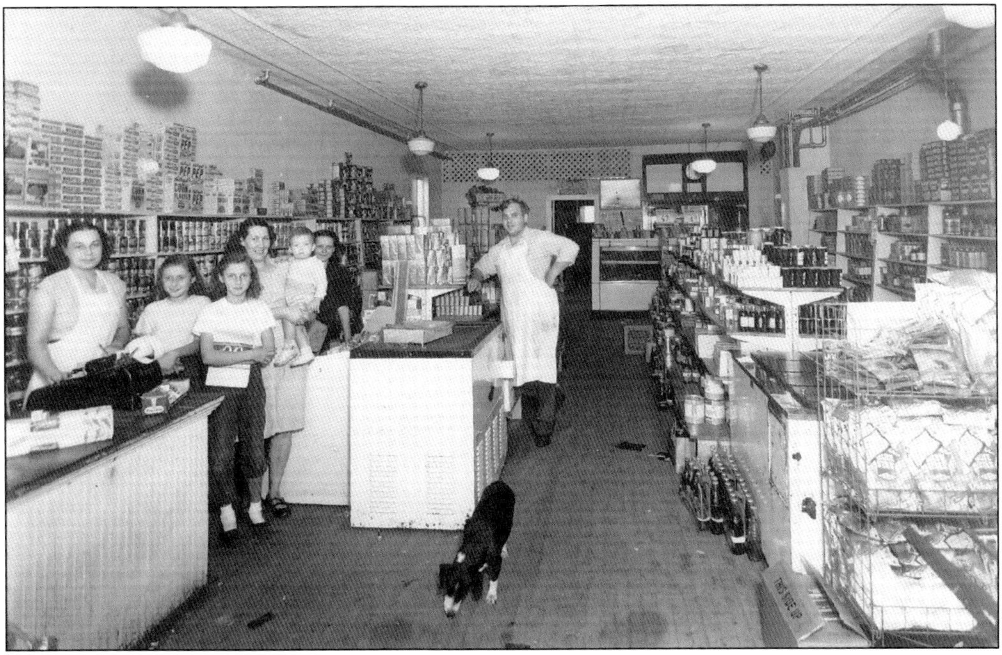

This photograph was taken inside the Grobarcik Royal Blue grocery store around 1948. Irvin Howe inhabited 11028 Front Street for a period, and his wife and sister-in-law operated a Royal Blue store here during the World War II years. Upon his return from national service, Howe sold the business to Joe Grobarcik (pictured at far right), whose respected store remained in business well into the 1970s.

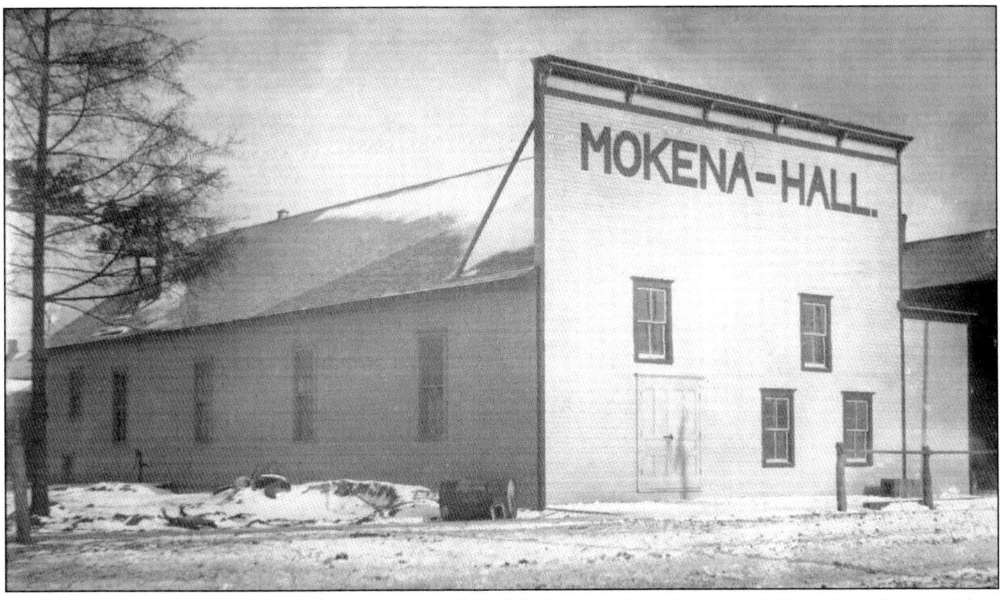

Completed in January 1913, the Mokena Hall filled a void in the social life of Mokena. After the burning of a previous hall owned by John Martin at this location, local businessmen George Hacker and Emil Krapp erected this building, which contained a stage, dining room, and kitchen. Mokena's first moving pictures were shown here, with the equipment operated by Krapp's sons Milton and Roy. (Photograph courtesy of Richard Quinn.)

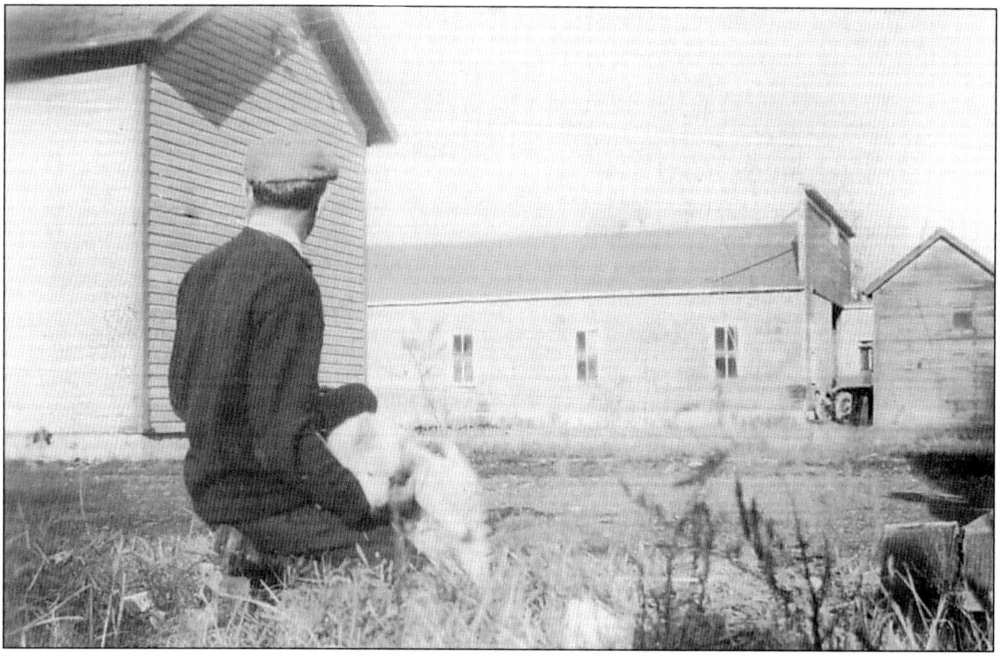

Facing east in this photograph from around 1925, a Mokenian looks toward the first garage of the prominent local Ford agency of Cooper and Hostert. Elmer Cooper and Barney Hostert established their original place of business on First Street in 1916, directly north of what is now 11018 Front Street. Aside from doing repairs, the firm also sold Ford cars, trucks, and tractors, which were originally shipped to Mokena by railroad and assembled at this location.

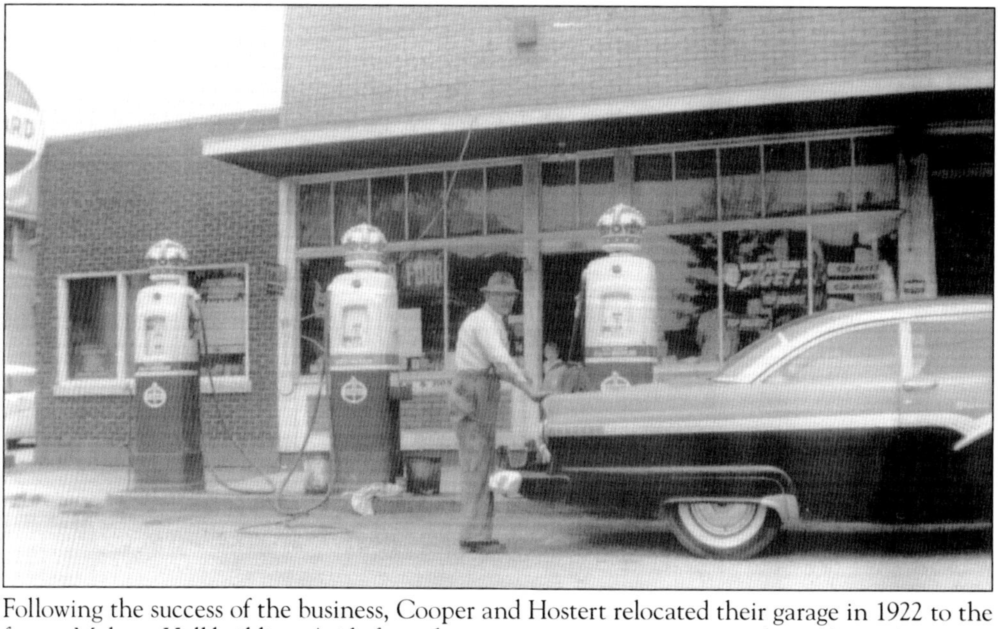

Following the success of the business, Cooper and Hostert relocated their garage in 1922 to the former Mokena Hall building. Aside from the automotive transactions conducted here, the garage was an informal city hall of sorts—a spot where locals came to discuss village issues. Seen here with a 1956 Ford Fairlane gassing up in front, this Mokena landmark was lost in a 1993 fire. 11018 Front Street now stands at this location. (Photograph courtesy of Richard Quinn.)

Mokenians gather for a photograph outside of Front Street's Cooper and Hostert Ford agency in June 1954. Shown here are, from left to right, Fred Clark, Lester Brownlee, Barney Hostert, Irv Howe, Art Hostert, Joe Grobarcik Jr., and Tony Dina Jr. In 1974, the agency was sold to the Show family, of Frankfort, and in 1976, it was granted the honor of being the oldest Ford dealership in Will County.

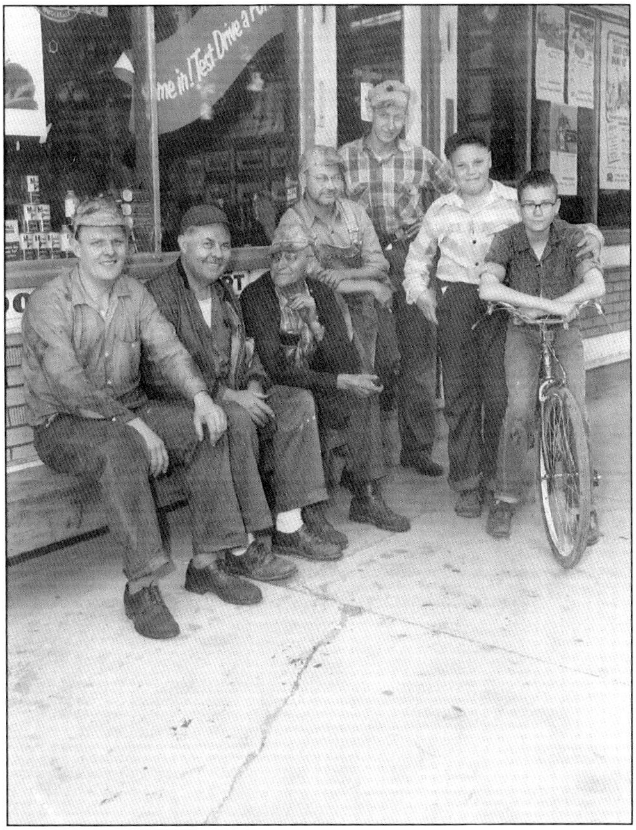

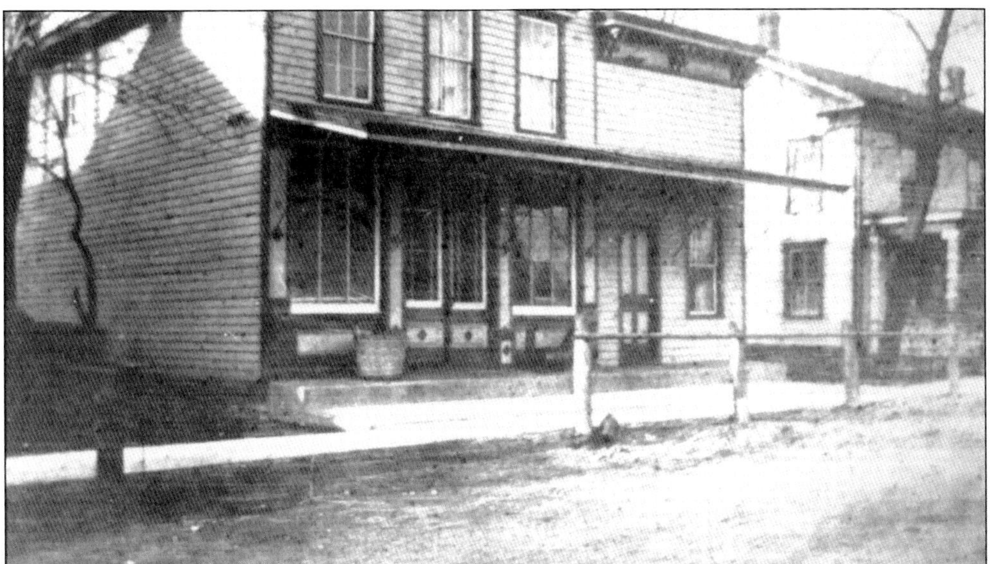

Yet another forgotten visage of Mokena was this Civil War–era building that formerly stood on the site of 11014 Front Street. Walter Fisher, of Joliet, opened a general merchandise store here in 1922. Deputized by the Will County Sheriff to help uphold Prohibition laws, Fisher was shot and killed in 1926 as he bravely pursued a mail bandit in an automobile chase.

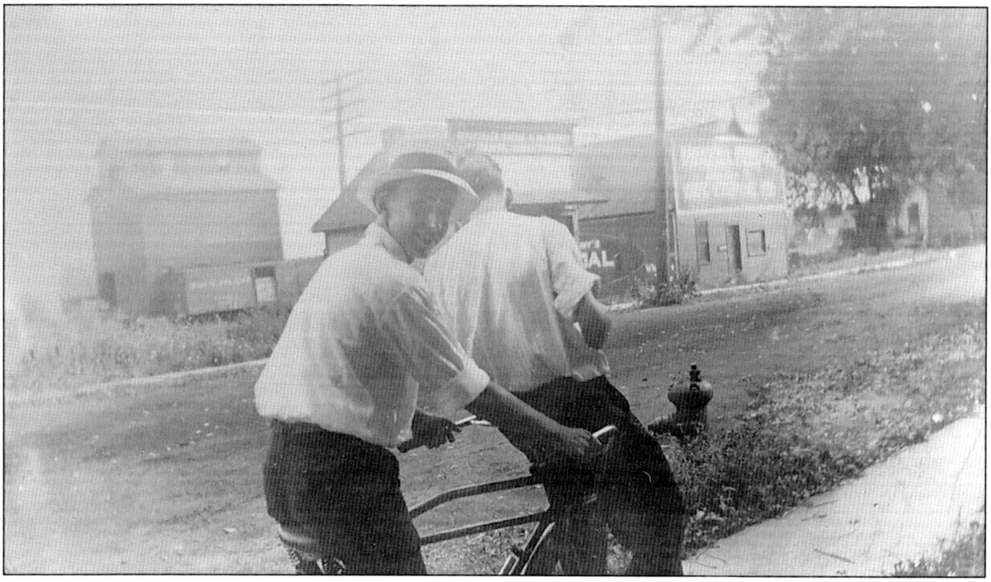

Best friends Roy Kropp (left) and Hugo Niethammer share a lighthearted moment on Front Street around 1913. Looking southwest from near the present-day 11014 Front Street, the Bechstein grain elevator can be seen in the background at left; the building in the center belonged to Wunderlich, Harris, and McGovney Undertaking; and at right is the Mokena Feed Company. (Photograph courtesy of David Kropp.)

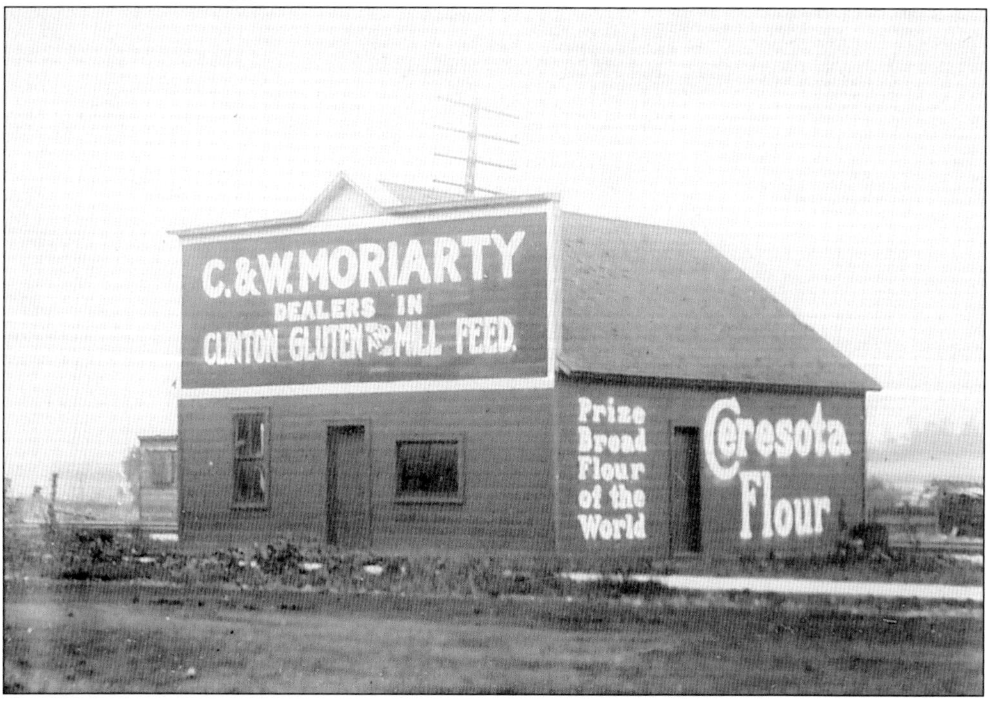

With a unique painted advertisement for Ceresota Flour on its western face, the feed store of Charles and W. Moriarty is depicted here around 1910. Within this shop were a very large scale and other associated instruments used for weighing feed and grain. Having since disappeared to history, this building stood near the present-day 11019 Front Street.

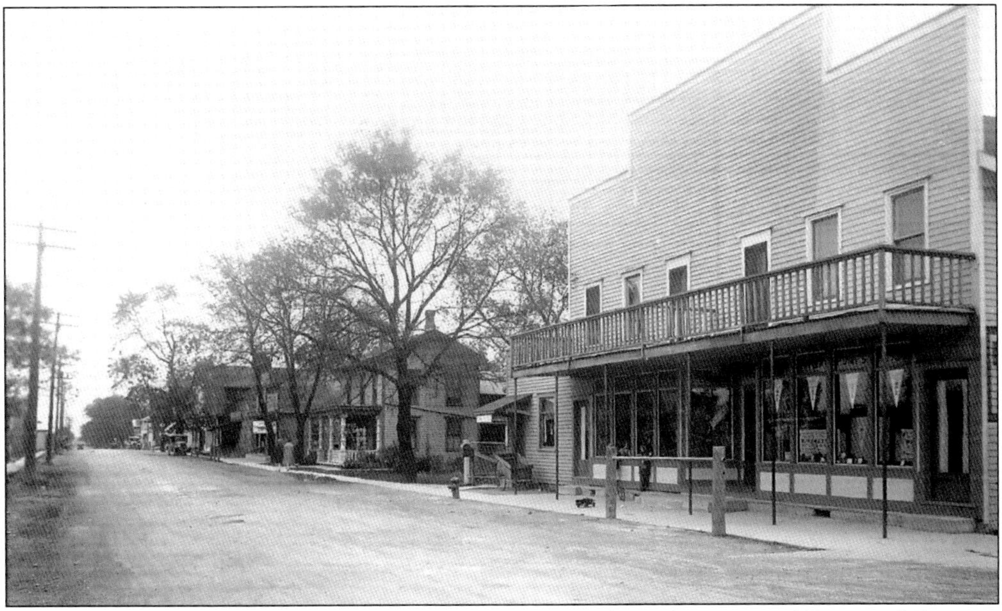

This marvelous view of foregone Mokena is looking west from the corner of Front and Division Streets around 1925. The prominent edifice at right was the hardware store of Mokena brothers Milton and Roy Kropp. Founded in 1921, the entrepreneurs bought and greatly expanded the former saloon of John Groth in 1924. A small section on the left side of the hardware store, seen here at left, served as the Mokena Post Office.

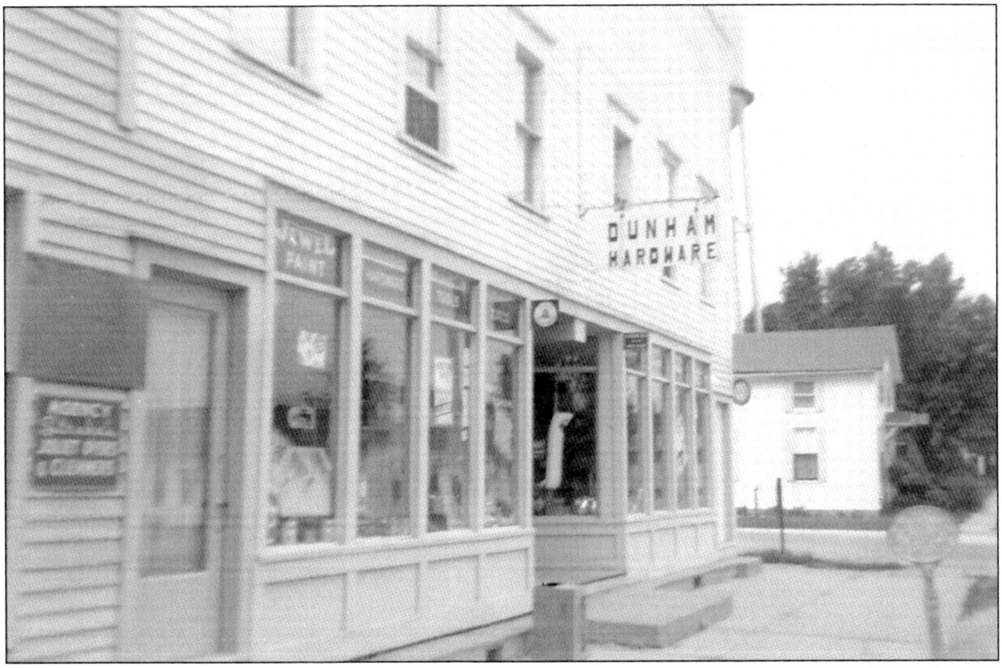

The Front Street hardware store of Ed Dunham is seen here around 1955. Formerly a Chicago telegrapher, Dunham purchased the former Kropp hardware store in 1945. The century-old store burned in a ruinous 1974 fire in which exploding ammunition proved a great peril to attending firefighters. This corner is the present-day location of 11000 Front Street.

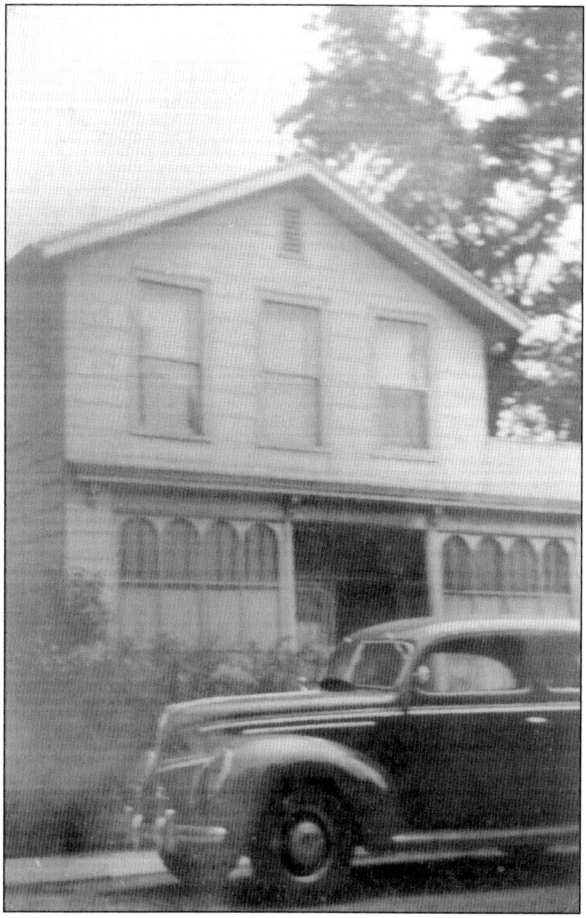

Complete with vintage auto, today's 10931 Front Street is seen here around 1940 as Muehler's Meat Market. Known during the World War I era as the Wishnick General Store, the Wishnick family sold scrap iron during the war years, when metal was scarce. Martin Muehler purchased this building in 1926 for use as a meat market. A native of Saxony, Germany, Muehler served in the German army before immigrating to the United States in 1910.

This image shows a serene Front Street, looking west about 1930. At left is the current 10931 Front Street. Note the barn at far left. In years past, nearly every house in the village had some sort of barn on its property, owing to the fact that many residents kept chickens and, in earlier days, horses. Although many of these barns have since disappeared, some home owners converted them to garages.

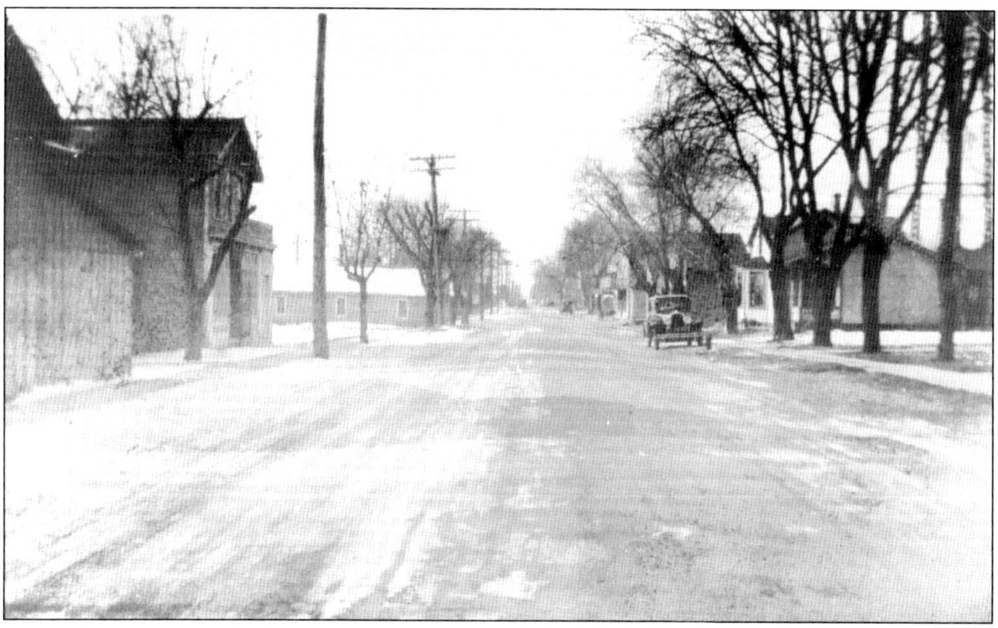

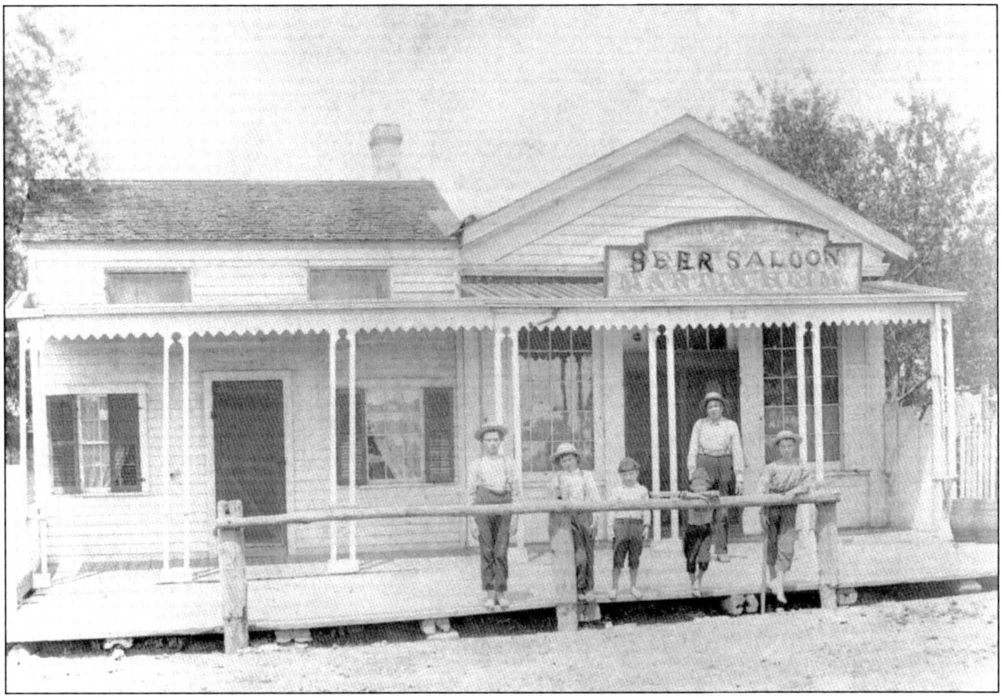

The saloon of Martin Heim is seen here around 1880. Heim, standing in the doorway, arrived in this area from Hessen-Darmstadt, Germany, in the 1840s, as part of the first wave of Germanic immigrants to the region. Originally a farmer near Wolf Road, Heim grew physically unable to perform farm work and founded this saloon after the construction of the Rock Island Railroad.

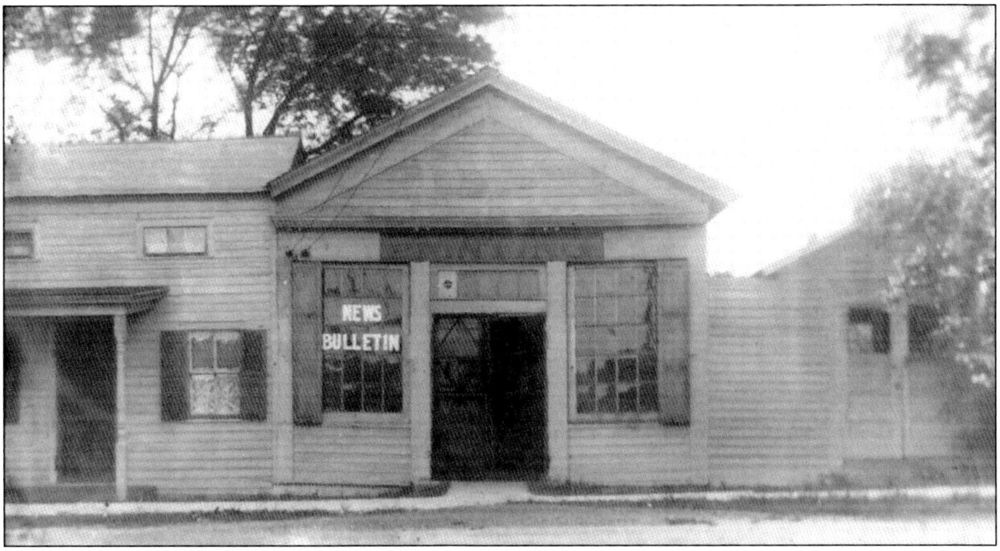

Heim's grandson William Semmler opened a print shop in the building in 1916. A reporter for the *Joliet Herald-News*, Semmler founded Mokena's own newspaper, the *Mokena News-Bulletin*, in 1919. The Semmler family printed the most interesting publication at this location for decades before ultimately ceasing in 1958, when it was sold to a Lemont, Illinois, firm. Seen here around 1925, this historic structure was torn down in the late 1970s. 10842 Front Street occupies this location today.

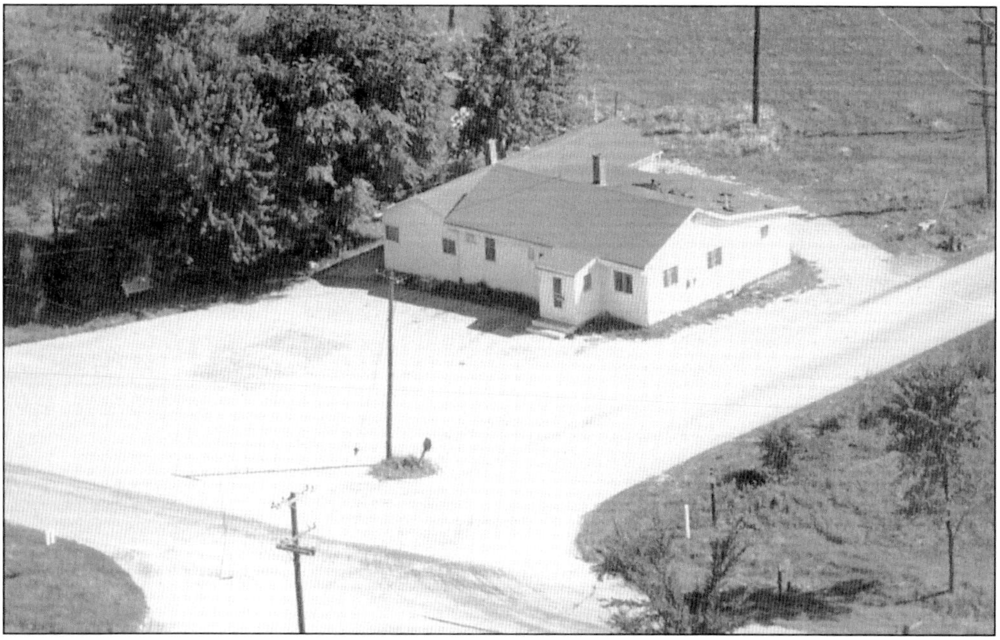

This aerial view of the northeast corner of Wolf and LaPorte Roads, dating from around 1950, shows the Robinson Tavern. The Green Gables, a restaurant here, was rumored to have been a speakeasy in the 1920s. In 1938, Fred J. Robinson acquired the property and opened a tavern. Robinson also installed gas pumps; during the 1940s, this was the only spot in Mokena where one could buy fuel on a Sunday.

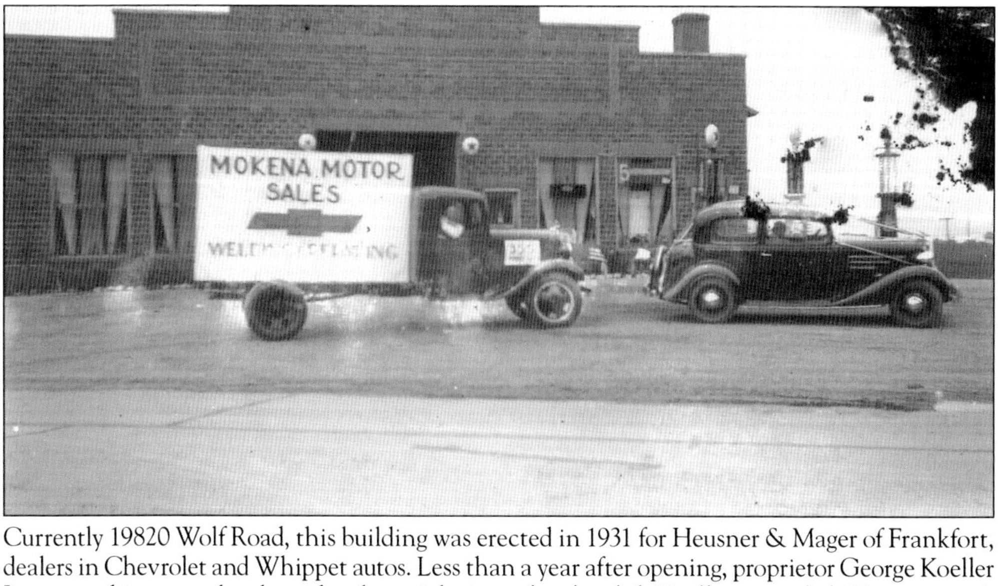

Currently 19820 Wolf Road, this building was erected in 1931 for Heusner & Mager of Frankfort, dealers in Chevrolet and Whippet autos. Less than a year after opening, proprietor George Koeller Jr. engaged in a gun battle with a late-night intruder that left Koeller wounded. He recovered, and the would-be burglar was never apprehended.

Two

The Fountain of Knowledge

Education, the portal through which liberation is offered, has a long history in Mokena. The beginnings of organized education in Mokena can be traced to the classes of a Mrs. Knight and Mrs. Hiram Wood, who taught in a primitive log structure that stood near the southwest boundary of today's village. Not long after the birth of Mokena and the arrival of the Chicago, Rock Island & Pacific Railroad in 1852, a schoolhouse was built in the young community. Local resident James Pierce taught the first classes in the small wooden building, which was constructed in 1855 on the public square.

By 1870, the school was bursting at the seams and a grand, new school was erected at the eastern edge of town. So dire was the need for this new building that class was being conducted there before the structure was even complete. Serving the town from 1872 to 1929, this stately building lent its name to one of Mokena's most well-known thoroughfares—Schoolhouse Road.

In days of yore, physical punishment of students was common, and Mokena was no exception. In 1874, teacher Harris Smith was fined $25 for striking a student with a hickory stick, proving that our forefathers saw a boundary to what was considered acceptable reprimand. Until relatively recent times, the village was of such a size that mischievous students understood the risk of trouble at school; a mother would likely have heard about the incident before the student came home.

The construction of the Carpenter Street School in 1929 included Mokena's first gymnasium, offering the opportunity for students to participate in school-sponsored athletic events for the first time, with basketball being a perennial favorite. Willowcrest School opened in 1957, shifting the location of Mokena's schools to their current location west of Wolf Road. Throughout their long existence, thousands of students have passed through the community's schools, learning the skills that have guided many to great heights.

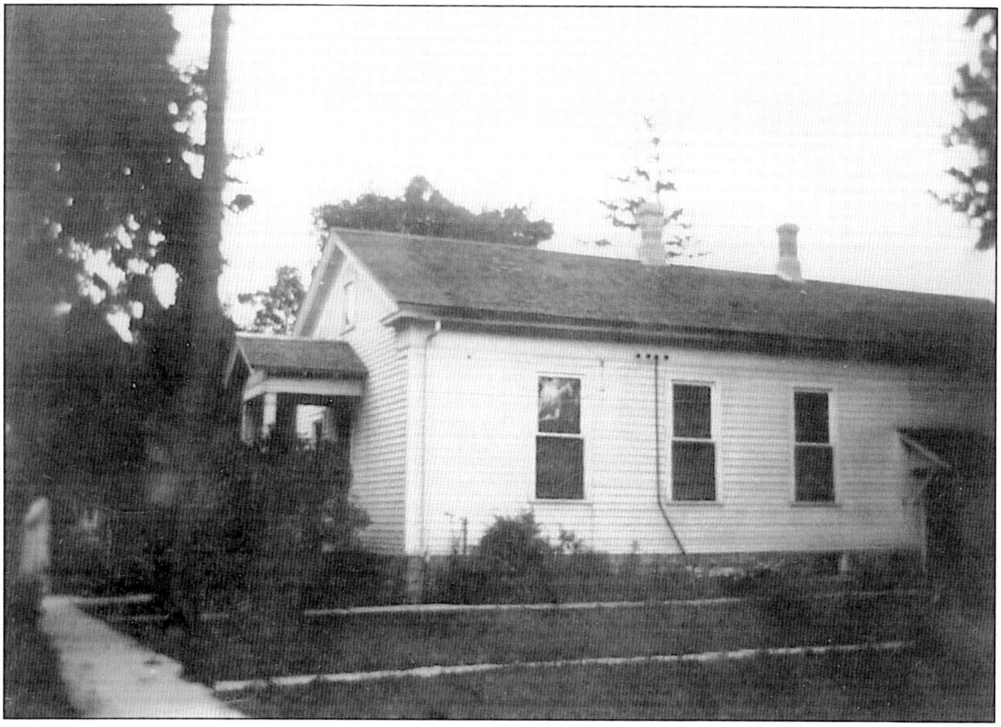

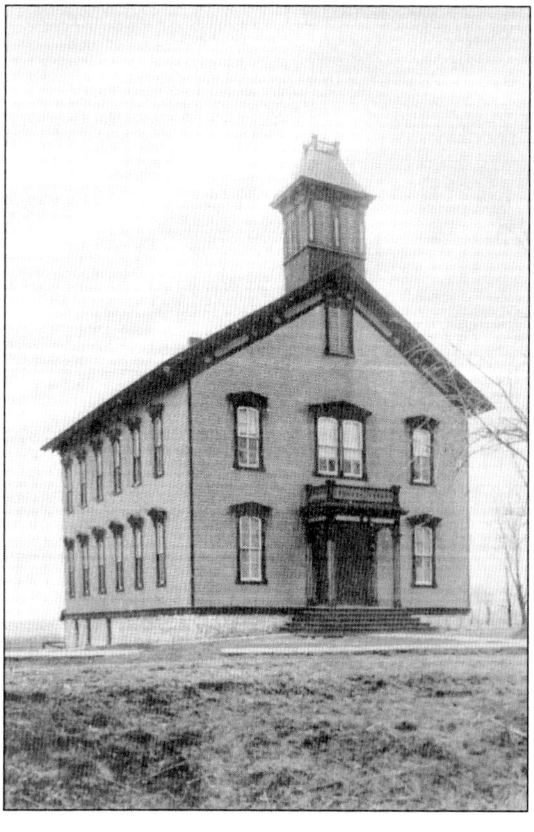

Built in 1855 at a cost of $1,000, this small clapboard structure was the first schoolhouse constructed in Mokena. Originally located about 75 feet west of Union Street, the building was purchased by St. John's church in 1873 and attached to their parsonage on Third Street. Seen here in 1926, the former schoolhouse has since been converted to a private residence and stands today at 11121 Third Street.

Erected in 1872, Mokena's second schoolhouse was aesthetically regarded as one of the finest in Will County. Schoolhouse Road got its name from this building, which formerly stood at the northwest corner of that thoroughfare and Front Street. Used by Mokena's students until 1929, the school was torn down in 1934 and its remnants were used to construct several local homes. (Photograph courtesy of Richard Quinn.)

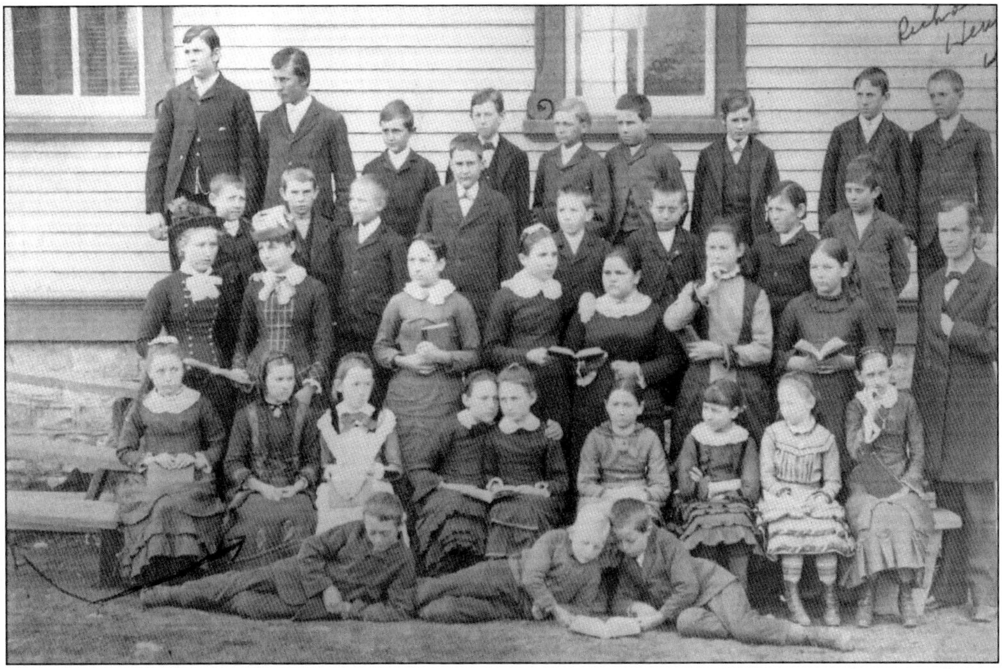

This image from around 1875 is the oldest known class photograph depicting Mokena students. With their backs to the schoolhouse, these children represent a microcosm of the village in this era. They are the children of farmers, grain traders, clergymen, and veterans of the Civil War. More often than not, they had German-born parents. These are the faces of their generation.

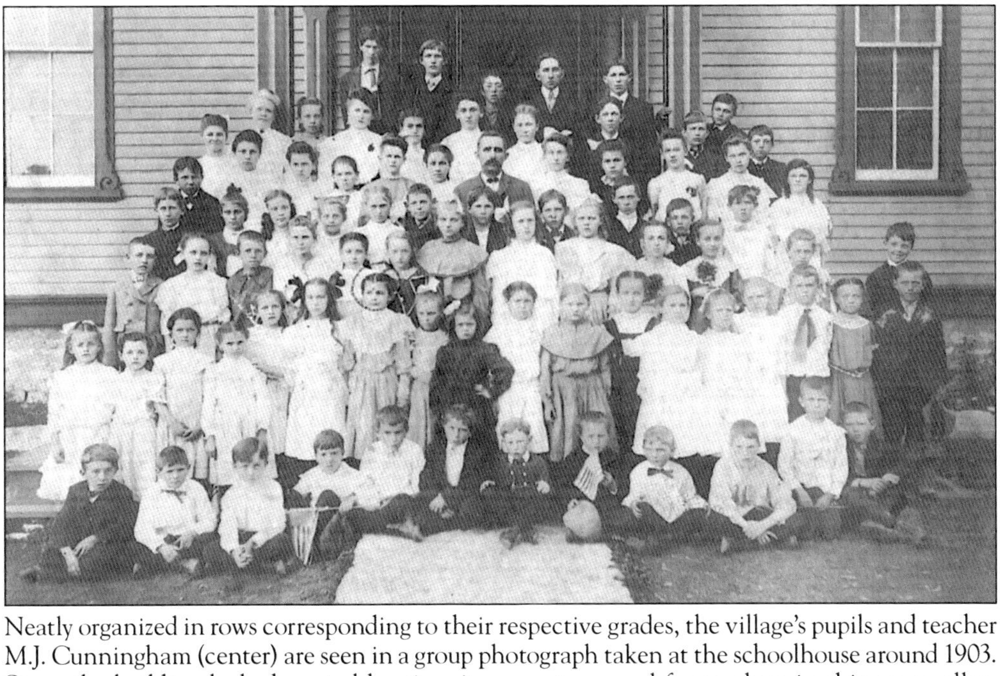

Neatly organized in rows corresponding to their respective grades, the village's pupils and teacher M.J. Cunningham (center) are seen in a group photograph taken at the schoolhouse around 1903. Since the building lacked central heating, it was not unusual for teachers in this era to allow students to eat homemade lunches around the school's wood-burning furnaces on frigid days. Wet and muddy boots were also known to be replaced with warm house slippers.

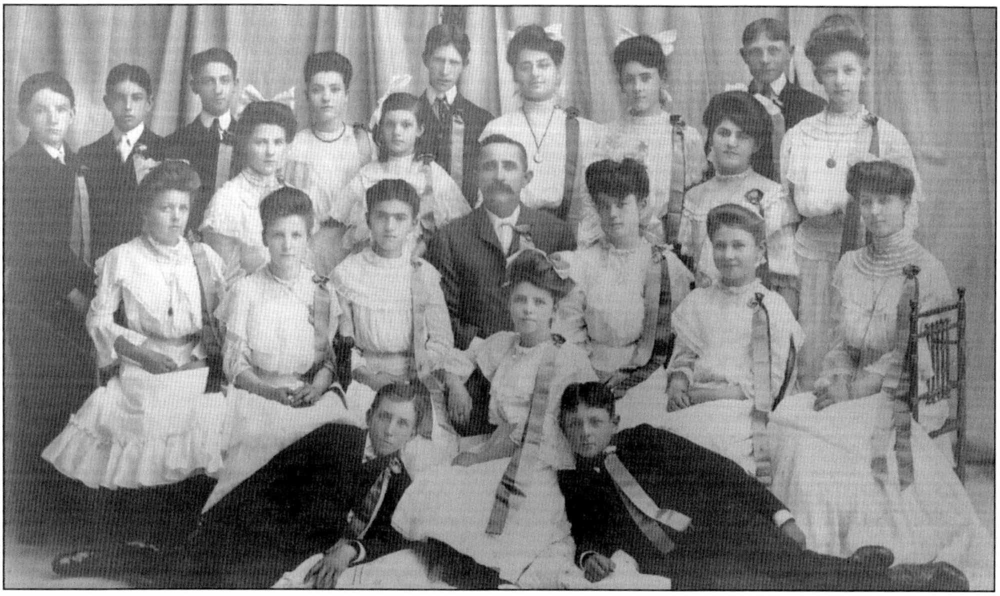

This image depicts the Mokena Public School graduating class of 1904. Posing proudly are, from left to right, (first row) Frank Brinkerhoff, Edith Lynk, and Albert Cappel; (second row) Ionia Haines, Mildred Brinkerhoff, Frieda Liess, teacher M.J. Cunningham, Sadie McGraw, Ida Cappel, and Frieda Weitendorf; (third row) Helen Erickson, Amanda Hohenstein, and Caroline Knater; (fourth row) Ernest Tonn, Alfred "Joe" Hatch, Frank Hirsch, Mary Bigger, Glen Rouse, Amanda Braun, Phoebe Lynch, Fred Cappel, and Bertha Zumstein.

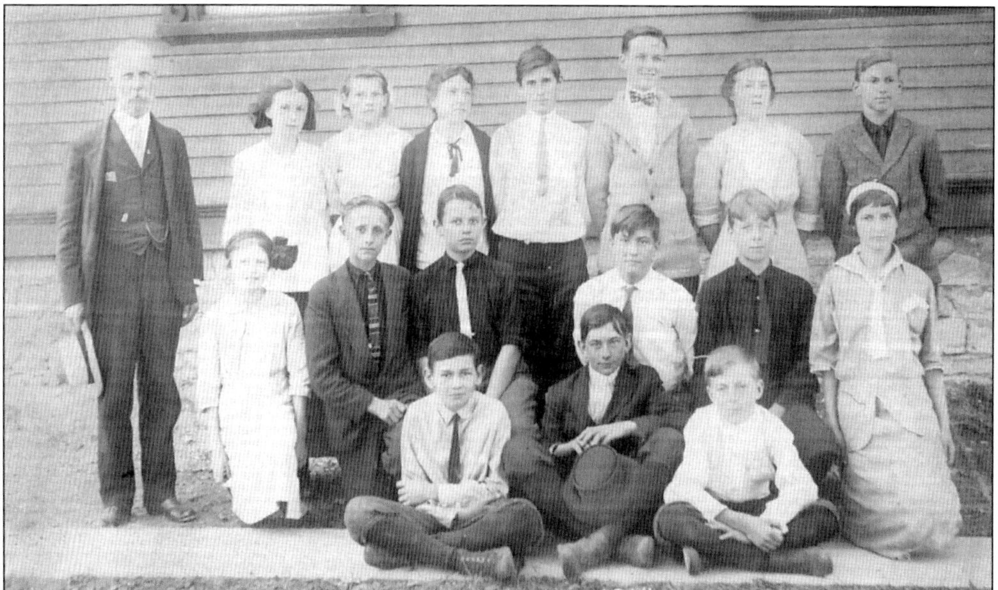

Pictured here in 1914 is the first class to graduate from the Mokena School's two-year high school program. Shown here are, from left to right, (first row) Milton Geuther, Lester Schiek, and George Rinke; (second row) Wanita Oswald, Milton Voss, Carl Hirsch, Lester Lauffer, John Marti, and Mildred Shevlin; (third row) Prof. S.J. Eakle, Myrtle Werner, Alfee Anderson, Alma Bechstein, Harvey Frick, Warren Norris, Clara Newson, and A.C. Woods.

These two pose in front of the Mokena schoolhouse around 1925. Once a crown jewel in Will County's school system, by the late 1920s many considered the Mokena building to be outdated. In 1922, a defective furnace set fire to an upstairs room, and in the same year it was discovered that the school's foundation was bulging considerably. The residence at 10810 Front Street now stands at the site of the former schoolhouse.

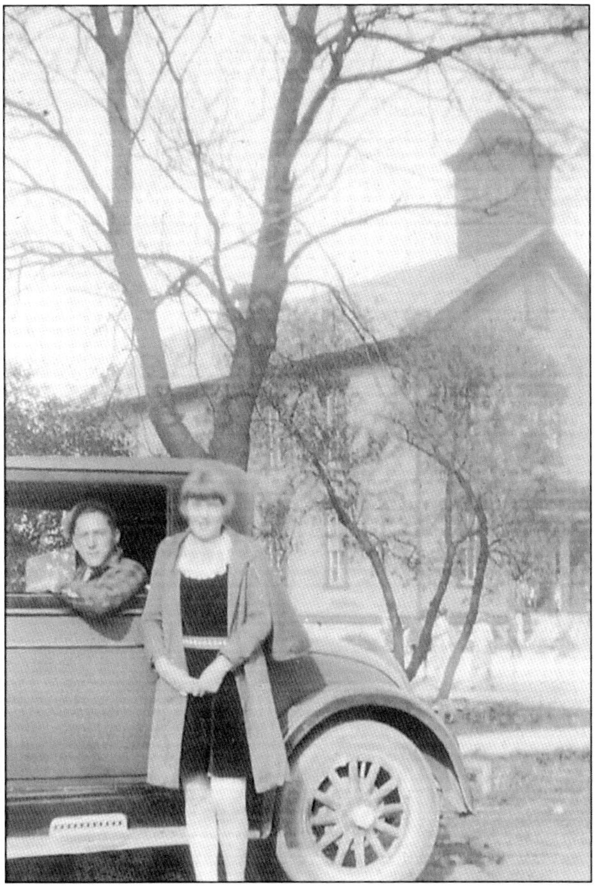

This image shows Mokena Public School around 1935. Known formally as Carpenter Street School, this picturesque building housed grades one through eight, and, until 1944, a two-year high school. Prior to this point, students wishing to finish their final two years of high school would commute by train or automobile to Joliet Township High School, or alternately to Blue Island. Since 1976, this building has housed the Mokena Village Hall.

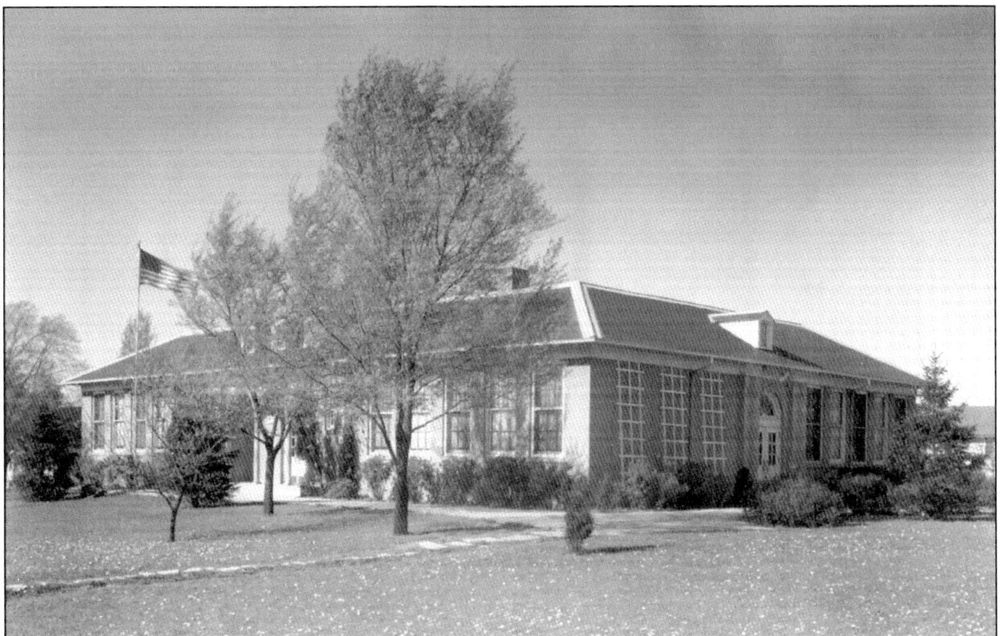

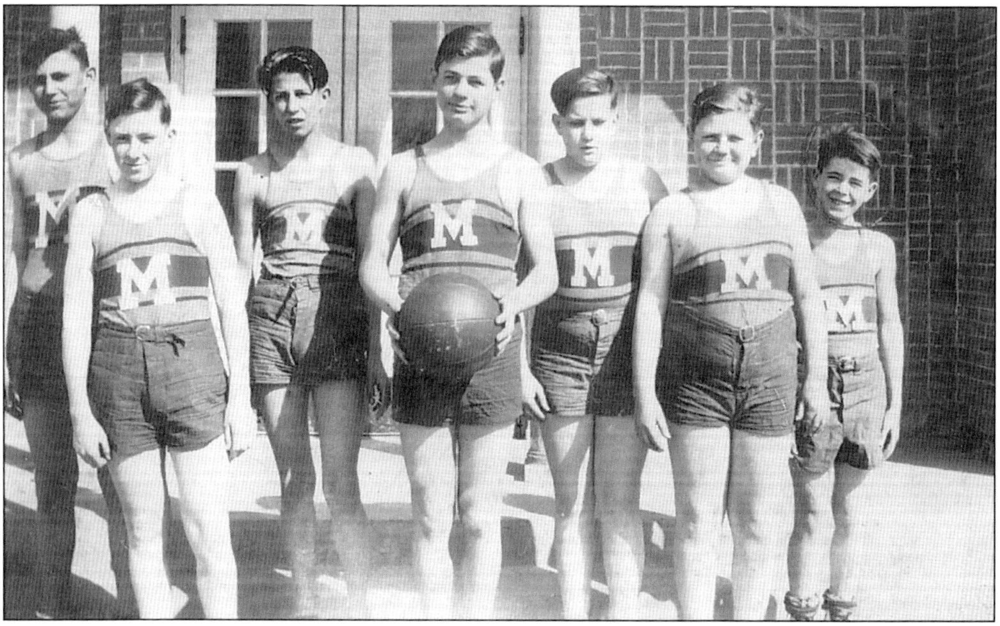

This image, taken March 19, 1931, at the Carpenter Street School, shows the seventh and eighth graders who made up the first Mokena basketball team. Over the years, basketball has proven to be a popular local sport. The players are, from left to right, Edwin Yunker, Gerald Carey, Richard Walsh, Wesley Cappel, Erwin McGovney, Harold Cappel, and Michael MacPherson.

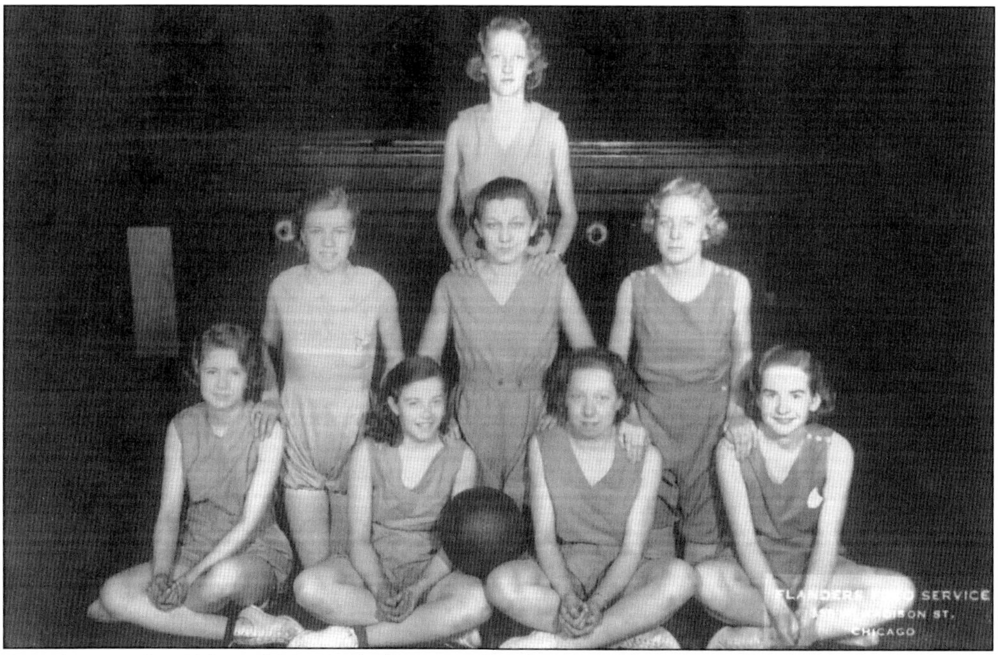

Seen here is the 1934 girls' basketball team of Mokena Public School. Nearly half of the high school girls were on the team, with the total number of female students amounting to only 18 that year. Pictured here are, from left to right, (first row) Dorothy Hall, Eileen Walsh, Alice Lauffer, and Grace Moriarty; (second row) Virginia Brown, Dorothy Homerding, and Edna Lorenz; (third row) Bernice Hostert.

The first student council of the Mokena Public School represented the interests of the student population during the 1938–1939 school year. The student council members are, clockwise, president Robert Homerding, secretary Katherine Reed, Pat Bennett, Gordon Spiess, Bill Homerding, George Merrick, Ed Tierney, Jean Shevlin, treasurer Corinne Marti, and vice president Virginia Nebeker.

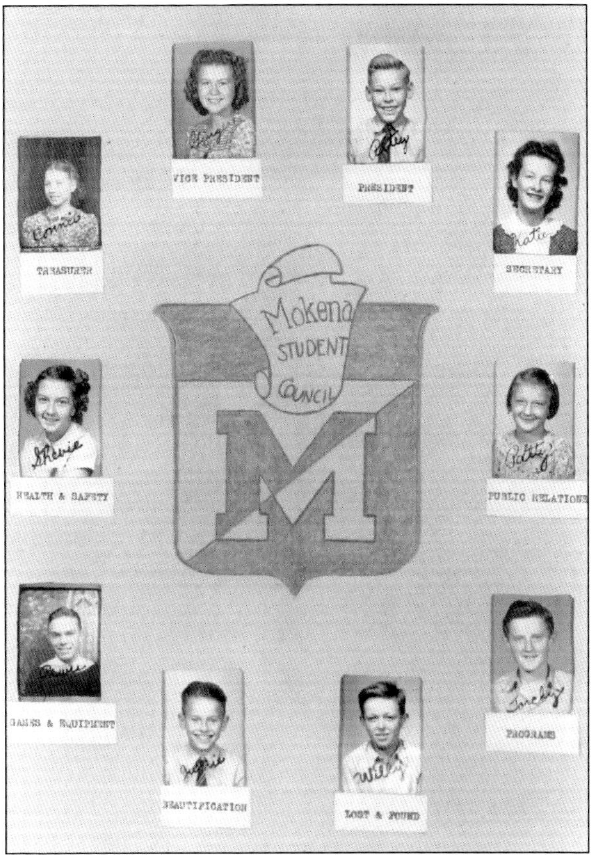

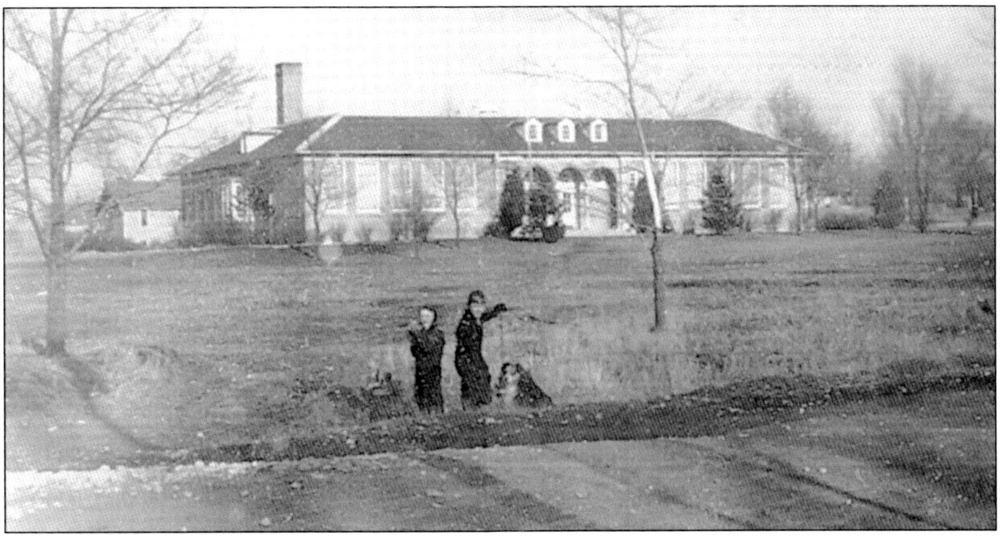

This is Mokena Public School, seen looking eastward from Division and Third Streets, as it was in March 1938. In the days when trapping was a popular area pastime, many Mokena boys checked their traps before the start of the school day. It was not unusual to occasionally trap an angry skunk, resulting in local youth heading to class covered in their sharp aroma. Ron and Bill Steen are visible in the foreground.

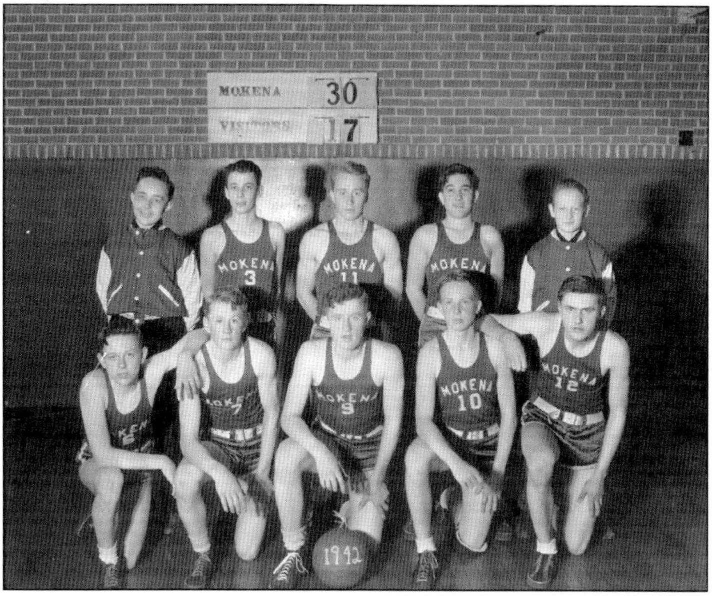

Members of the 1941–1942 boys' basketball team pose for a group photograph in the gymnasium of the Mokena Public School. One of the last teams formed before the abolishment of Mokena high school in 1944, shown here are, from left to right, (first row) George Rinke, Stan Baudry, Bud Hudson, Schatzie Mueller, and Art Benson; (second row) Bill Homerding, Ed Abbe, Gordon Spiess, Bob McGregor, and Melvin Kropp.

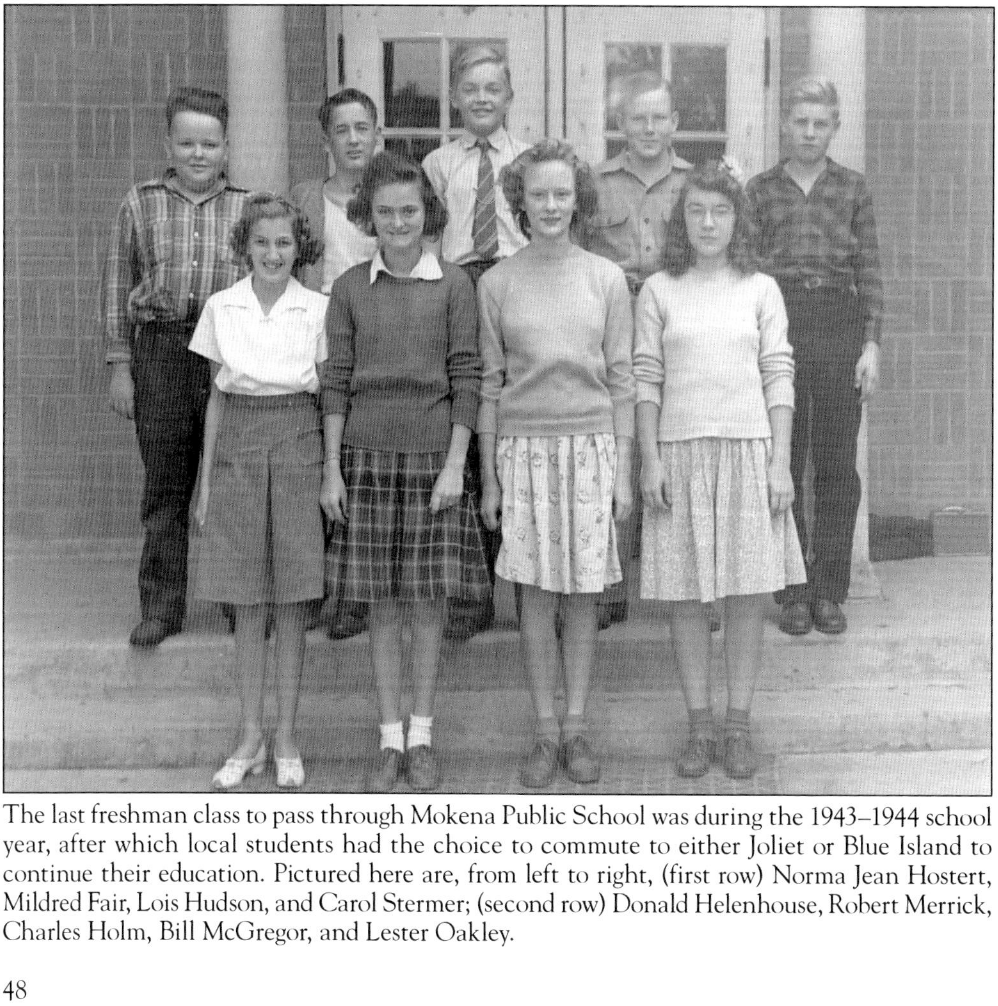

The last freshman class to pass through Mokena Public School was during the 1943–1944 school year, after which local students had the choice to commute to either Joliet or Blue Island to continue their education. Pictured here are, from left to right, (first row) Norma Jean Hostert, Mildred Fair, Lois Hudson, and Carol Stermer; (second row) Donald Helenhouse, Robert Merrick, Charles Holm, Bill McGregor, and Lester Oakley.

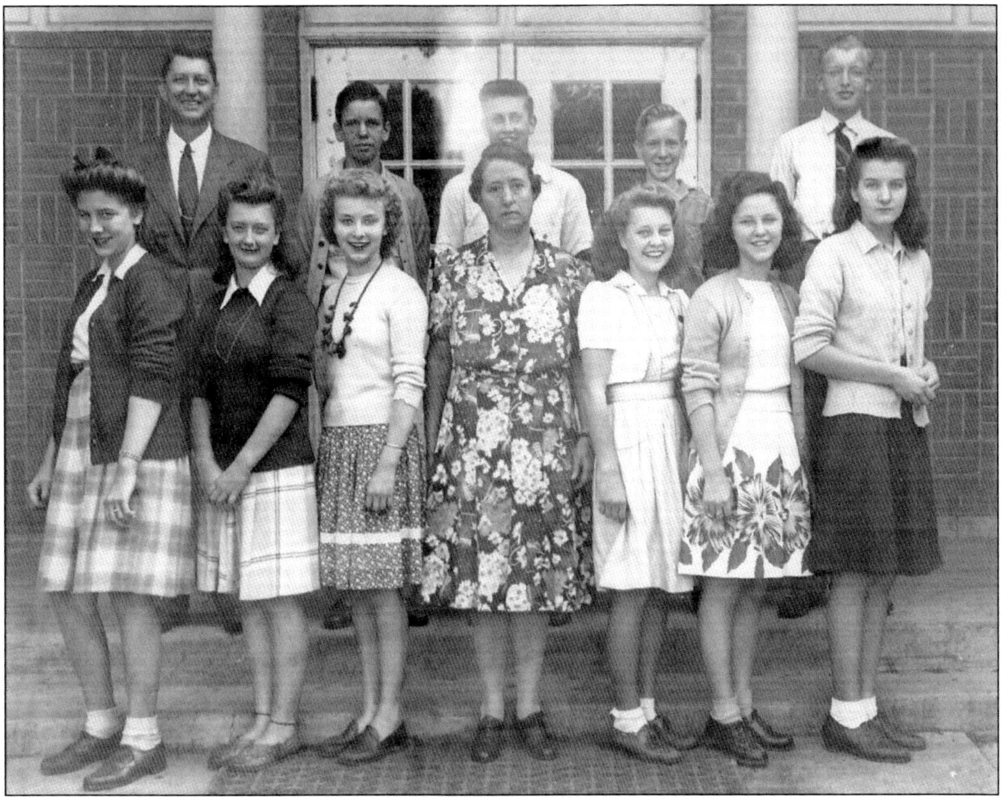

Shown here at the main entrance to the Carpenter Street School during the 1943–1944 school year is the last sophomore class of Moken'as two-year high school program. The students and teachers are, from left to right, (first row) Doris Spiess, Patricia Bennett, Carol Reihn, Mrs. Knader, Marion Sizer, Donna Bueschel, and Harriet Calder; (second row) Principal Dunn, Andrew Bueschel, Frank Sizer, Walter Olson, and Irvin Holm.

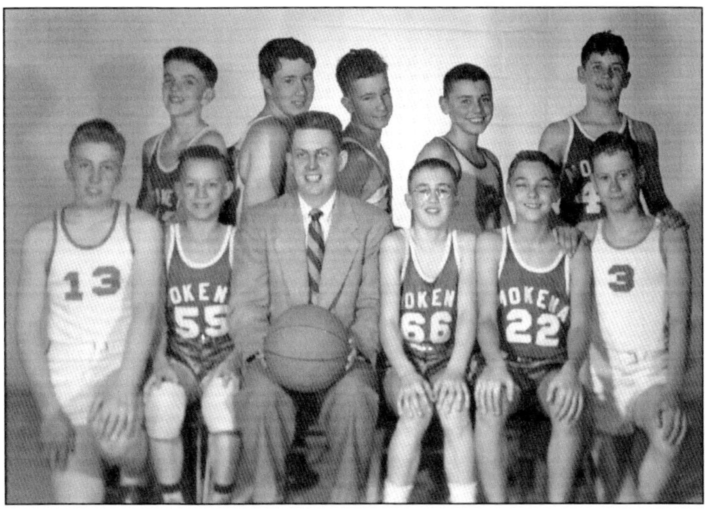

This 1954–1955 Mokena Meteors boys' basketball team won a spirited March 1955 game against the Mokena school board. Shown here are, from left to right, (first row) John Lavezzi, Allen Schuldt, coach Herbert Wrath, Joe Kruzich, Douglas Porick, and Anthony Dina; (second row) Billy Sayers, Ronald Daugherty, Louis Johnson, Lee Yunker, and Jerry Haehnlein.

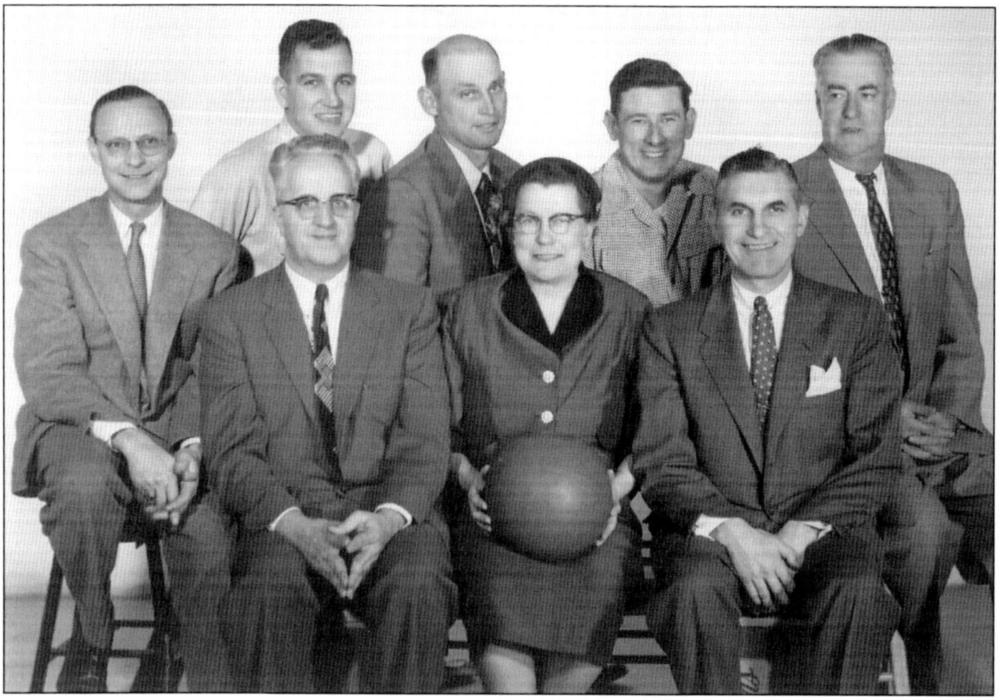

Composed of school board members, this basketball team challenged the Mokena Meteors to a lighthearted match at Mokena Public School on March 19, 1955. Fashioning themselves the Vagabonds, they are seen here in a contemporary photograph. The Vagabonds are, from left to right, (first row) Lyman Teague, Elizabeth Cappel, and Tom Powers; (second row) Robert Geuther, Hans Mueller, Edwin Yunker, Gordon Bruce, and John Scarth.

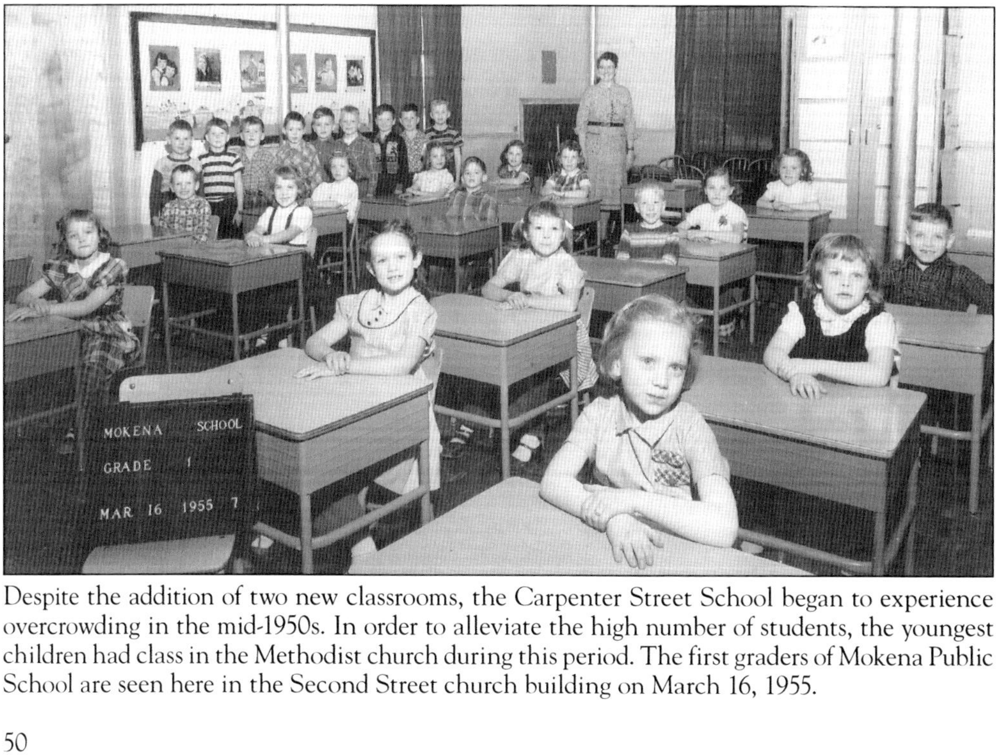

Despite the addition of two new classrooms, the Carpenter Street School began to experience overcrowding in the mid-1950s. In order to alleviate the high number of students, the youngest children had class in the Methodist church during this period. The first graders of Mokena Public School are seen here in the Second Street church building on March 16, 1955.

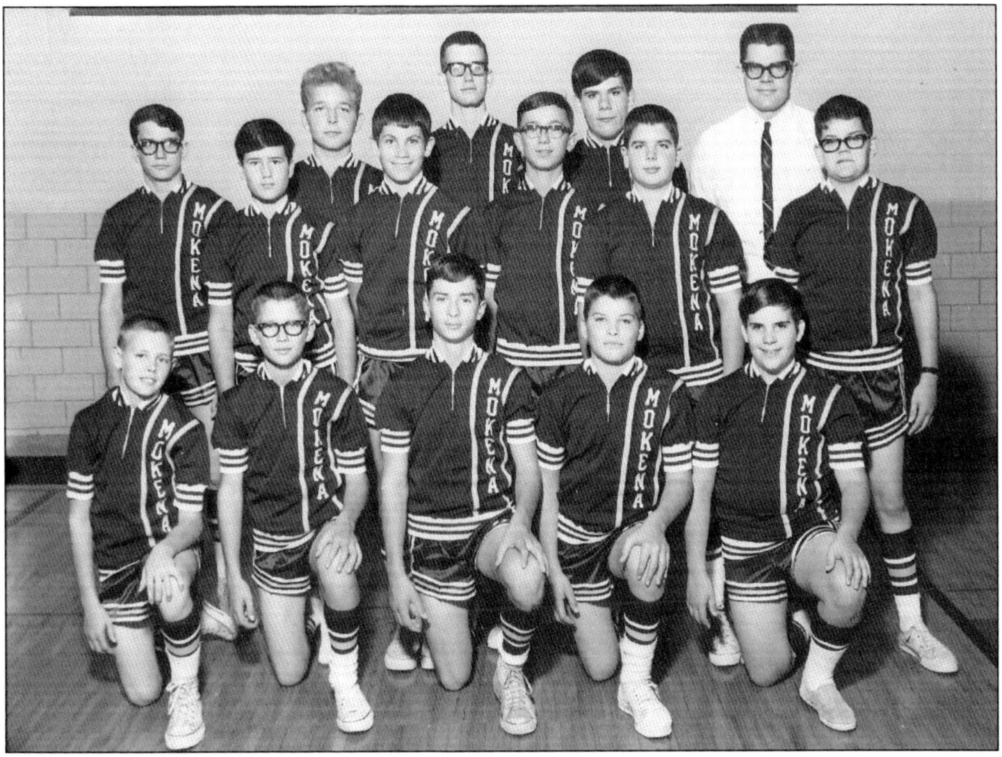

By the end of the 1968 basketball season, the eighth-grade Mokena team had achieved a perfect winning record of 23-0 and emerged victorious from two major tournaments. The winning team is shown here around April 1968, with coach Richard T. Quinn at top right. Quinn would go on to serve as mayor from 1981 to 1983.

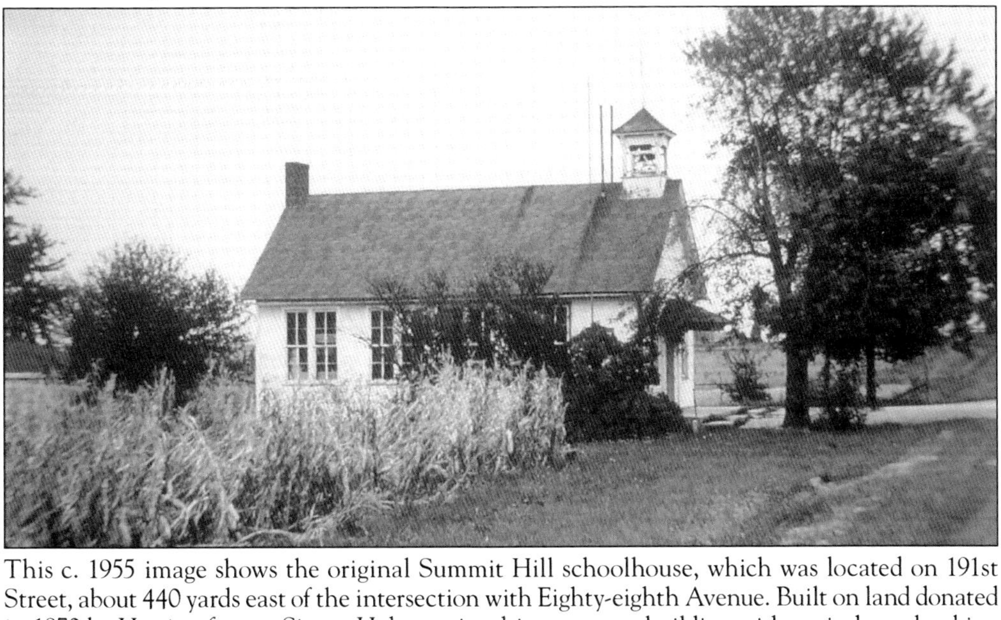

This c. 1955 image shows the original Summit Hill schoolhouse, which was located on 191st Street, about 440 yards east of the intersection with Eighty-eighth Avenue. Built on land donated in 1870 by Hessian farmer Simon Hohenstein, this one-room building with no indoor plumbing was used by generations of farm children until being abandoned around 1960.

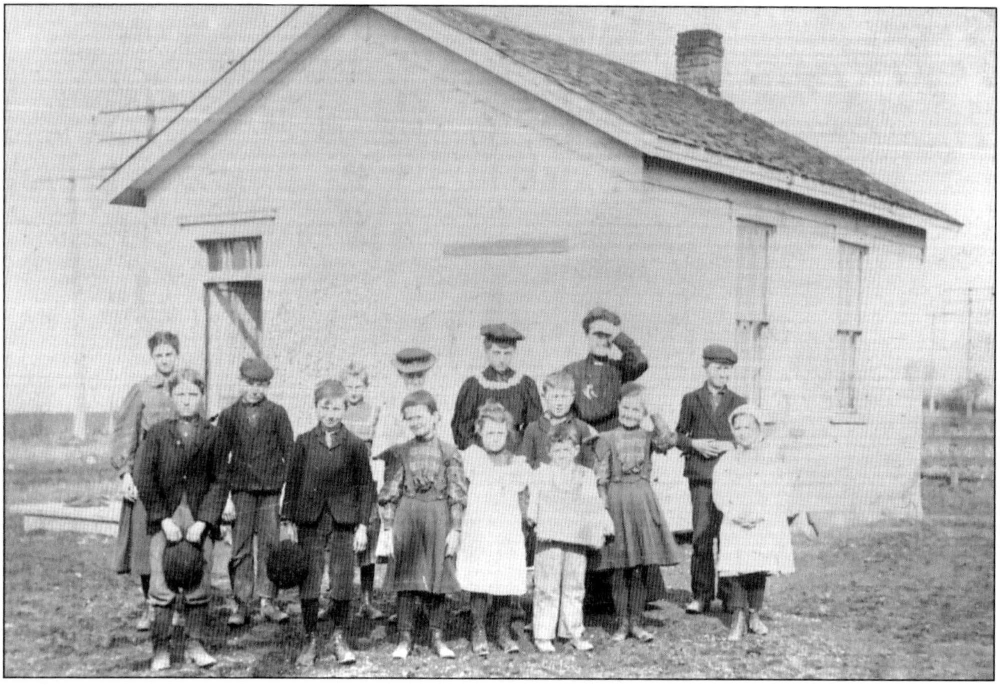

Built in 1861 at the southeast corner of Wolf Road and 187th Street, this tiny schoolhouse north of Mokena was known as the Marti School. Housing small classes for many years, the old building was sold to Walter Haas for $77 in 1934, at which time the students from this rural district then attended school within the village. This photograph, taken around 1906, shows teacher Alma Mast (shielding her eyes) with her class.

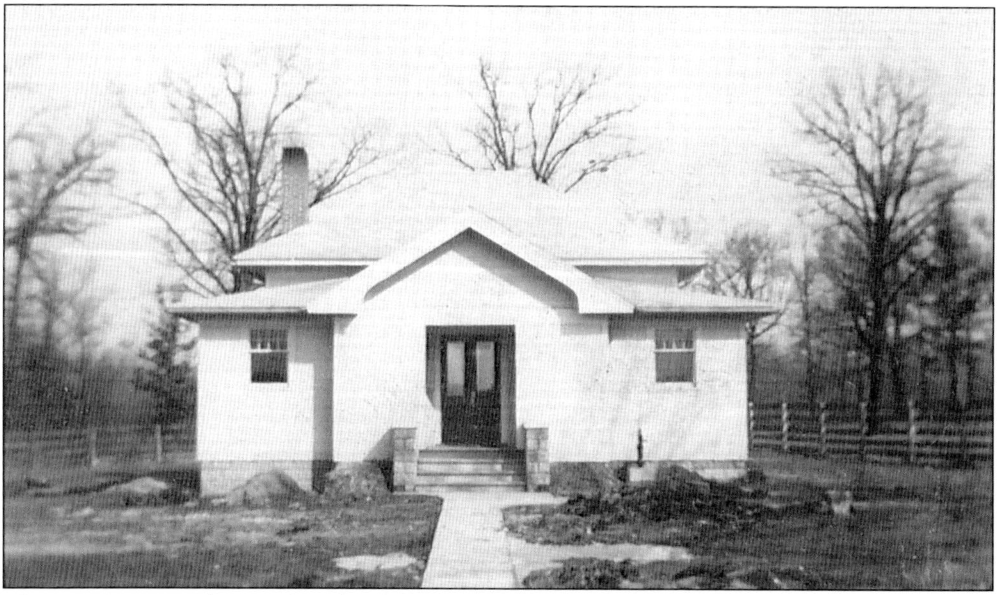

This c. 1930 image depicts the Cleveland School, which stood at the present-day intersection of Route 30 and Wolf Road. This school was named for the Cleveland family, who lived on a farm a few yards west of this location. Originally designated as District 1, this district, although shown here in a later iteration, was the oldest in Frankfort Township until it disbanded in 1943.

Three

A Symbol of Spiritual Fact

Religious institutions have often been the common root from which many American communities have grown. In the days of the pioneers, before Mokena was established, a group of German Lutheran farmers and their families worshipped in a small frame church on the property of Johann Georg Geuther. Located on the present-day St. Francis Road, this group called themselves the German Evangelical Lutheran Immanuel congregation and was formally established in November 1850. Not long after this formation, a division in the group erupted and several members severed ties.

By 1858, the newer collection of the evangelic faithful was meeting in the Mokena schoolhouse and, after forming a constitution in March 1862, was known as the German United Evangelical St. John's Church. Construction began on a quaint church on the Public Square; bounded by Second Street, Union Street, and Third Street, the Public Square was set aside by Allen Denny in 1855 as a space for churches and schools. In 1923, the St. John's congregation constructed a magnificent new church that is still in use to this day.

After the 1850s schism, the Lutheran Immanuel flock initially stayed at their location before moving to Mokena generations later, in 1916. The oldest religious organization in Mokena, it has truly survived the test of time. After Prussian immigrant Matthias Enders donated a tract of land near Wolf Road to the Chicago Archdiocese, the local Catholic congregation was formed. Founded in 1864 as St. Mary's German Catholic Church, this assembly has since become one of the Chicago suburbs' foremost Catholic parishes.

Not to be forgotten, Mokena's Methodist Episcopal Church can trace its beginnings to 1866, and within the next year, they constructed their own church on the Public Square. Along with a small local Baptist assemblage that seems to have disbanded around 1900, these worshippers differed from their neighbors in that they were generally of American origin. From these humble beginnings, Mokena's churches have transcended the ages to stand for solid living.

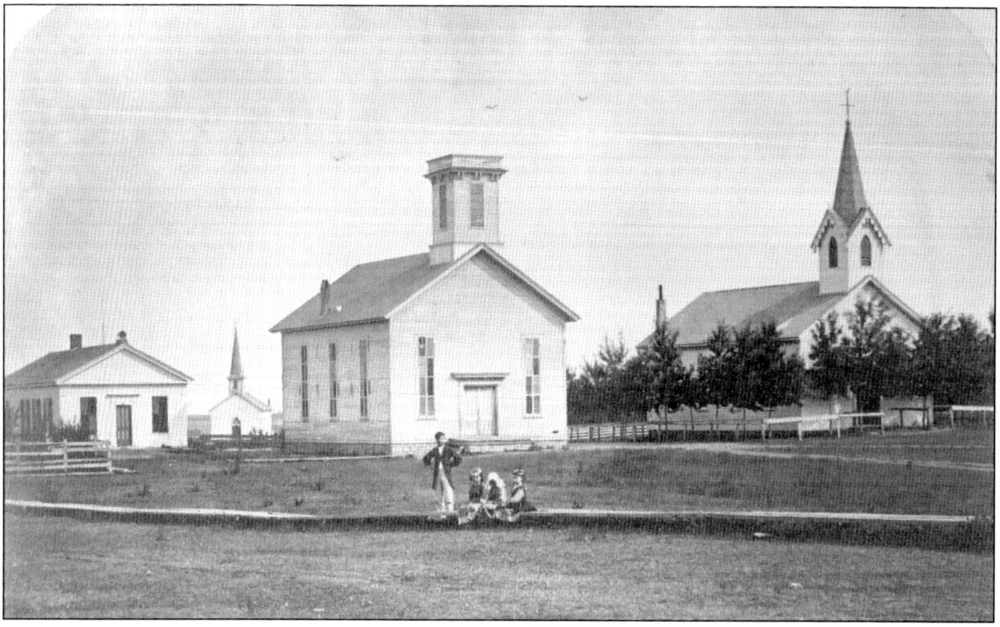

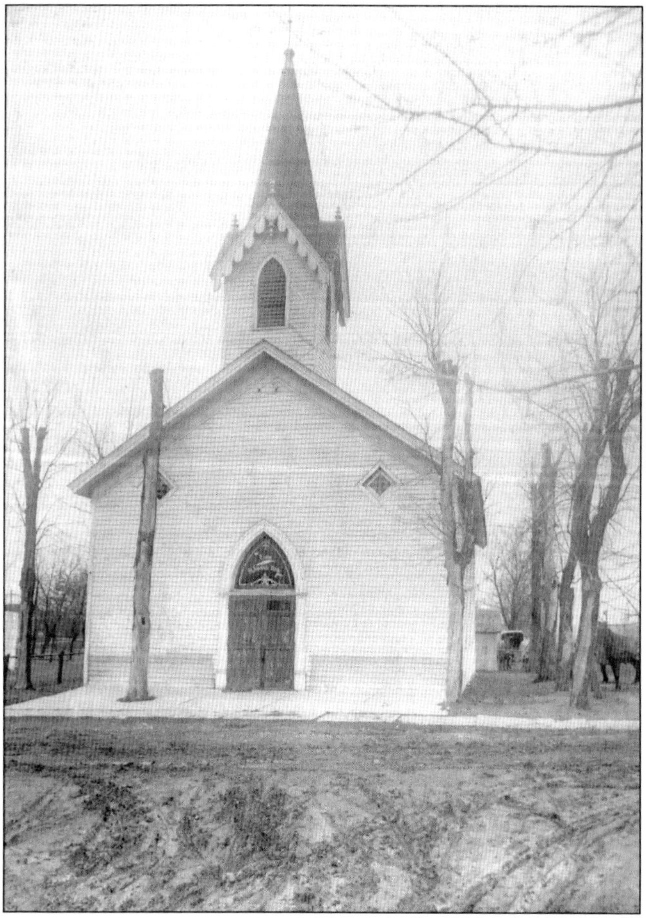

Taken around 1870, this is the oldest known photograph of Mokena. Facing north from the photographer's standpoint at roughly Mokena and First Streets, from left, a viewer can see the village's first schoolhouse, St. Mary's German Catholic Church, the Methodist Episcopal Church, and the German United Evangelical St. John's Church. Note the plank sidewalk in the foreground.

Originally formed in March 1862 as the German United Evangelical St. John's Church under the guidance of Rev. William Meyer, this congregation traces its beginnings to 1851, when a group of local Germanic citizens broke ties with nearby Lutheran worshippers. Having built their first church in 1862 on the northwest corner of Second and Union Streets, the structure is seen here c. 1910.

Much of St. John's early growth can be attributed to Rev. Carl Schaub. Born in 1843 in Ramlinsburg, Switzerland, Schaub took over pastoral duties at St. John's in 1873 and led the flock until his retirement in 1907. A deeply pious man who held his congregation as near as his own family, Schaub was known to venture miles into the surrounding countryside to visit an ill parishioner.

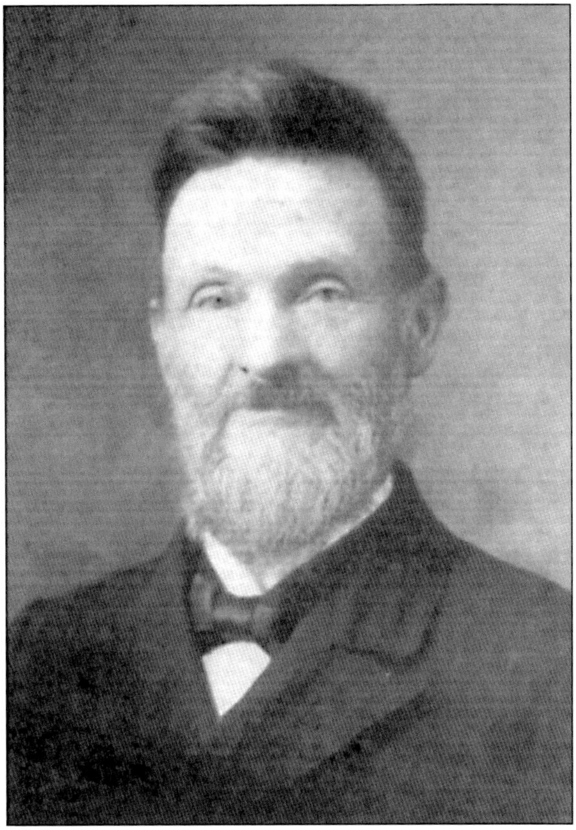

A vintage interior view of the St. John's church at Second and Union Streets is pictured below. Dedicated in September 1862, this structure cost $1,500 to construct and was built by church members. Reflecting the heritage of parishioners, services were conducted entirely in German until 1907. In 1925, local brothers Milton and Roy Kropp moved the old church to the southwest corner of Division and First Streets and converted it to duplex housing.

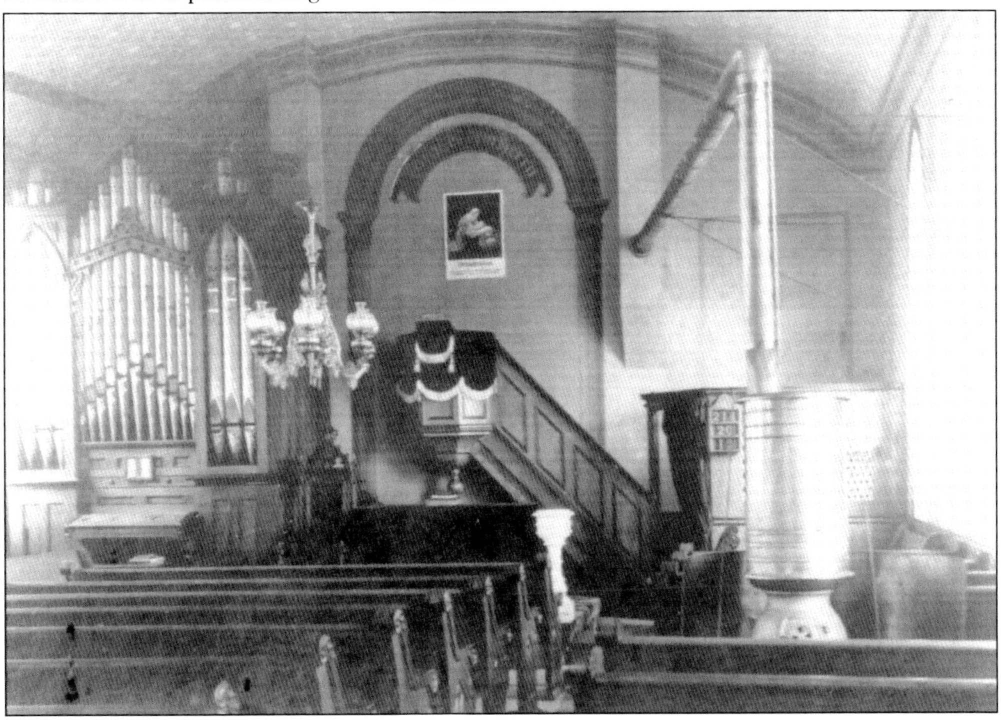

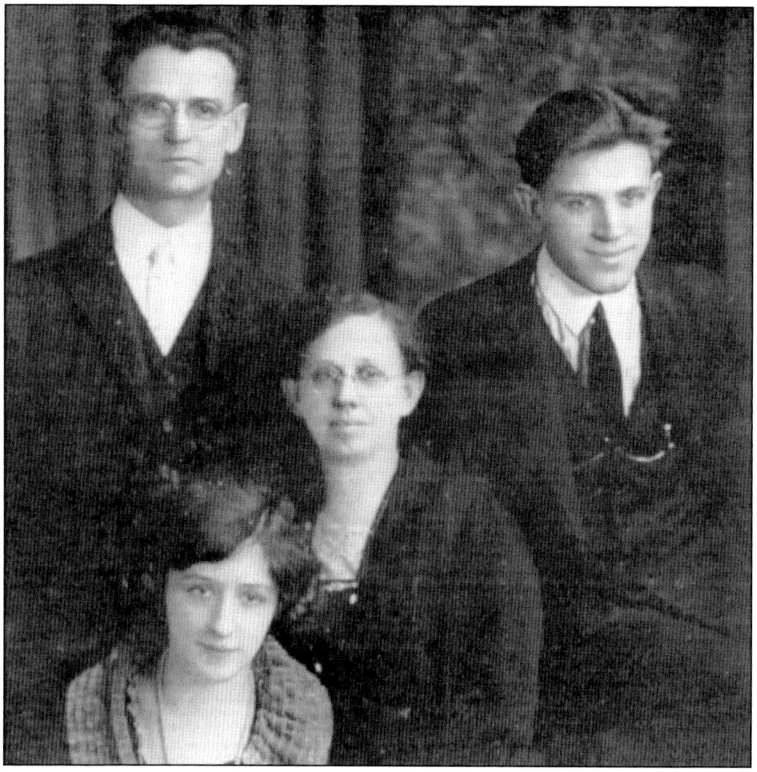

The family of Rev. William Kreis (top left) is shown here around 1923. A native of Germany, Kreis immigrated to America in 1895 and came to Mokena in 1917 to assume religious duties at St. John's church. A friendly and much-beloved spiritual guide, Reverend Kreis's legacy in Mokena was the construction of the new church edifice in 1922. Also pictured are, from left to right, daughter Elfriede Kreis, Marie (Freytag) Kreis, and son Arthur Kreis.

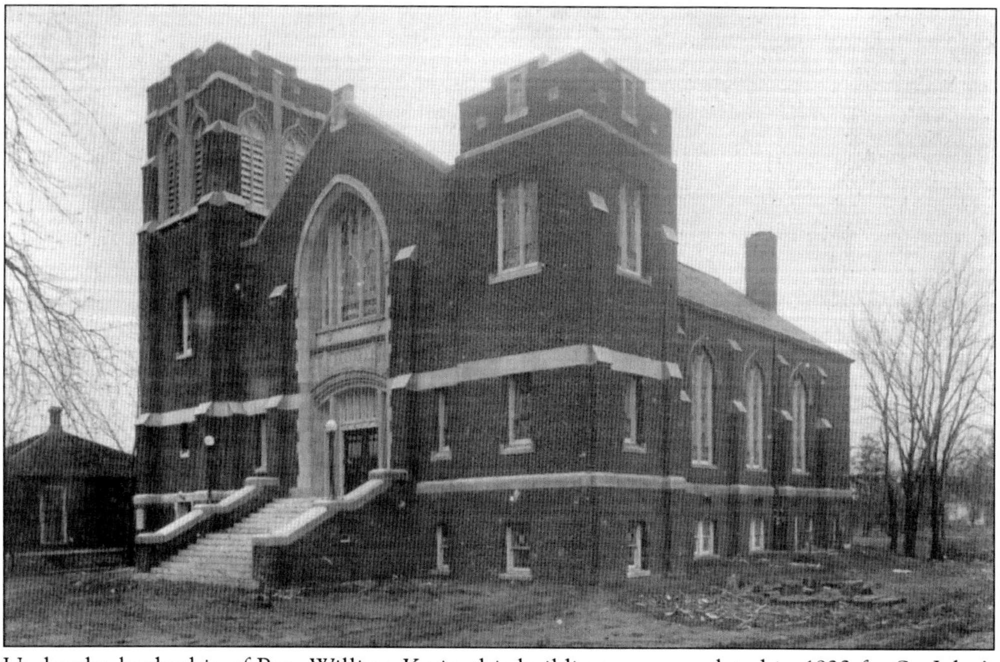

Under the leadership of Rev. William Kreis, this building was completed in 1923 for St. John's German Evangelical Church. Built on the old Noble Jones property on Second Street after three years of planning, the new church's dedication was one of the largest events to occur in Mokena. The church's magnificent English Gothic architecture stands triumphant to this day.

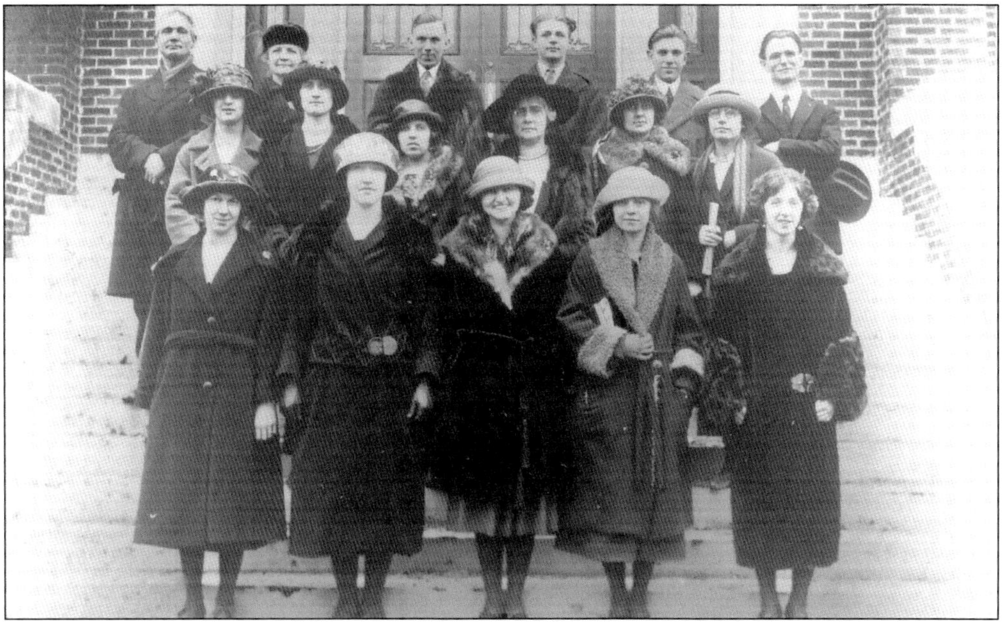

The Sunday school officers of St. John's pose at the new church in 1923. Pictured here are, from left to right, (first row) Laura Eggers, Edna Spiess, Olive Geuther, Wanita Oswald, and Elfriede Kreis; (second row) Florence Shevlin, two unidentified individuals, Rose Bechstein, Edna Bechstein, and Clara Woodrich; (third row) William Yunker, Helen Scheer, Roy Kropp, unidentified, Arthur Kreis, and Rev. William Kreis.

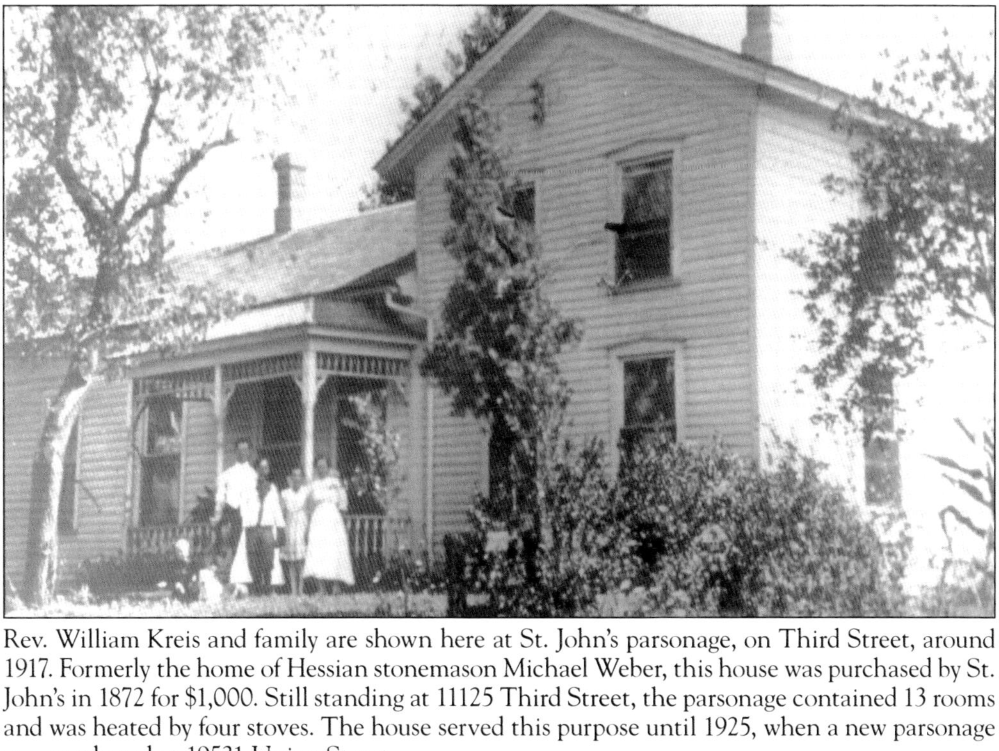

Rev. William Kreis and family are shown here at St. John's parsonage, on Third Street, around 1917. Formerly the home of Hessian stonemason Michael Weber, this house was purchased by St. John's in 1872 for $1,000. Still standing at 11125 Third Street, the parsonage contained 13 rooms and was heated by four stoves. The house served this purpose until 1925, when a new parsonage was purchased at 19531 Union Street.

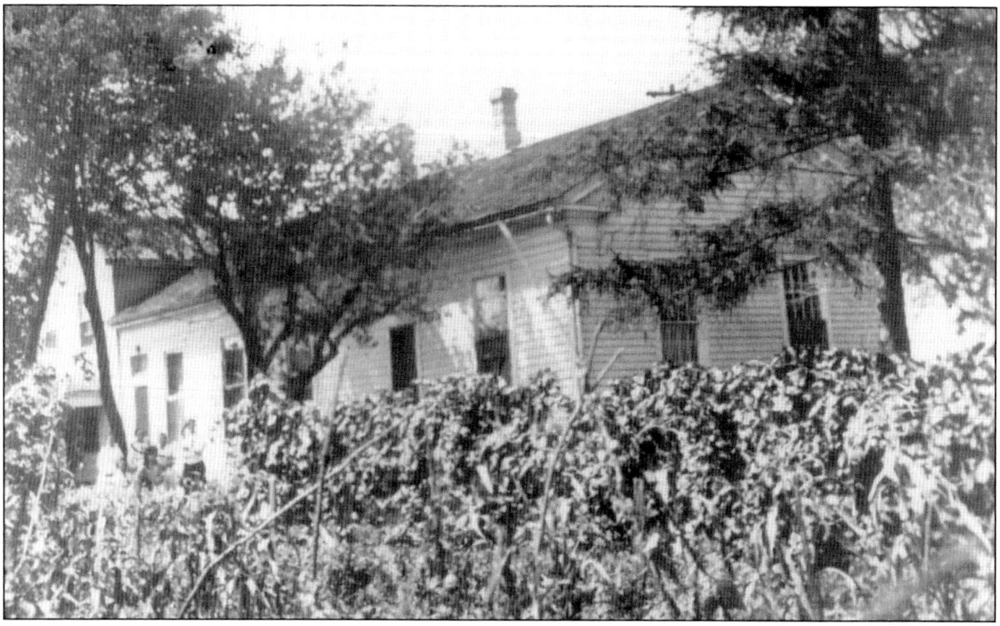

St. John's parsonage is depicted about 1917 with the viewer facing westward. Prominent on the image's right is the parsonage's eastern wing; it served as Mokena's first schoolhouse, originally built a few yards south of this location in 1855. Moved and attached to the parsonage in 1877, the old schoolhouse was used alternately for German language instruction, the pastor's study, choir rehearsal space, and a Sunday school. The old school was detached around 1926.

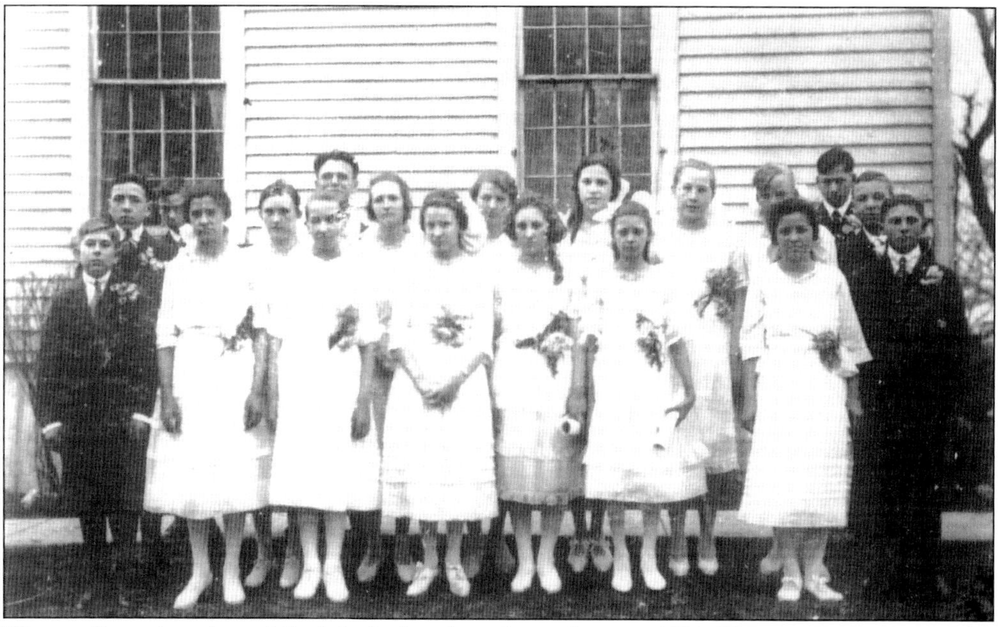

The confirmation class of St. John's church is shown here in 1921. They are, in no particular order, Philip Hacker, Clarence Groth, Henry Weiland, Elizabeth Heines, Elda Schenkel, Laura Eggers, Reverend Kreis, Alma Yunker, Lydia Bettenhausen, Lucille Hinspeter, Mable Schoeneck, Julia Hirsch, Ruby Oswald, Alice Lorenz, Florence Warning, Margaret Maue, Walter Groth, Ben Yunker, and Elmer Cappel.

Two unidentified people share a fun-spirited moment at the old entrance to St. John's Cemetery on Wolf Road. Originally composed of five acres in the southernmost area of the current cemetery, this land was purchased by St. John's in 1863. Bavarian-born Philippine Laufer was the first known burial in May of that year, although a handful of graves date to the late 1850s. Numerous German-language monuments in the cemetery silently attest to Mokena's past.

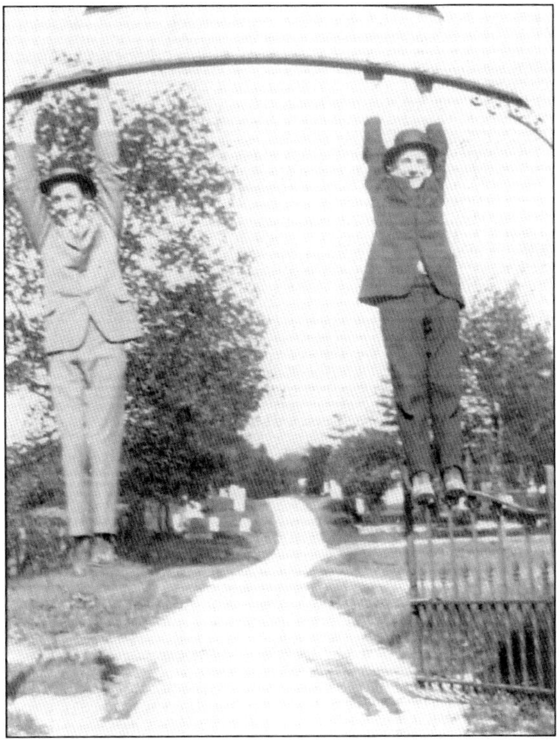

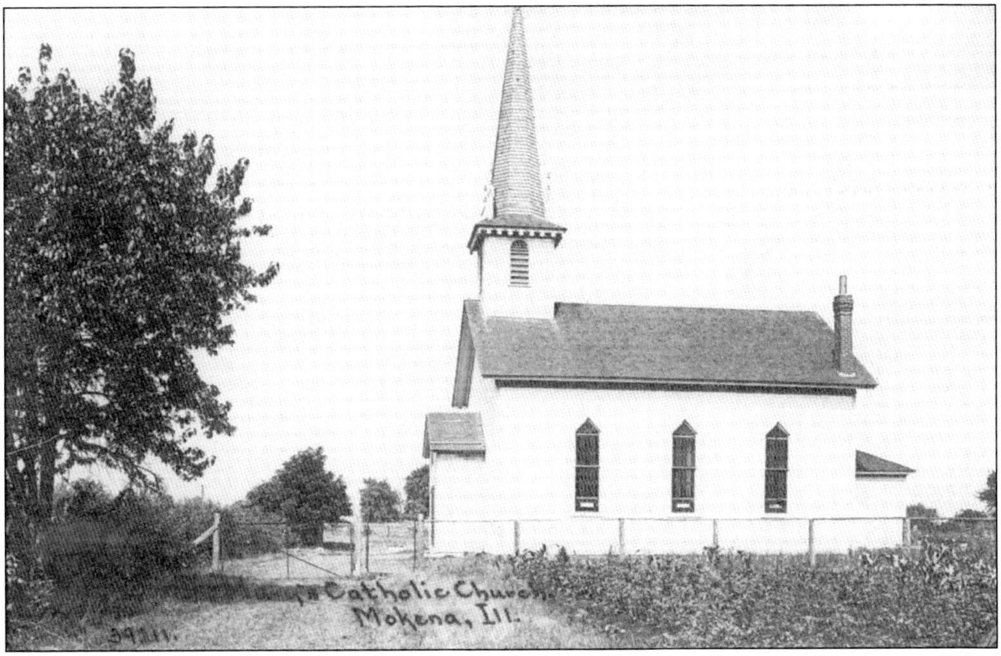

Founded in 1864 by nine Catholic families, St. Mary's German Catholic Church—the smallest Catholic congregation in Will County—was built the same year by Bernhard Folman, a local carpenter and parish member. Shortly thereafter, the church's adjoining cemetery was founded upon a plot of land donated by Matthias Enders and Johann Schmidt. Services were originally held here every other Sunday.

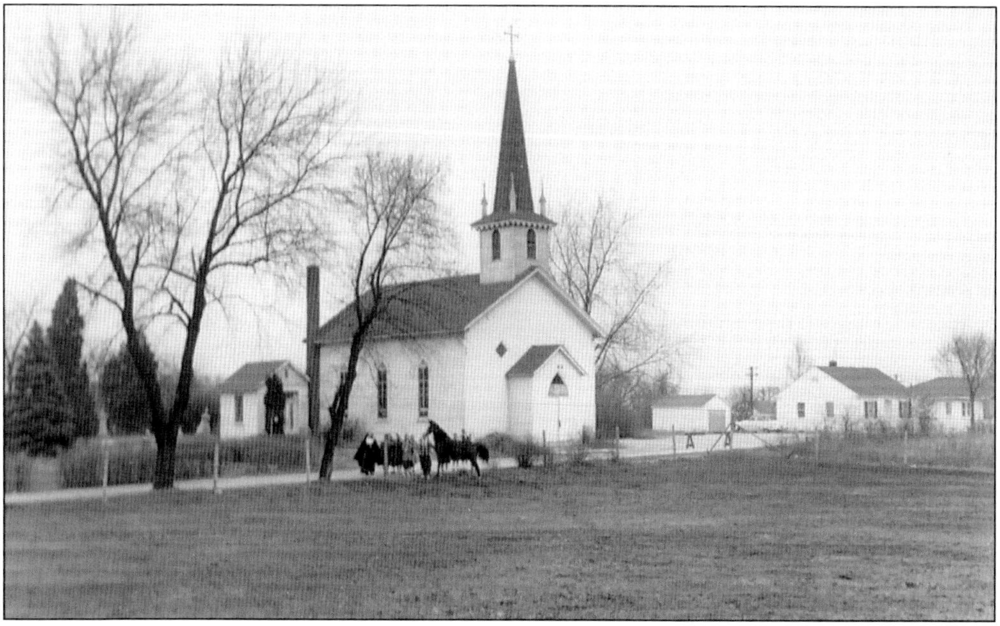

Still standing on Koop Lane (named for St. Mary's first resident priest, Fr. Cecil Koop), St. Mary's Church has become one of Mokena's most distinguished historical landmarks. Slightly damaged in 1921 during what may have been a small tornado and struck by lightning two years later, this edifice was in regular use until the 1950s. The tides of time wore strongly on the church until 1976, when it was lovingly restored.

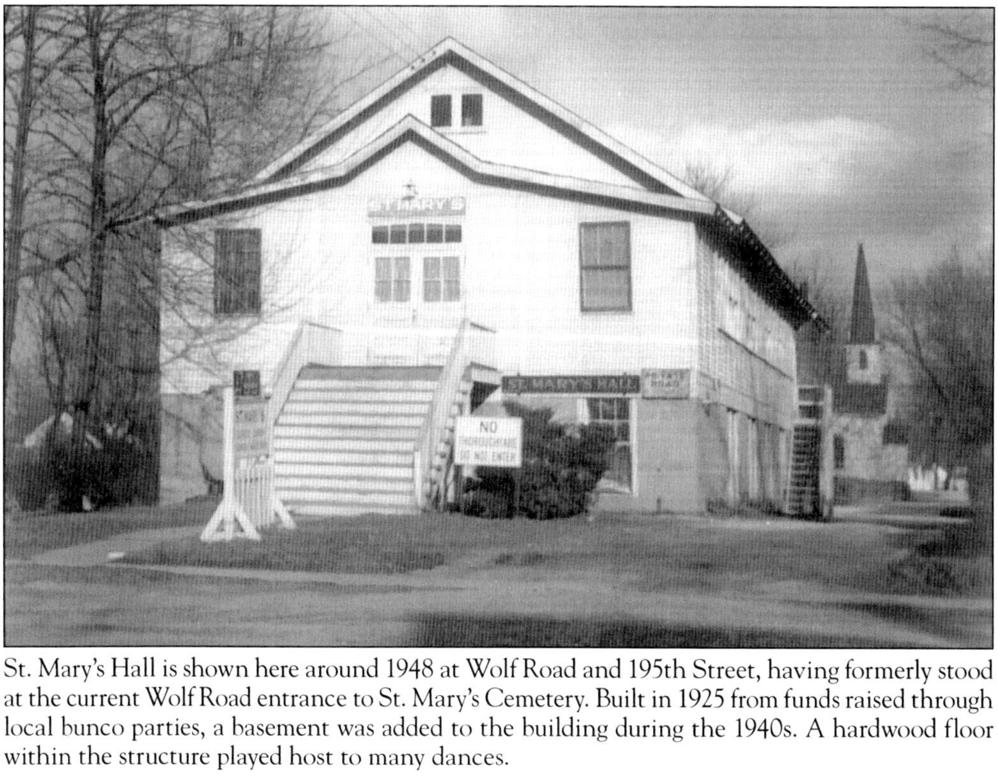

St. Mary's Hall is shown here around 1948 at Wolf Road and 195th Street, having formerly stood at the current Wolf Road entrance to St. Mary's Cemetery. Built in 1925 from funds raised through local bunco parties, a basement was added to the building during the 1940s. A hardwood floor within the structure played host to many dances.

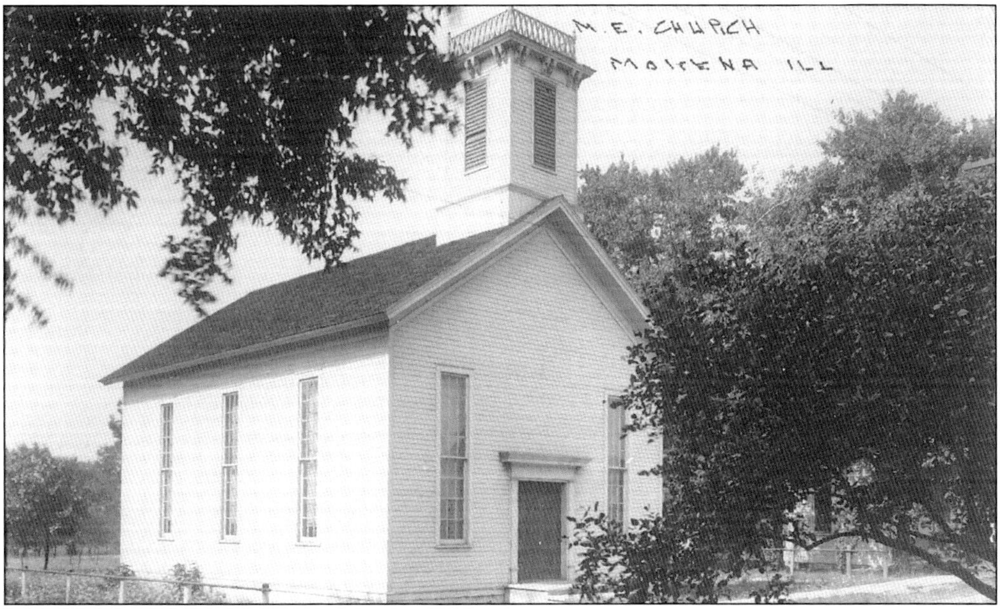

Since its organization in 1866, the Mokena United Methodist Church has long been a part of village life. Seen here about 1915 and known originally as the Methodist Episcopal Church, this building on Second Street was dedicated on December 15, 1867. According to legend, the sale of a stray horse provided the funds to construct this church. Every other Sunday, the local Baptist society worshipped here.

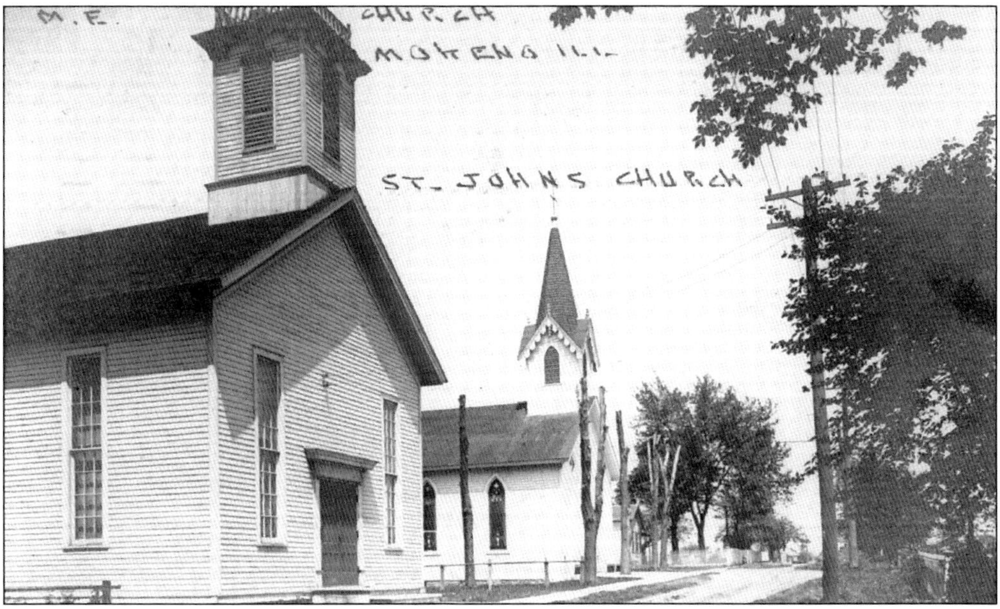

This 1920 postcard of Second Street depicts two of Mokena's churches. The Methodist church is prominent in the foreground, with St. John's church farther down the street. Having been shared with the small Baptist congregation, a lengthy dispute over ownership of the church building developed with the Methodists, and after an 1899 lawsuit, the Methodists were declared the lawful owners of the structure. St. John's Christian Community Center now stands at this site, 11046 Second Street.

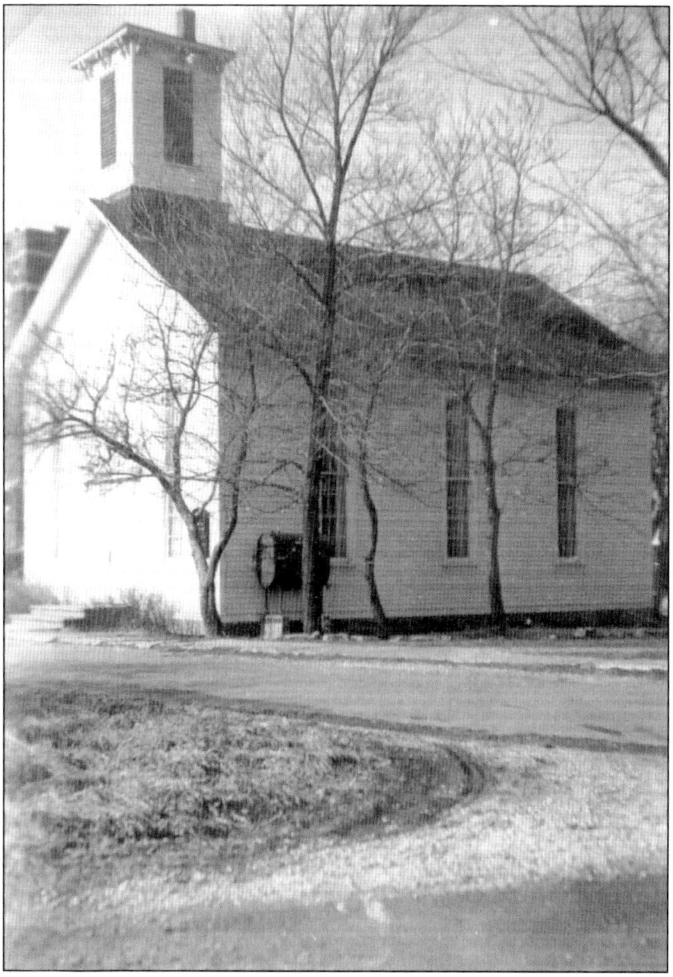

This image, taken around 1950, depicts the Methodist Episcopal Church shortly before the large addition of a new sanctuary on its eastern side. During the late 19th century, this church had its own resident pastor, something of a rarity for a community of such a small size. St. John's Christian Community Center at 11046 Second Street now stands at this site; this historic structure was demolished in 1999.

The new Immanuel Lutheran Church is seen here in 1917, facing west from the intersection of Cross and Union Streets. Established in 1850 near present-day Frankfort, this congregation relocated to Mokena in 1915 under the guidance of Rev. Elias Hieber. Within a year, this structure was completed. From 1967 until 1978, the village's first proper library was housed in this building's basement.

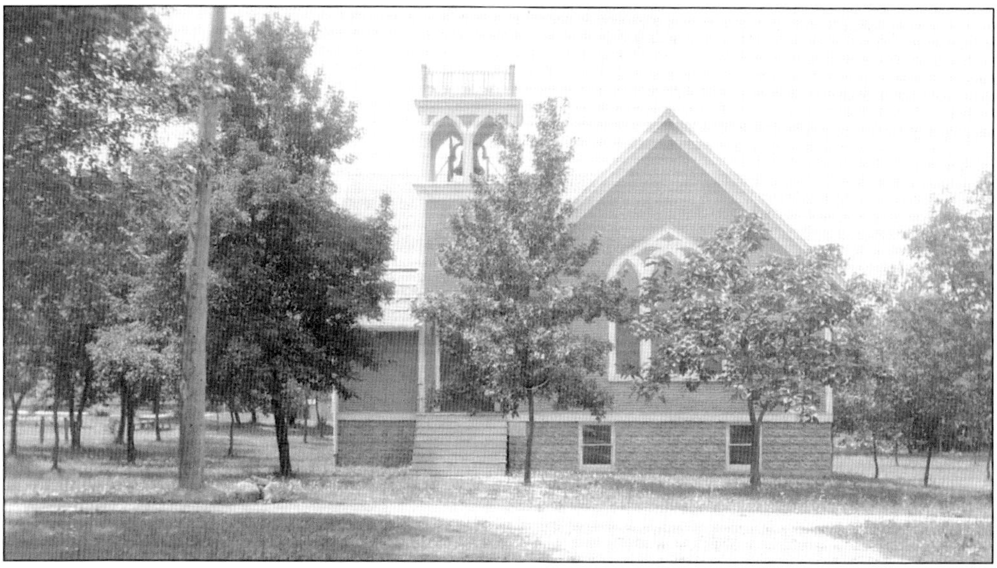

Four

Home Is Where the Heart Is

A home is more than simply a place to live. Be it a plain cottage or stately mansion, a home must be a sanctuary, a location where peace and harmony reign. Mokena has provided this to generations of residents for more than 150 years. The first home of frame construction that was built in the village was finished in 1853 by German hotelkeeper Carl Gall. Within several years, a carpenter of Luxembourgian origin named Bernhard Folman had settled in Mokena and completed many dwellings in this early period.

The simple utilitarian homes of early Mokena reflected the lives of Mokena's forefathers. Several log cabins of a much earlier, likely pre–Civil War style were allegedly incorporated into modern homes and are said to still remain in the inner portions of a few local houses. Even though no established architect seems to have designed any of Mokena's initial domiciles, prior to 1900, elements of the popular Greek Revival, Italianate, and Queen Anne styles were incorporated into contemporary homes.

The arrival of the stylish bungalow during the 20th century's interwar years presented a sharp difference in the appearance of Mokena's houses. As of this writing, at least a few structures still stand that are believed to be Sears catalog homes. After the end of World War II in 1945, development began on two new subdivisions that reflected the prosperity of the United States in this era. Located off Wolf Road to the northwest of the village and between Denny Avenue and LaPorte Road on the southern edge, Sunny Acres and Mineral Springs remain respectful and serene neighborhoods to this day.

The end of the 20th century was a time of prosperity for Mokena. After the construction of a staggering 24 new subdivisions during the 1990s, Mokena rose to prominence as the comfortable Chicago suburb that it is today. Here, the village motto—"Planned Progress and Pleasant Living"—proves its meaning.

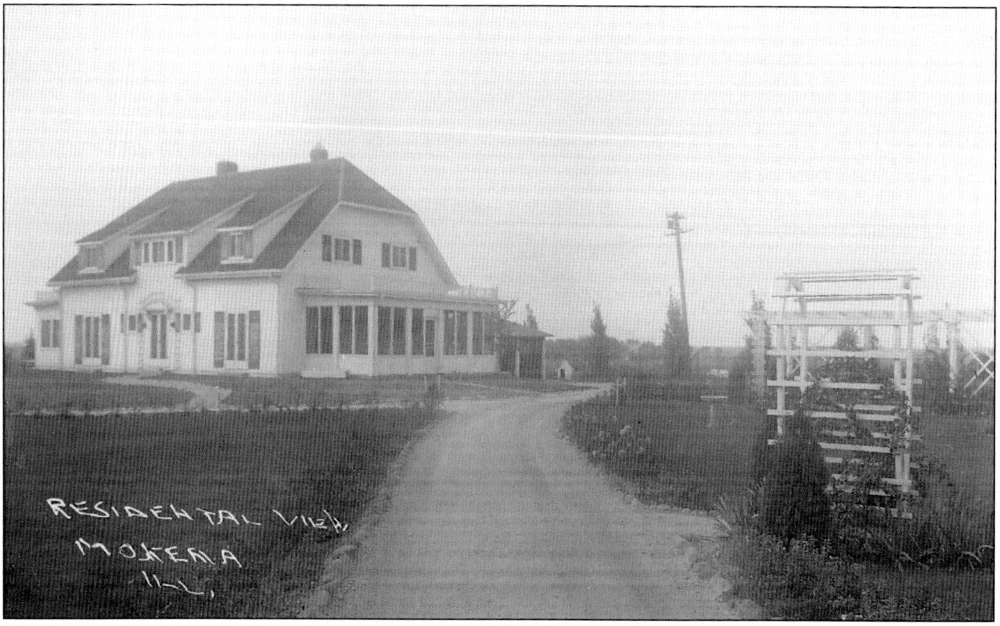

Constructed around 1930, this Parker Street residence remains one of Mokena's stateliest homes. Built for Chicago newspaper man F.A. Tooley, at one point this property boasted an in-ground pool near the southeast corner of today's Parker and Union Streets. In the early 1930s, around the time this photograph was likely taken, Parker Street was the northernmost street in the village.

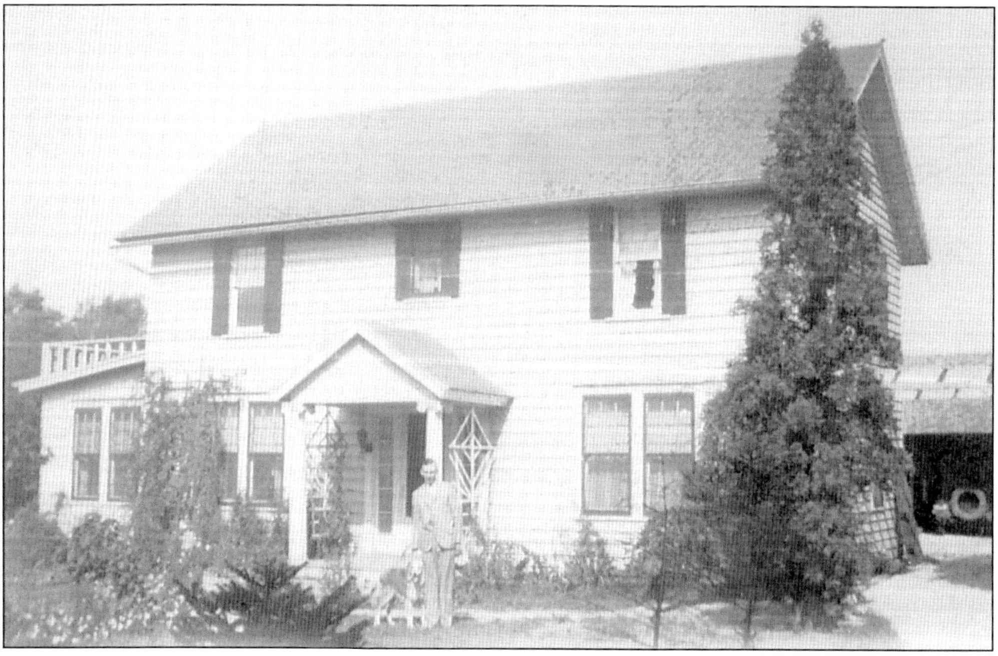

This home was built in 1925 for local newlyweds Roy and Elfriede (Kreis) Kropp. This picturesque house, which originally had a private tennis court to the west, is situated at the current 11132 Third Street. The home's aesthetic design was inspired by a contemporary dwelling in the Cherry Hill area of Joliet. Here, home owner Roy Kropp poses in front of his residence around 1930. (Photograph courtesy of David Kropp.)

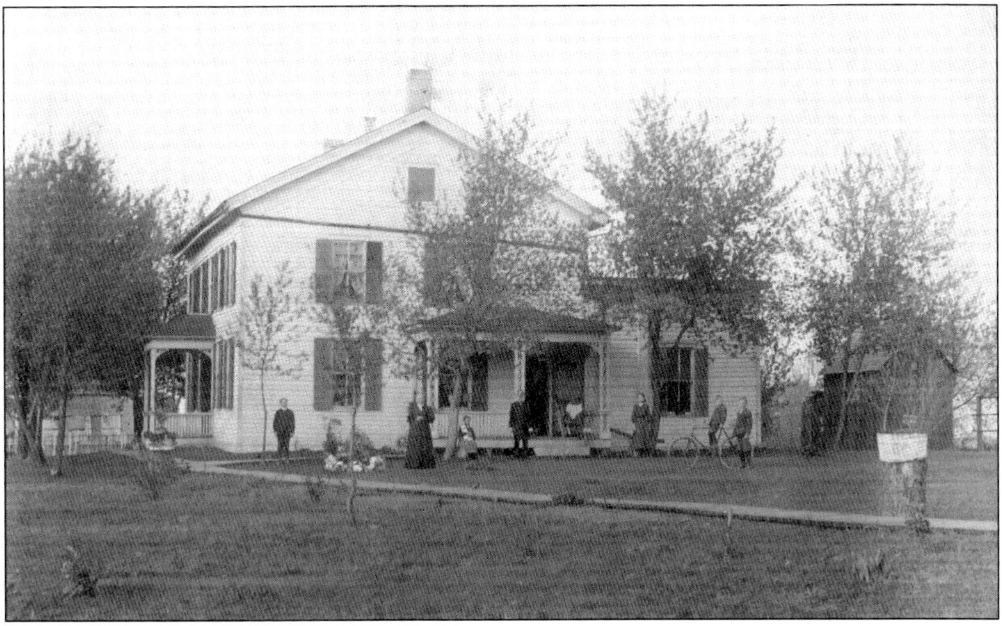

Built by early Mokena businessman James Ducker in the late 1850s, this home at 11122 Third Street is a beautiful representation of Greek Revival architecture, popular with affluent Mokena residents in the era before the Civil War. Rev. Carl Schaub moved his family to this house after his installation at St. John's church in 1873. Schaub's grandson Roy Kropp is seen on the bicycle in this image from around 1905.

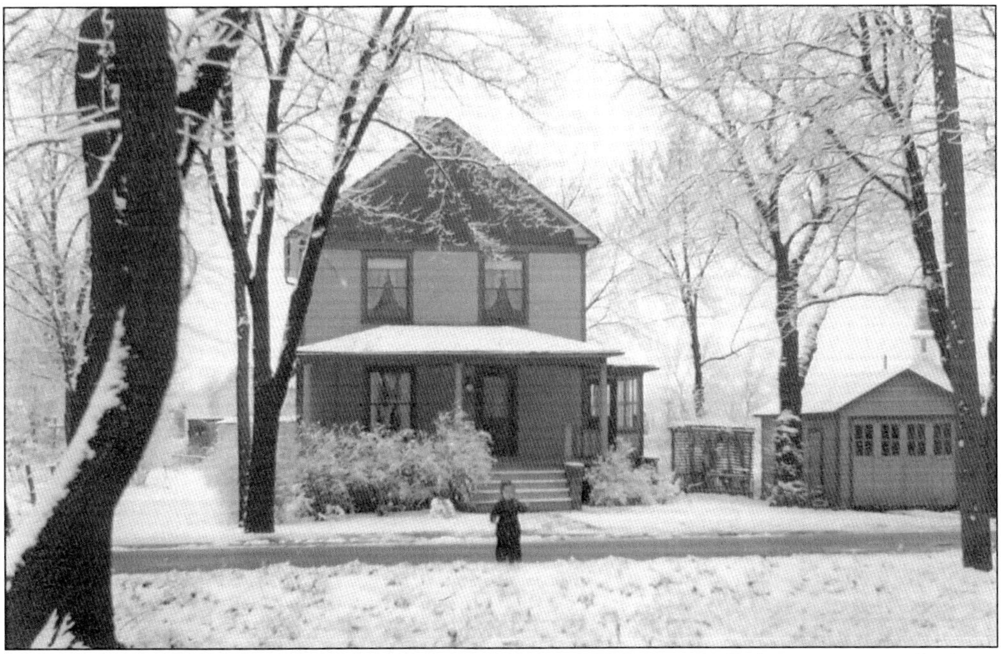

A wintry scene at 11110 Third Street is seen here around 1940. With the exception of a large addition to the north side of this home, this residence currently appears much as it did when this photograph was taken. Known in the 1920s as the Marks dwelling, this address is part of a large, spacious lot that is typical of neighboring homes on west Third Street.

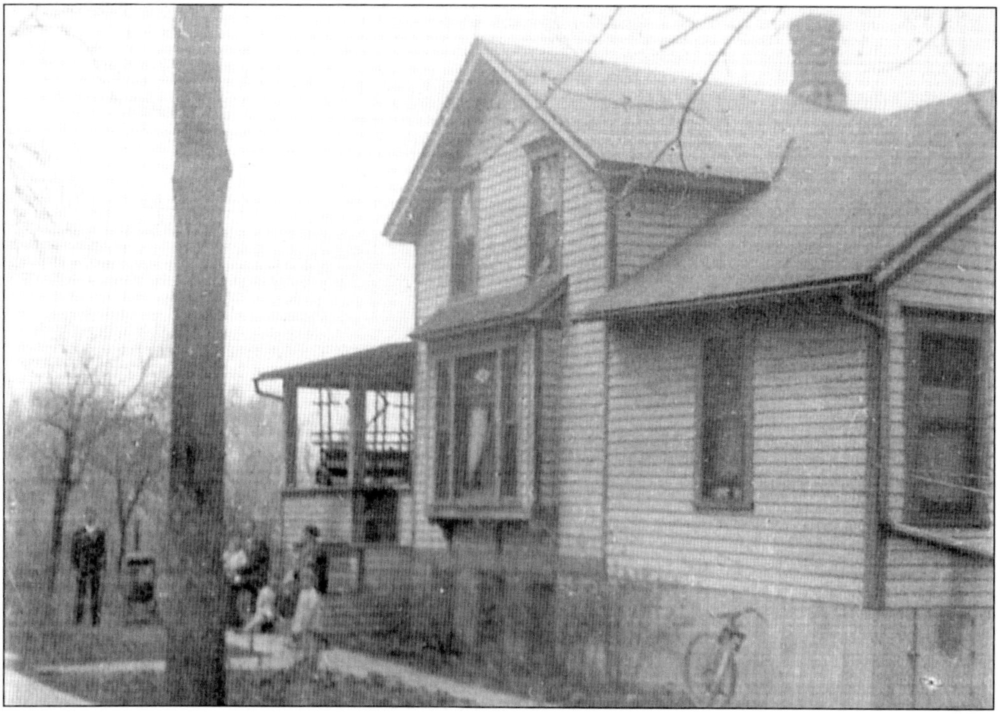

For decades, the former Walsh home has been a Mokena landmark. Standing today at 11042 Third Street, during the pre–World War II era, the choir of St. Mary's Church would occasionally rehearse here in winter months because the church was too cold. Visible here in the 1930s, attorney Arthur W. McGovney resided here in the early 20th century.

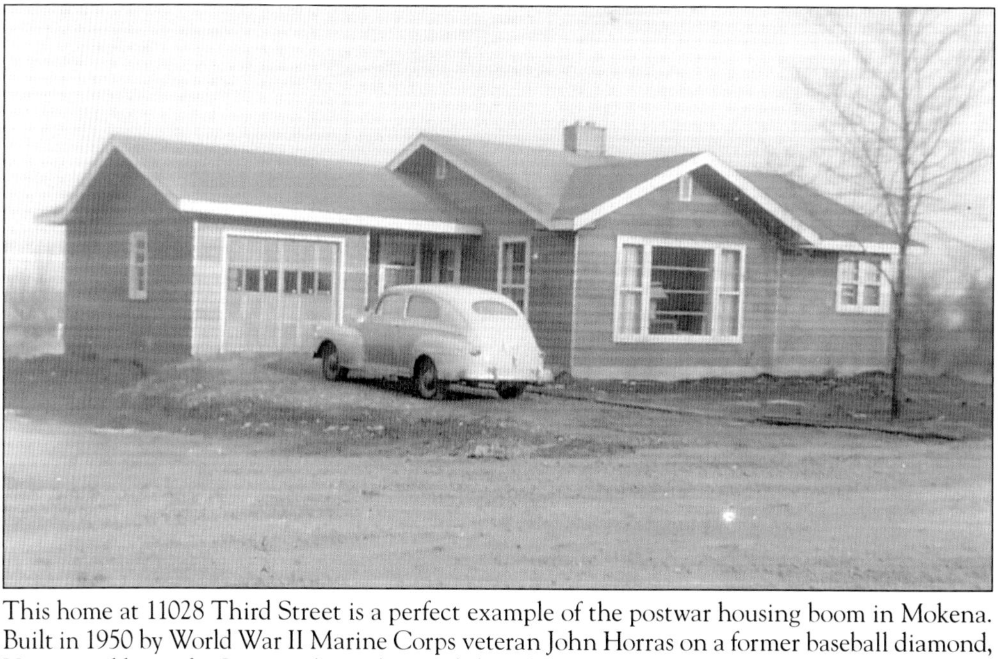

This home at 11028 Third Street is a perfect example of the postwar housing boom in Mokena. Built in 1950 by World War II Marine Corps veteran John Horras on a former baseball diamond, Horras and his wife, Corinne (Marti), raised their family here and later converted the garage at left into additional living space.

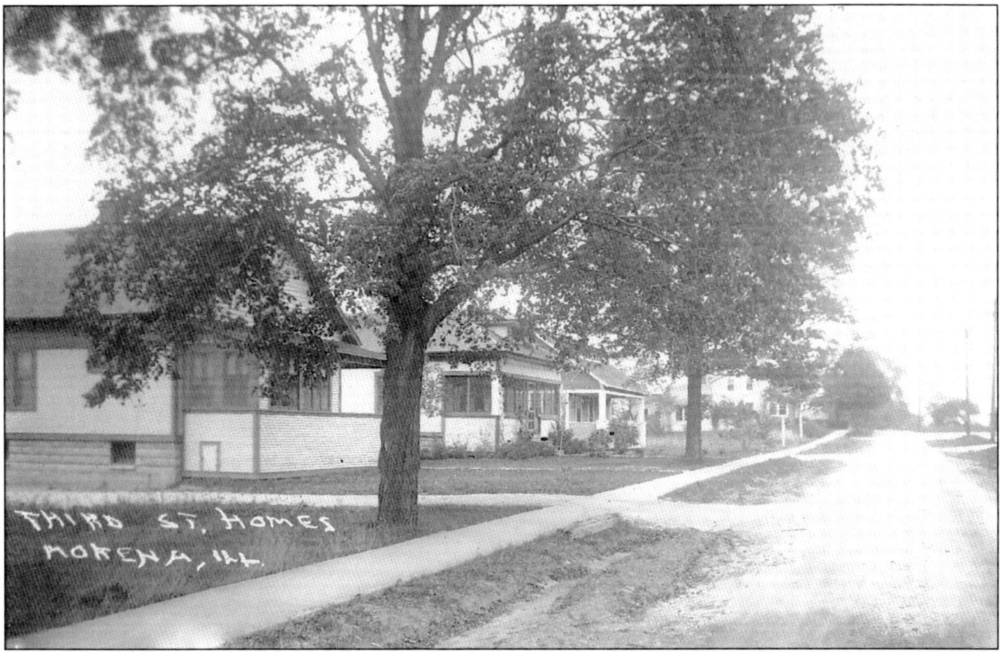

This section of Third Street was developed by local real estate man George Hacker in the 1920s. Looking east toward the intersection of Midland Avenue, at far left is the home of Harold Cooper, still standing at what is currently 11010 Third Street. In 1925, Hacker described this block to the *Mokena News-Bulletin* as containing "some of the choicest tracts in Mokena" and noted that they were "convenient to electric light."

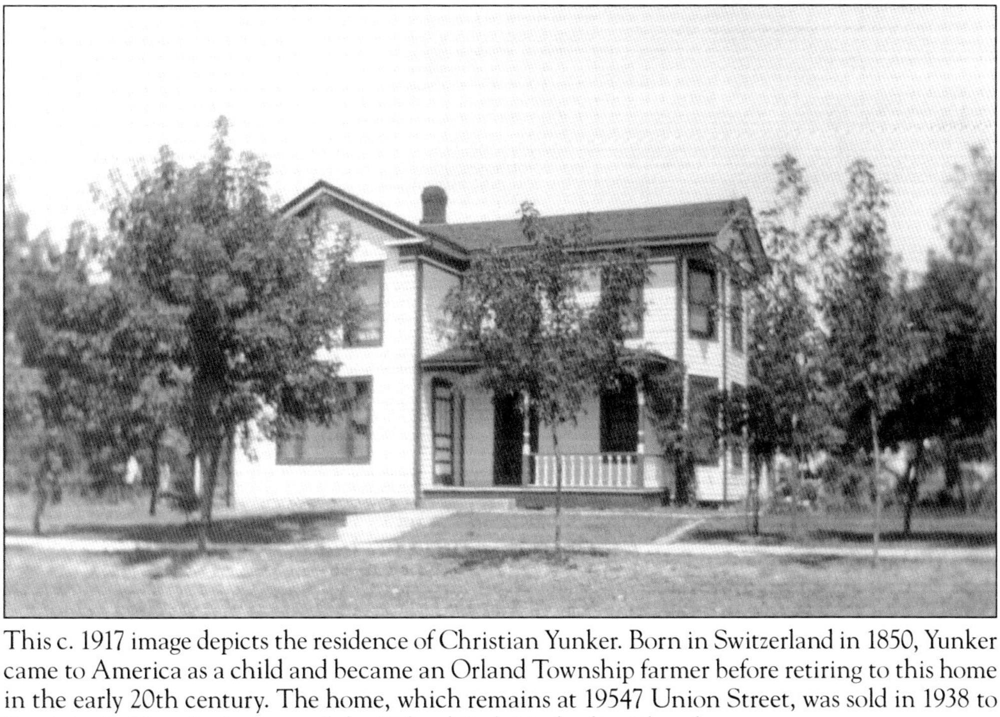

This c. 1917 image depicts the residence of Christian Yunker. Born in Switzerland in 1850, Yunker came to America as a child and became an Orland Township farmer before retiring to this home in the early 20th century. The home, which remains at 19547 Union Street, was sold in 1938 to Rev. Manly Mumford, pastor of the Orland Park Methodist Church.

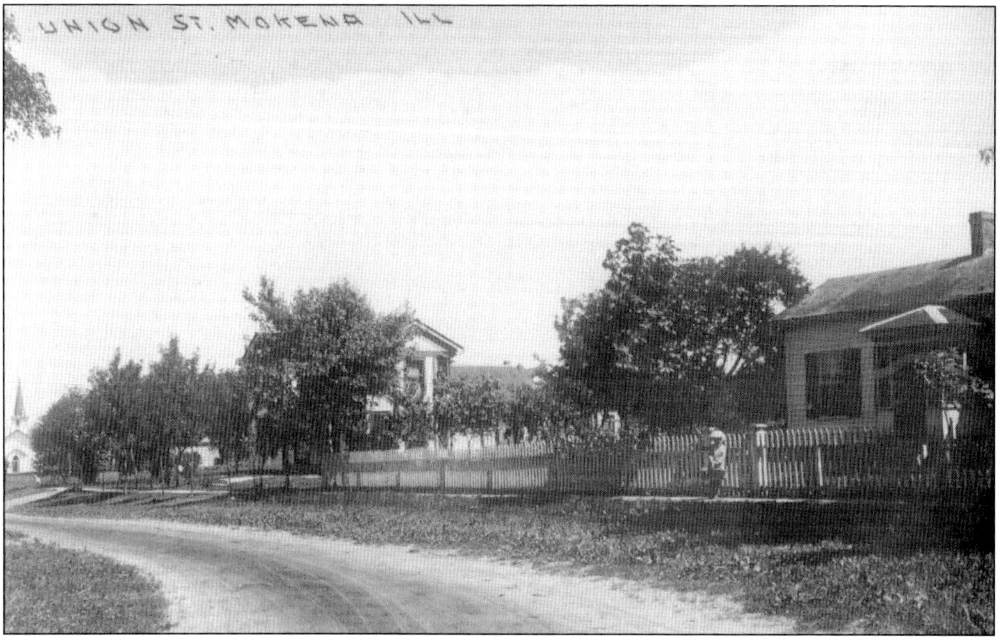

A rare c. 1910 postcard image of Union Street depicts it as nothing more than a winding path. Looking north from Second Street, the old cottage at right exemplifies the simple, utilitarian architecture of this region that was prevalent in the 19th century. St. Mary's German Catholic Church is visible in the background at left.

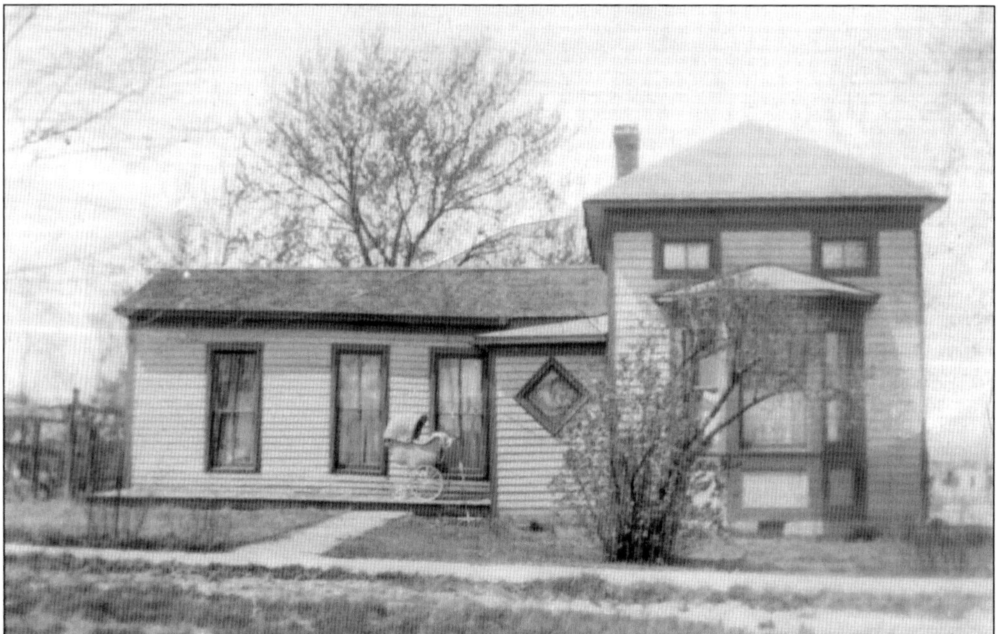

The western portion of this home at 11028 Cross Street is one of the oldest in Mokena, likely built prior to the Civil War. Within a few years of the war's end, it was inhabited by Francis Rook, a wounded veteran of the Union army. Pictured here around 1920, this house was inhabited at this time by the Roesner family.

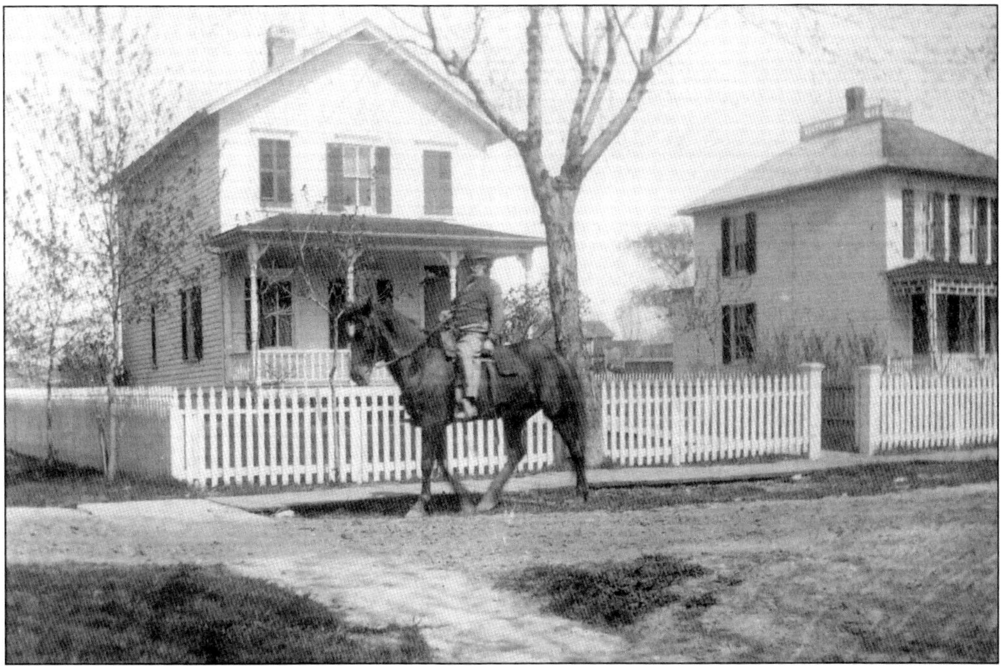

Local pioneer Charles Hirsch strikes an equestrian pose on Mokena Street around 1890. At left is the former Methodist parsonage, erected in 1873 at a cost of $1,000. The home at right was built in the same era for Clara Williams, one of the first teachers at the new Mokena Public School. Both homes still stand at 19617 and 19619 Mokena Street, respectively.

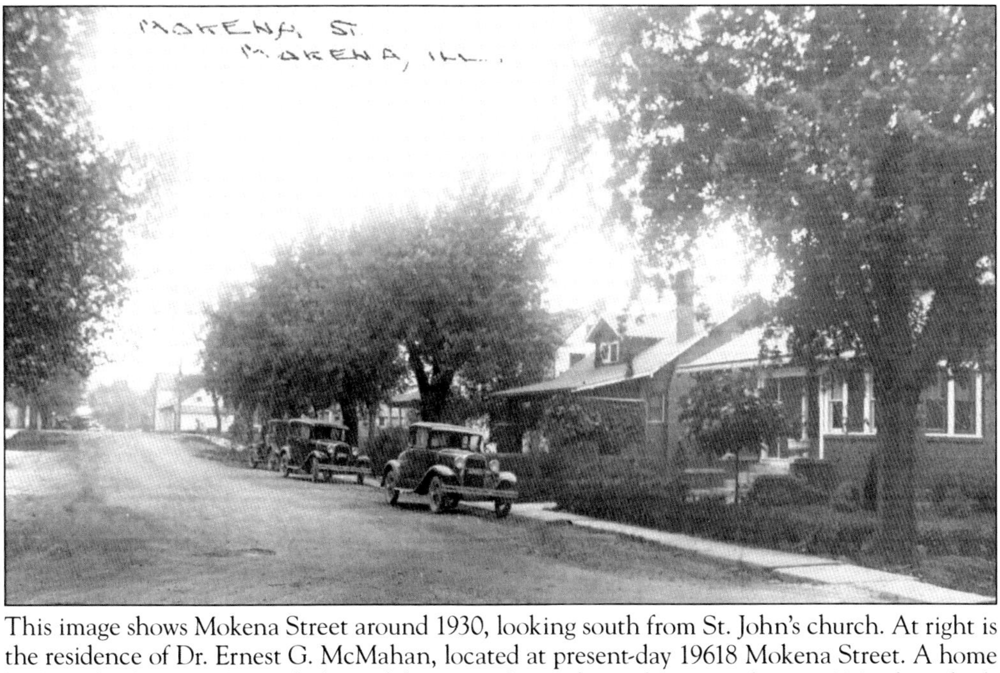

This image shows Mokena Street around 1930, looking south from St. John's church. At right is the residence of Dr. Ernest G. McMahan, located at present-day 19618 Mokena Street. A home built at this location by Nicholas Volck in 1883 burned in a disastrous fire in 1926, after which Dr. McMahan built the structure seen here. Born in Tennessee in 1892, McMahan began his medical practice in Mokena in 1923.

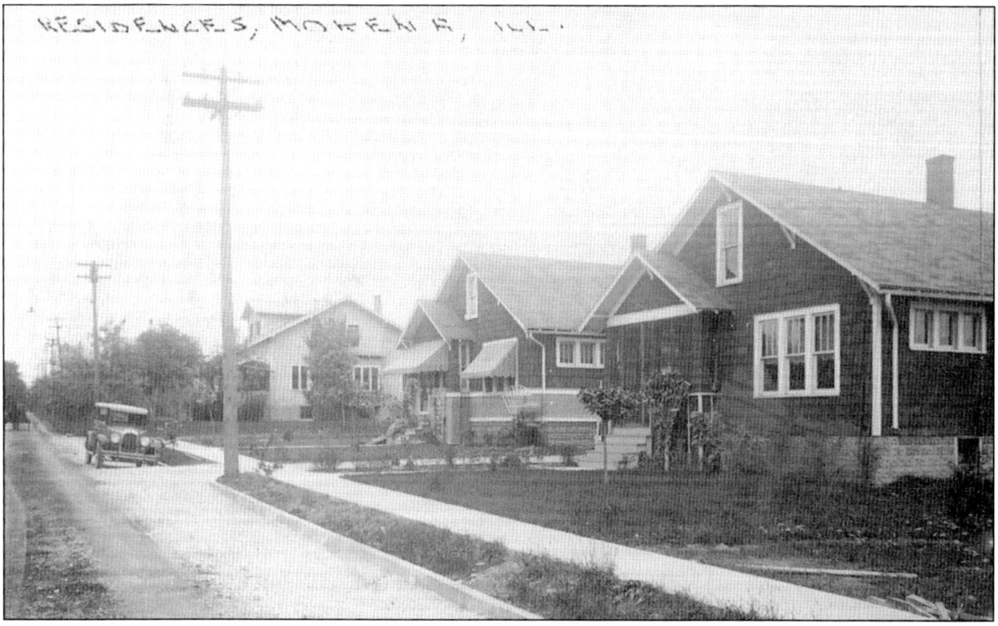

This c. 1930 photograph shows Midland Avenue, looking south towards Carpenter Street. Originally referred to as Niethammer Street, many fine examples of post–World War I craftsmanship can still be found here. According to legend, the identical houses in the foreground were built of materials salvaged from Mokena's second schoolhouse. Seen in the background at left is the beautiful stucco home of Erhardt Oswald Jr., which was completed in 1920.

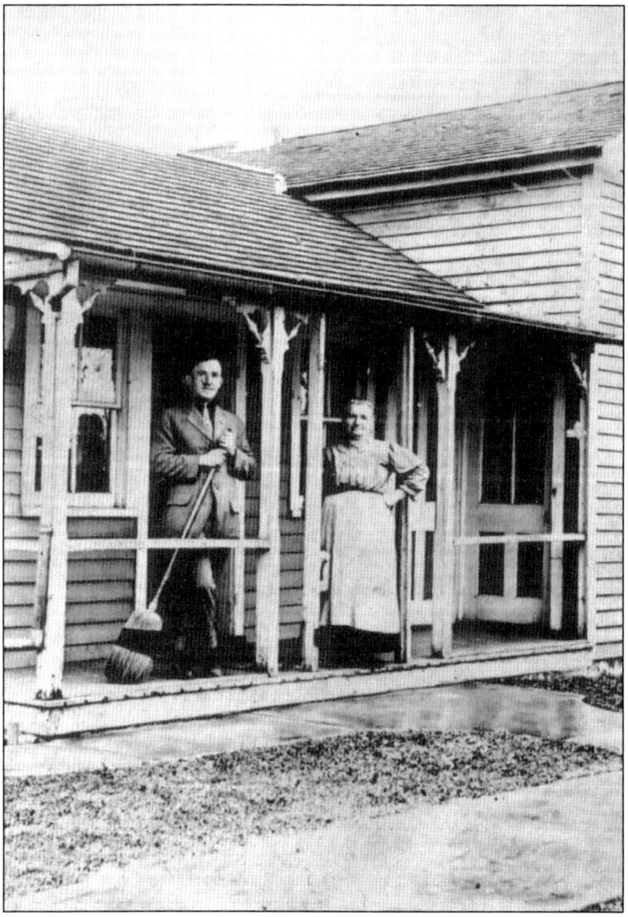

This First Street home, seen here in 1911, was the residence of the Ferdinand Tonn family from 1891 to 1950. Prior to this time, the Rinke family had a small meat market on these premises. On the porch are teacher Ernest Tonn and his mother, Edmunde Tonn. Demolished in the 1990s, this home stood at the present-day 11004 First Street. (Photograph courtesy of Richard Quinn.)

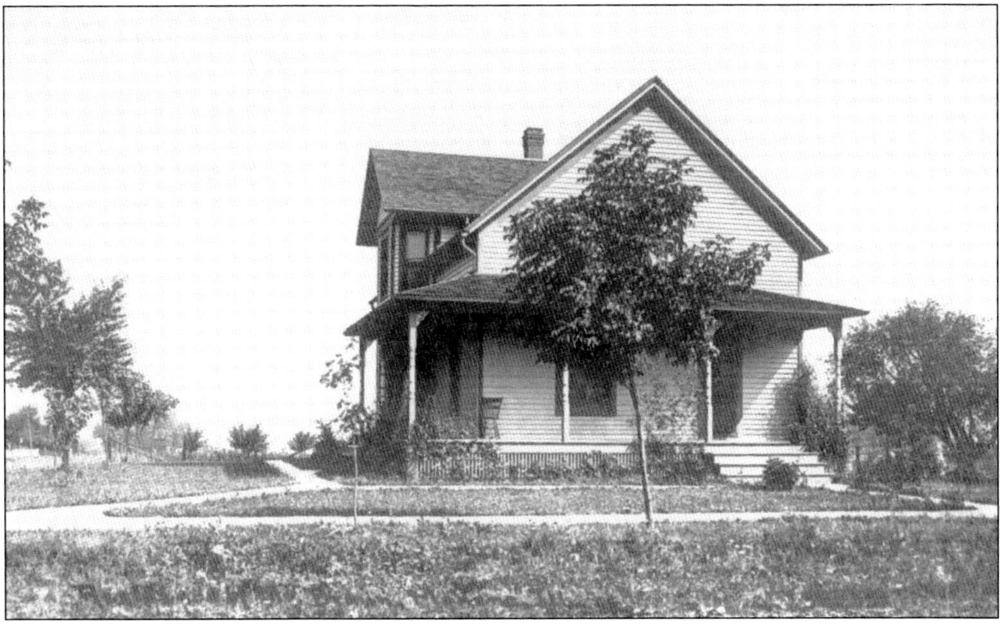

Located on the northeast corner of First Street, this grand home was formerly the residence of Herman G. Schweser. A resident of the Mokena area for his entire life, Schweser was born on August 25, 1880, to pioneers John and Barbara Schweser. An employee of Bowman Dairy, Schweser was also an early member of the Mokena Fire Department, where he served as chief from the 1920s through the early 1940s. (Photograph courtesy of Richard Quinn.)

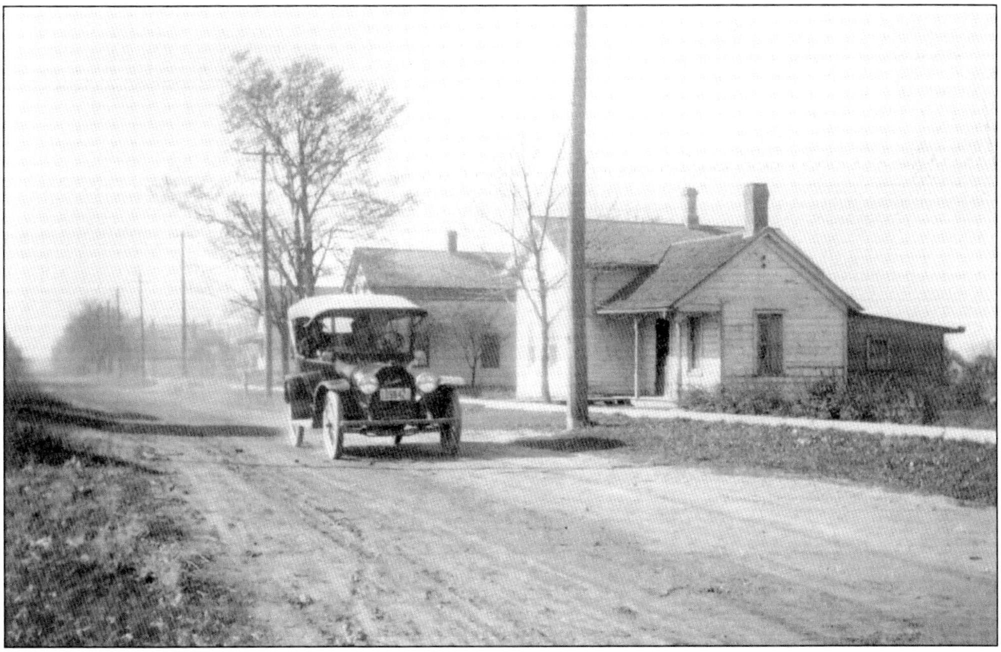

The small home at right, built around 1860 and located at 10934 First Street, is among the oldest in the village. In the fall of 1911, the family of George M. Kraus moved into this house, having recently arrived from the Chicago area. Kraus ran a barbershop on Front Street until his death in 1946.

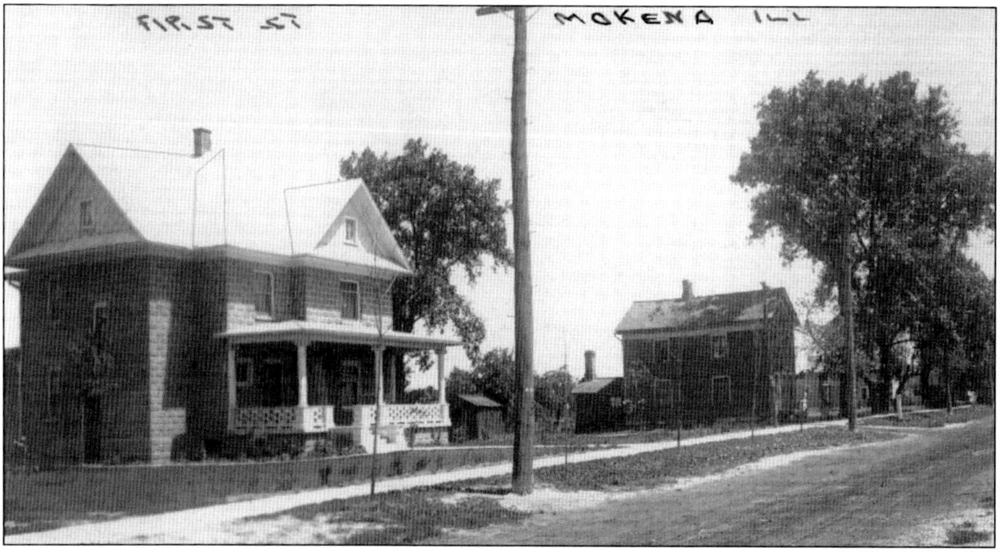

One of Mokena's most unique homes stands at 10928 First Street, visible here at left around 1920. Built by concrete manufacturer Valentine H. Scheer in the years before America's entry into World War I, this home has long been rumored to be a Sears catalog home. After being ordered from a catalog, the building components would have been shipped to Mokena by railroad and then constructed following a company blueprint. (Photograph courtesy of Richard Quinn.)

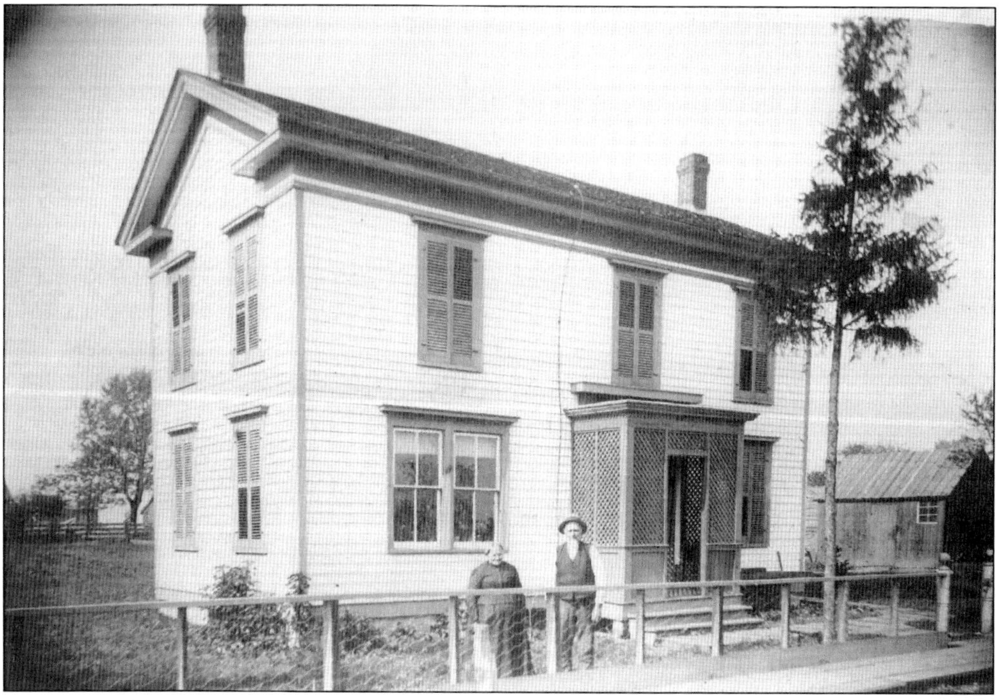

Nicholas and Maria (Baumgartner) Marti are pictured here at their First Street residence around 1900. Still standing at 10904 First Street, it is said that portions of the home depicted here were originally constructed with wooden logs. Nicholas Marti, of Swiss descent, settled in Frankfort Township in 1851, where he farmed in the Mokena area for decades. From 1868 to 1876, Marti owned a large farm on today's 191st Street.

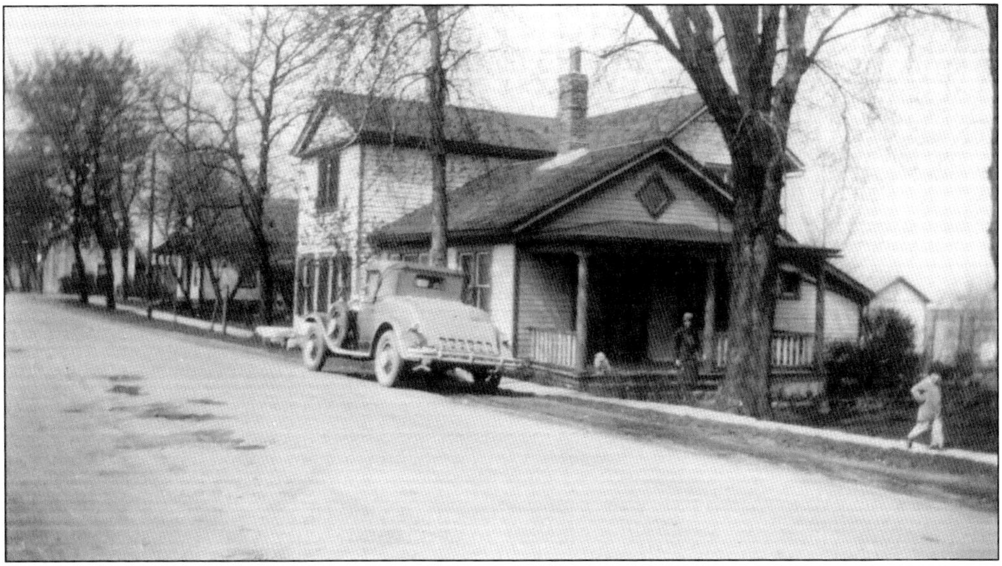

Reflecting the resourcefulness of Mokena's forefathers, several additions to this Front Street home are apparent in this image. The residence of Caroline Braun (known locally as "Grandma Braun") is seen here in August 1929, complete with Chrysler Roadster and Danny the dog relaxing on the porch. This home stood just west of the present-day 11134 Front Street.

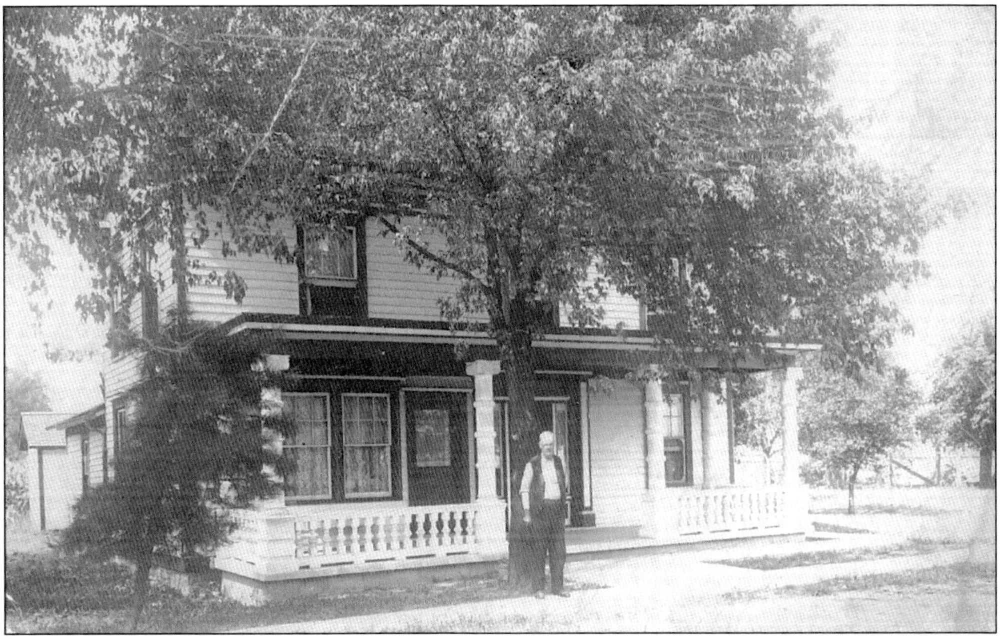

Charles Moriarty, lifelong resident of the Mokena area, poses on a warm day around 1909. Born in 1847, Moriarty served in the Union army at the end of the Civil War and later became a well-known auctioneer, crying sales in both English and German. Likely manufactured by local man J.G. Oswald, this home's beautiful concrete columns are preserved to this day at 11008 Front Street.

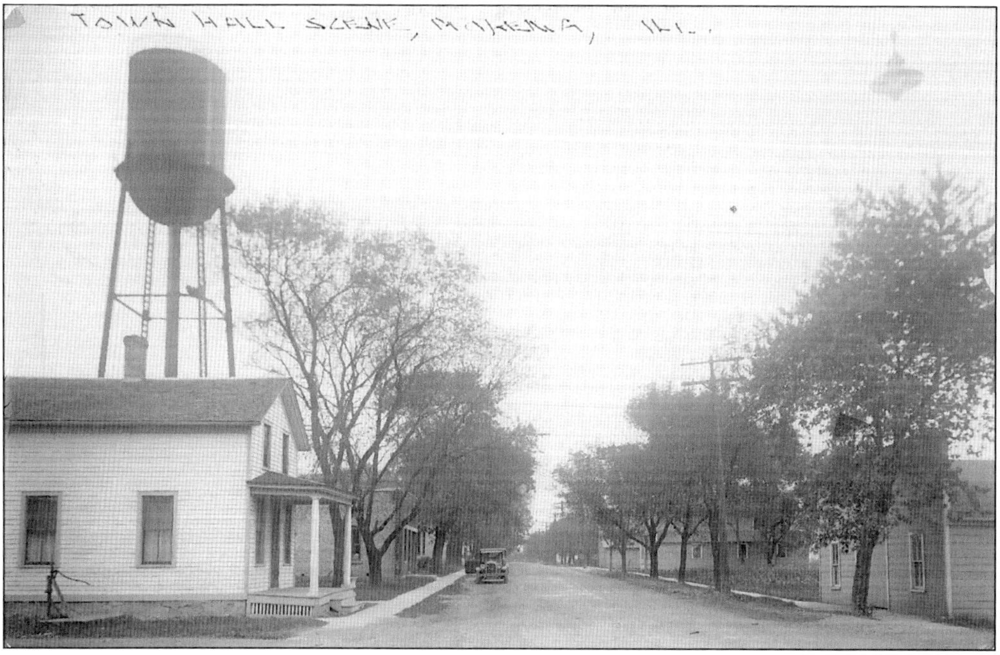

This image, looking east from Division Street, shows a tree-lined Front Street around 1918. Mokena saloon owner Simon Hohenstein Jr. purchased the home at left from Michael Enders around 1905. The outdoor well was a common sight in this and previous years, accessible by hand pumps like the one visible in the left foreground. At right is the former blacksmith shop of Bob Turner.

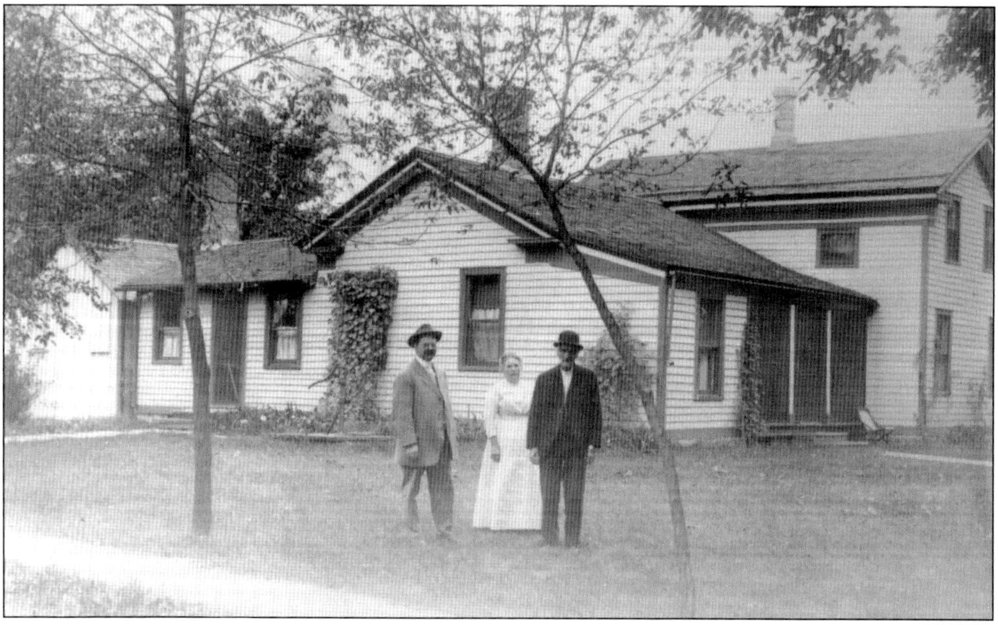

Situated at 10910 Front Street, this historic home was the McGovney residence for generations. Easily one of Mokena's oldest structures, legend has it that a portion of the house was built around a log cabin. Shown here around 1905 are, from left to right, Chicago attorney Arthur McGovney, Emma McGovney, and family patriarch Ozias McGovney. Ozias McGovney's father, John McGovney, was the first permanent white settler of Frankfort Township.

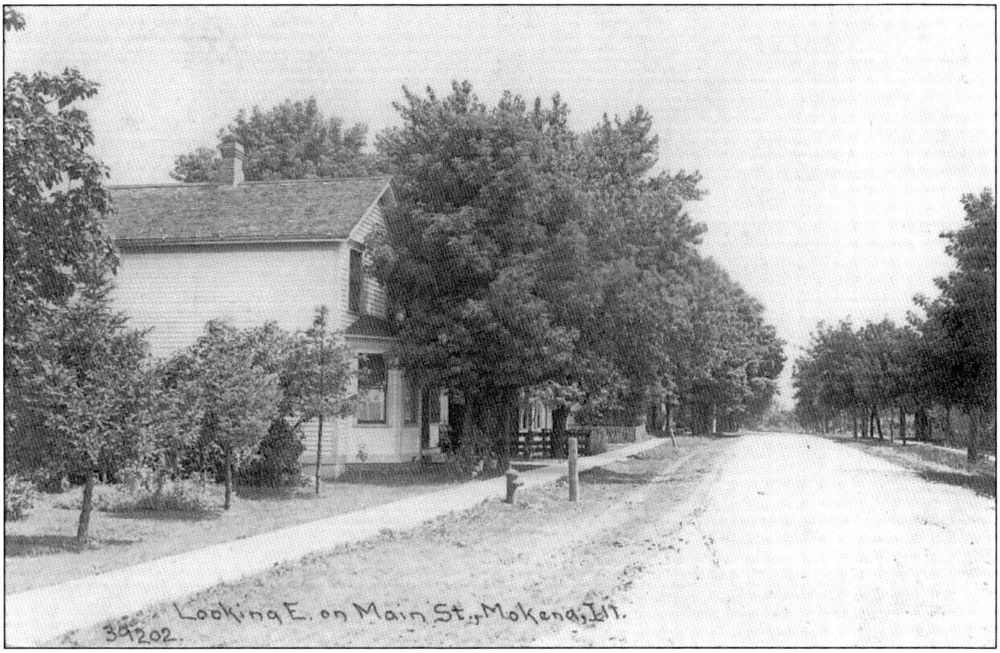

This home, which stood a few yards east of 10900 Front Street, was known for decades as the John Liess residence. Liess, who was born in Germany, was a successful area insurance salesman beginning in the late 19th century. Notable is the home's bay window, a common local trend around 1900, a few years previous to the taking of this photograph.

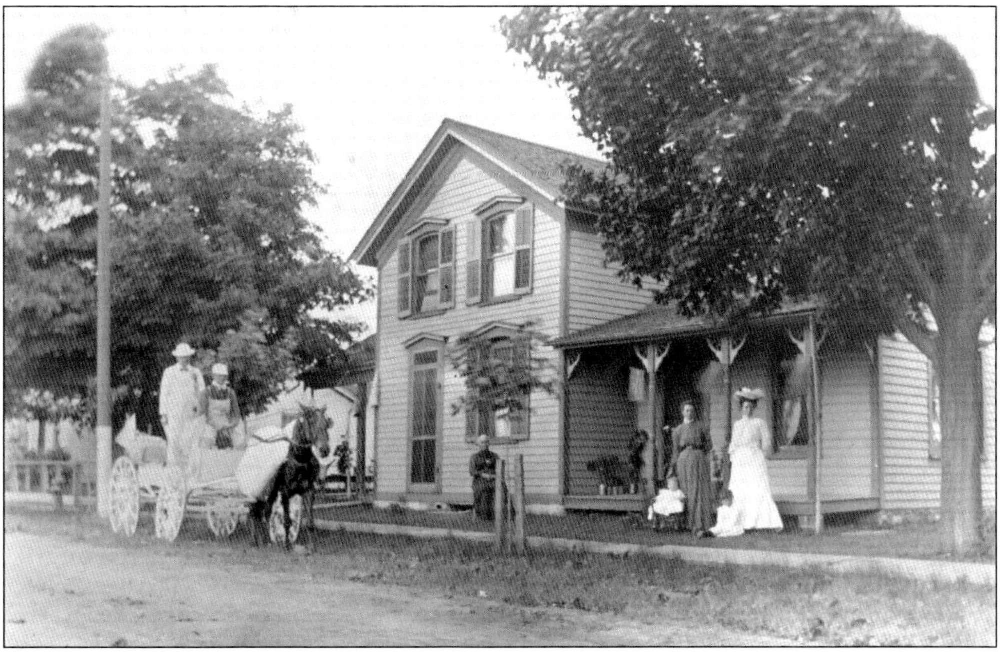

The chic Front Street residence of Julius G. Oswald is shown here about 1904. Oswald (standing in the wagon at left) manufactured concrete blocks, vases, and even coffin vaults in an outbuilding at the rear of this property. Aside from constructing many concrete farm silos, Mokena's first hard sidewalks were built by Oswald in 1911. This home still stands at 10836 Front Street.

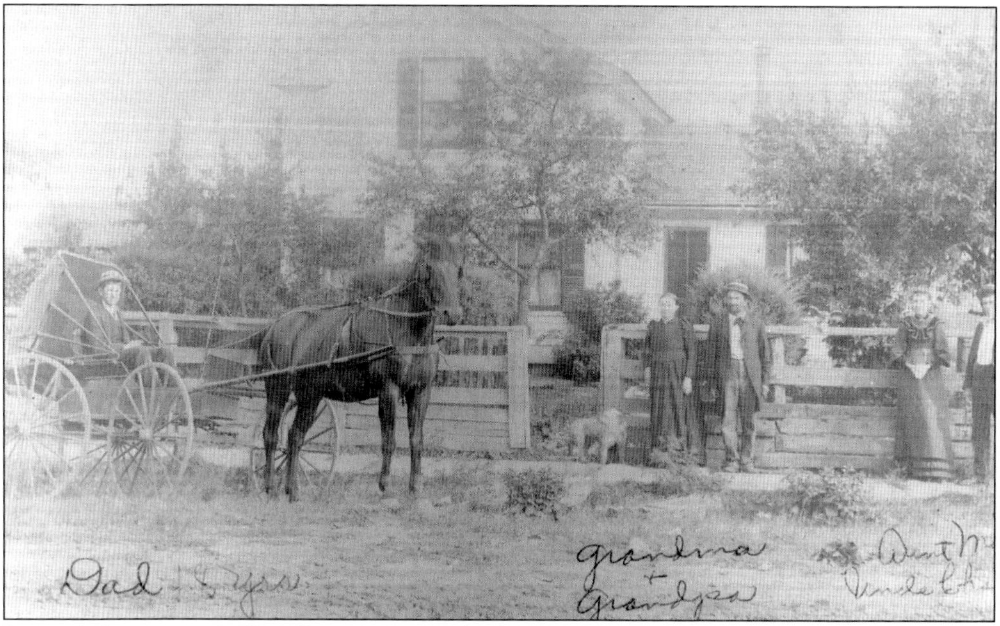

Presently known as 11107 McGovney Street, this historic home was, for many years, the homestead of the Hacker family. Patriarch Carl J. Hacker was employed by the Rock Island Railroad for 45 years. A hardened veteran of the Civil War, Hacker was wounded in 1864 during a North Carolina campaign. Seen here in 1898 are, from left to right, Phillip Hacker, Maria (Mau) Hacker, Carl J. Hacker, Minnie Hacker, and Charley Hacker.

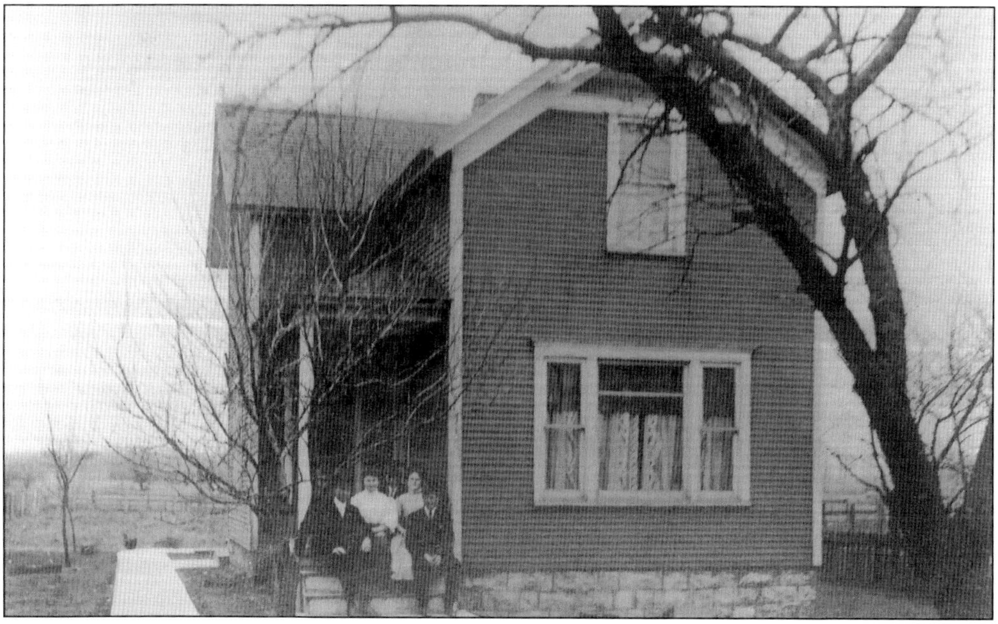

This home, situated at the present-day 11111 McGovney Street, was likely constructed around 1900 by local builder George Hacker. A man of great zeal, Hacker not only became a director of the Mokena State Bank, he also helped to establish banks in New Lenox and Orland Park. Also working as a lumberyard owner and realtor, Hacker developed a New Lenox subdivision and served as mayor of Mokena from 1915 to 1929.

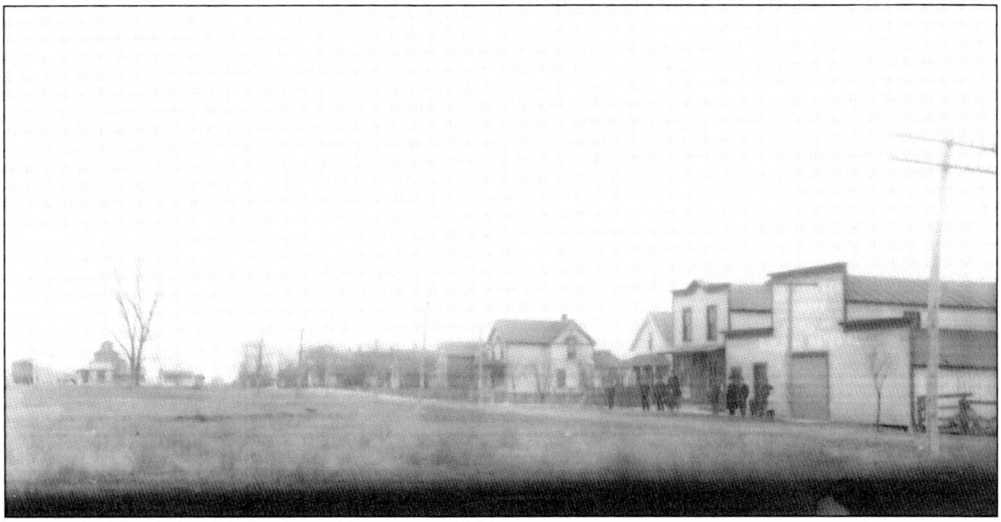

McGovney Street, unrecognizable compared to its present-day appearance, has undergone many changes in the years since this photograph was taken around 1903. Facing east, the lumberyard of George Hacker can be seen at right. The open expanse at left was for years the property of the Rock Island Railroad, where large events were occasionally held, such as the Seibel Bros. Dog and Pony Show in the early 1900s.

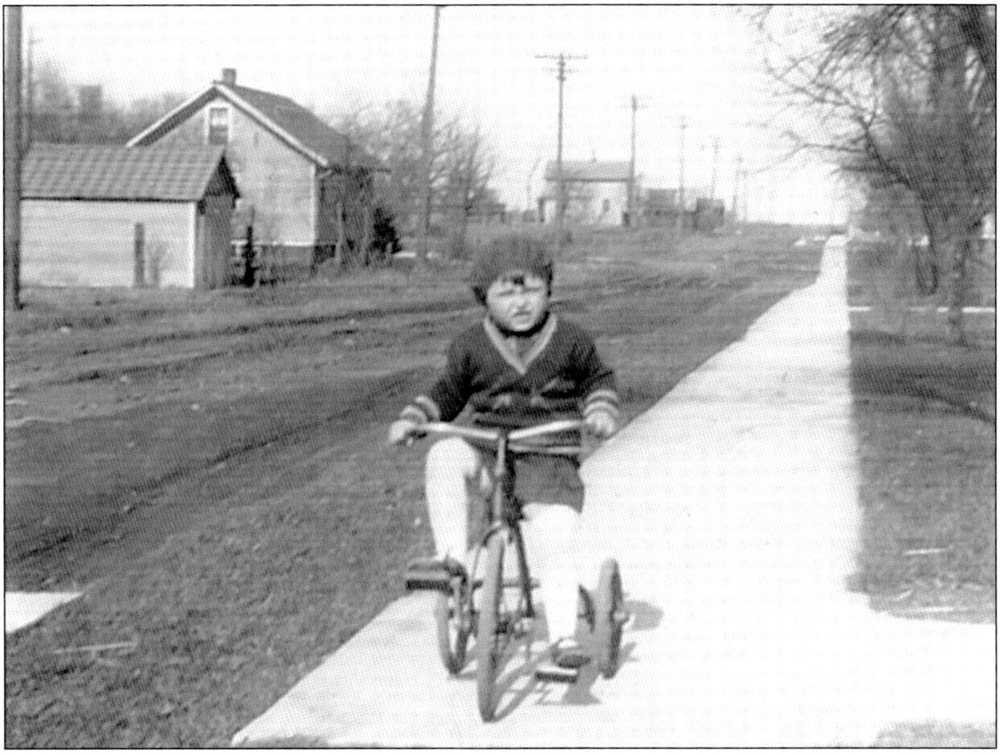

A youngster enjoys a tricycle ride on Denny Avenue around 1935. For nearly 100 years, this street was the southernmost in Mokena, with nothing beyond it but a vast stretch of farms and prairie. Denny Avenue's few residents often complained about the unimproved condition of their thoroughfare, as can be seen in this photograph.

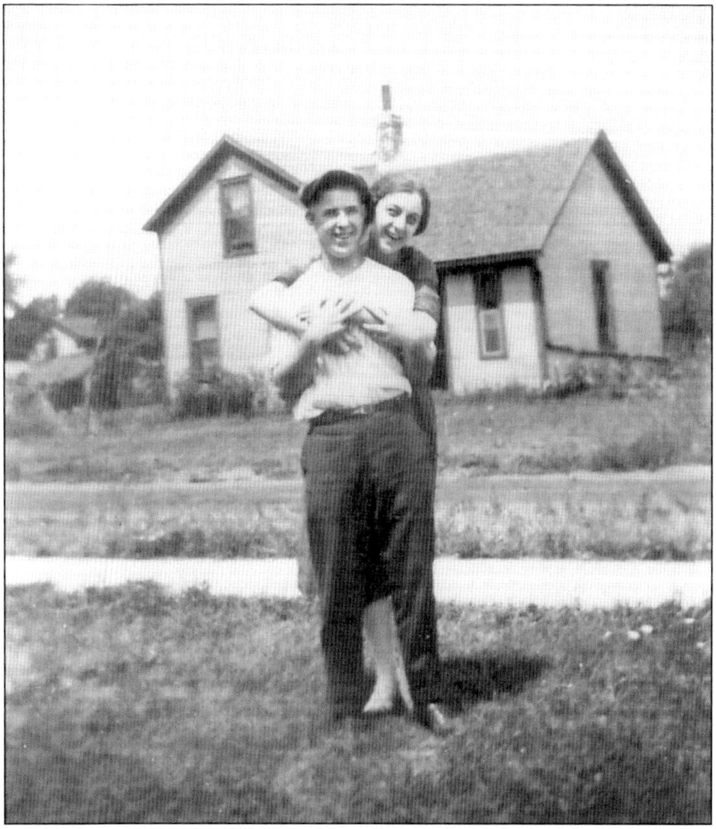

A happy moment on Denny Avenue is seen here around 1926. This section of the village was part of Allen Denny's second addition to Mokena, and the street appears to be named for him. One of the first settlers in the future Frankfort Township, Denny operated a stop on the Underground Railroad. The residence in the background still remains at 11040 Denny Avenue and is one of the oldest on the street.

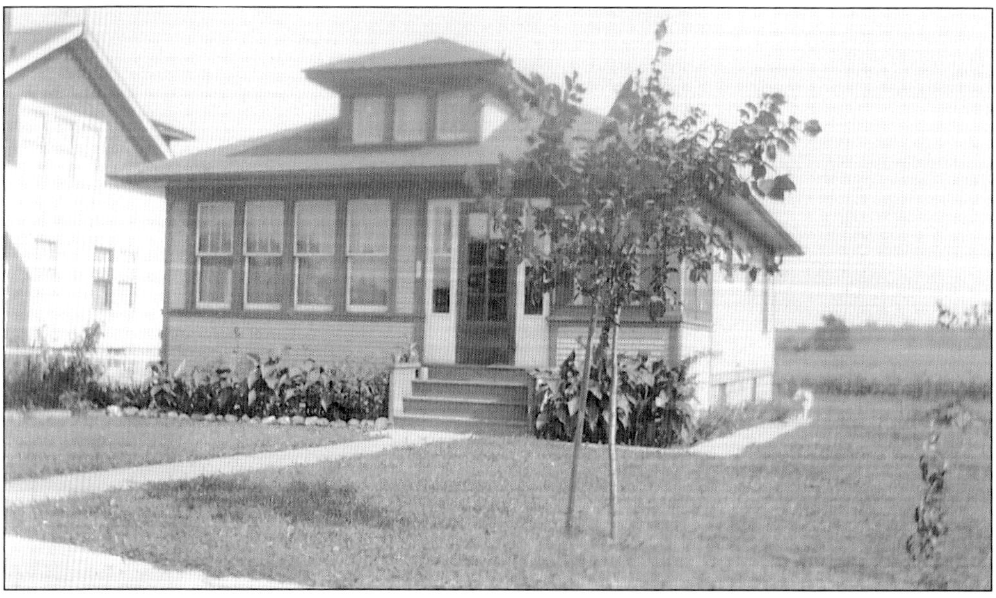

This image depicts 11047 Denny Avenue as it looked around 1926. A great example of the bungalow home style, this type of architecture was at the height of its local popularity during the 1920s. Although many bungalows can be found in Mokena and the surrounding region, this residence has since been altered by the addition of a second story.

Five

Thy Whistle Blowing

With the arrival of the steel rail across the prairie, Mokena was born into this world. The great railroad bought prosperity and fortune to the new community and it assured its future. Neighborhoods with no connection vanished and were scattered to the wind, such as the hamlet of Chelsea, which briefly existed between today's Frankfort and Mokena.

In the early 1850s, an immense building project on the virgin prairie busied many of Frankfort Township's early settlers—the Chicago, Rock Island & Pacific Railroad (CRI&P) was constructing a new line between Chicago and Joliet. The venture was not without its problems—several area residents lost large tracts of farmable land to the railroad bed, and part of the populace grew impatient with the company and demanded real evidence of a working train. On October 10, 1852, the festively decorated locomotive *Rocket* passed through town, ushering in a new era of success.

Around the same time, area farmer Allen Denny established a subdivision parallel to the Rock Island tracks, and Mokena was born. The English-born Samuel Tinley, whose family later lent its surname to the neighboring village of Tinley Park, was an early railroad agent in Mokena. In the 1870s, construction began on another proposed railroad through the Mokena region. For reasons since lost to time, this endeavor failed and was never finished.

The Rock Island Railroad benefited Mokena greatly; local farmers could now easily ship cattle, grain, and milk to city markets, therefore increasing their profits. Ironically, a different rail line brought about a temporary stunting of Mokena's economy. The completion of the Wabash, St. Louis & Pacific Railroad, around 1880, through the new communities of Marley and Orland Park drew much business to these areas and away from Mokena.

The legacy of the railroad in Mokena now belongs to the commuter, as it shuttles hundreds to and from Chicago daily. Mokena is a community with a long and illustrious railroad past. To this day, conductors still colorfully announce "beautiful downtown Mokena" as the metal behemoths lumber into town.

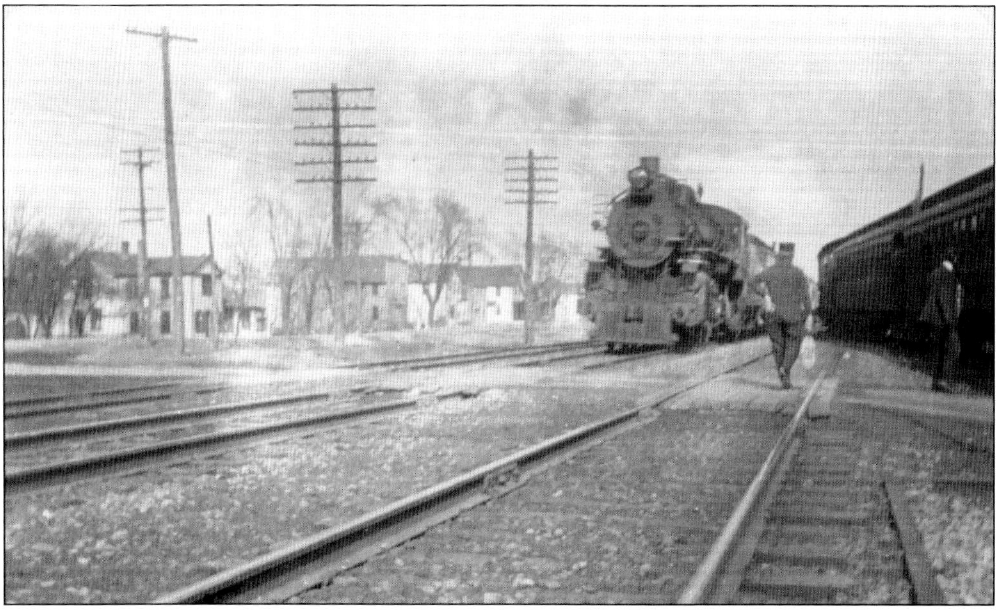

The Wolf Road railroad crossing, facing east with Front Street in the background, is shown here around 1935. The sound of locomotives and their heavy cargo rumbling through town has long been a part of Mokena. Around the turn of the 20th century, it was common for freight engineers to summon cattle buyers to the village stockyards by sounding the engine whistle.

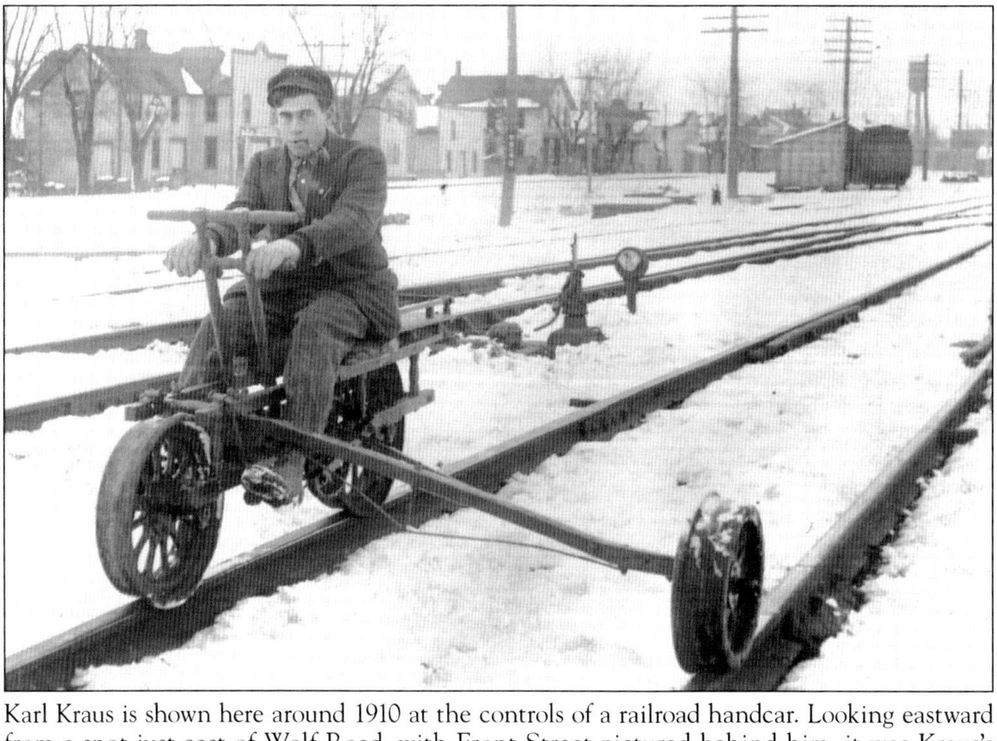

Karl Kraus is shown here around 1910 at the controls of a railroad handcar. Looking eastward from a spot just east of Wolf Road, with Front Street pictured behind him, it was Kraus's responsibility to travel up and down the local section of the Rock Island tracks and fill signal lamps with kerosene.

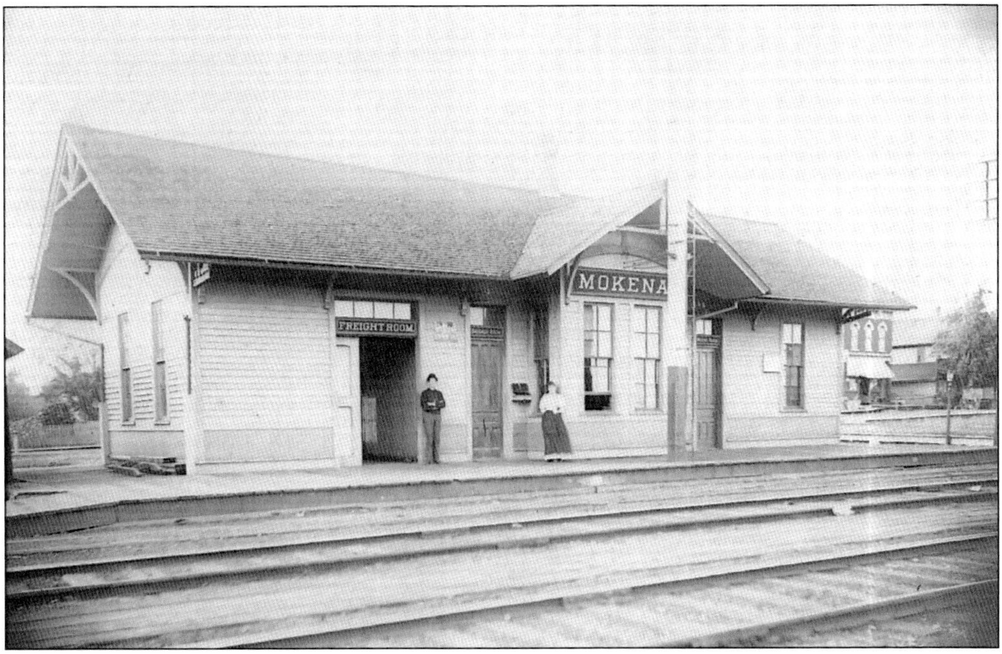

The Mokena depot of the CRI&P Railroad is shown here around 1895. Erected in 1852, this modest structure was not only one of the first built in the new village, it was also one of the earliest stations on the Rock Island line between Chicago and Joliet. In the background at right is the present-day 11034 Front Street.

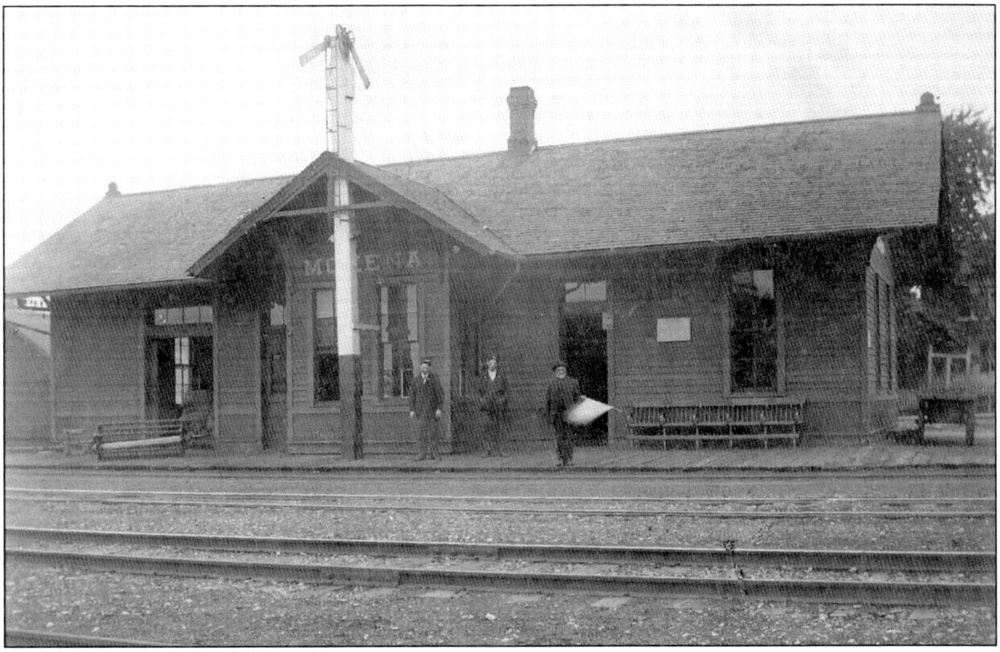

Pictured here around 1900, the Mokena Rock Island depot was a relatively simple building. The depot had no indoor plumbing but had a small wooden outhouse just west of the building and a coal-burning stove inside. At one point, in the 19th century, a small living space existed in the depot for the local Rock Island agent.

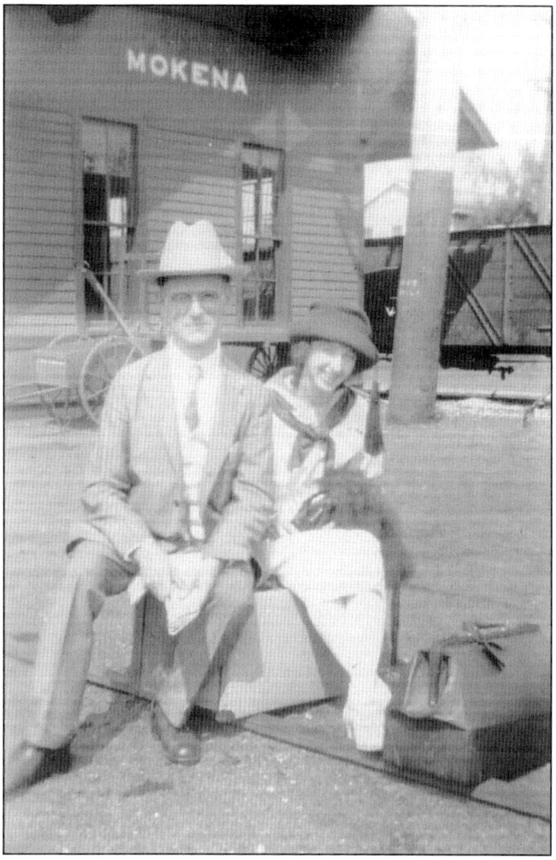

New arrivals to the village, Rev. William Kreis and his daughter Elfriede are pictured at the Mokena depot about 1918. After moving to Mokena from Iowa in 1917, the Kreis family found themselves in the unfortunate predicament of having arrived before their household furnishings. Because of this misfortune, the Kreises boarded temporarily with two local families. (Photograph courtesy of David Kropp.)

In April 1949, this new depot was completed directly to the south of its predecessor, which was relocated to Spring Valley, Illinois, and converted into a private residence. This station was regarded as a large improvement over its outdated forerunner. In 1993, this structure was demolished and replaced on the same site by the current depot, although a southern wall was incorporated into the new building.

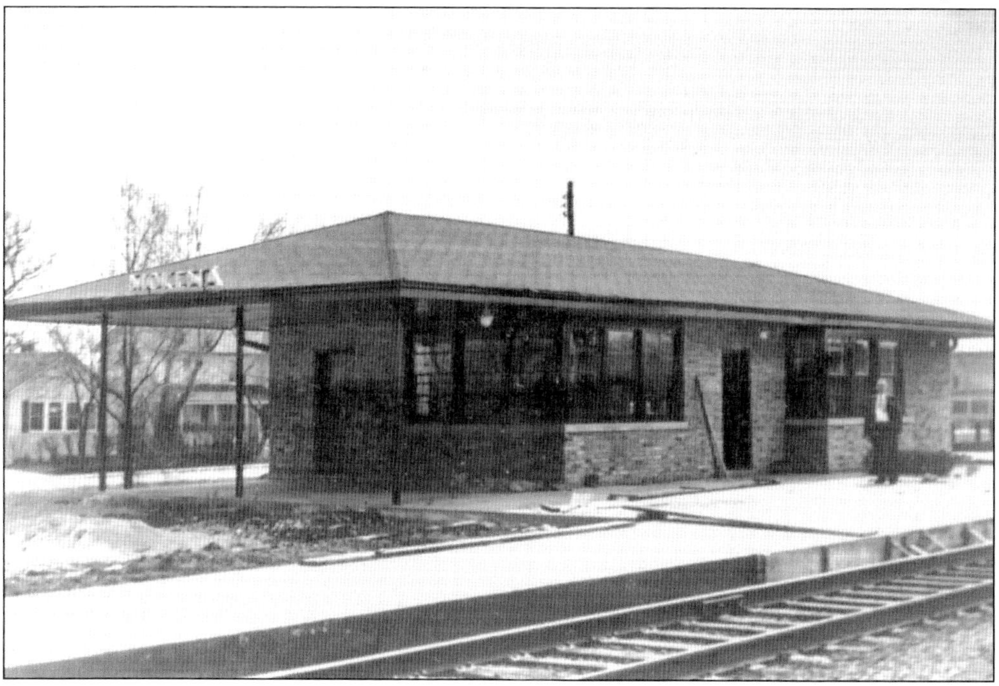

Local resident Charles Rinke is shown here atop the local mailbag platform around 1935. For years, a platform stood on the north side of the railroad tracks from which hung a mailbag. A skilled arm within a moving city-bound train snatched this bag and the contents were sorted in a special mail car.

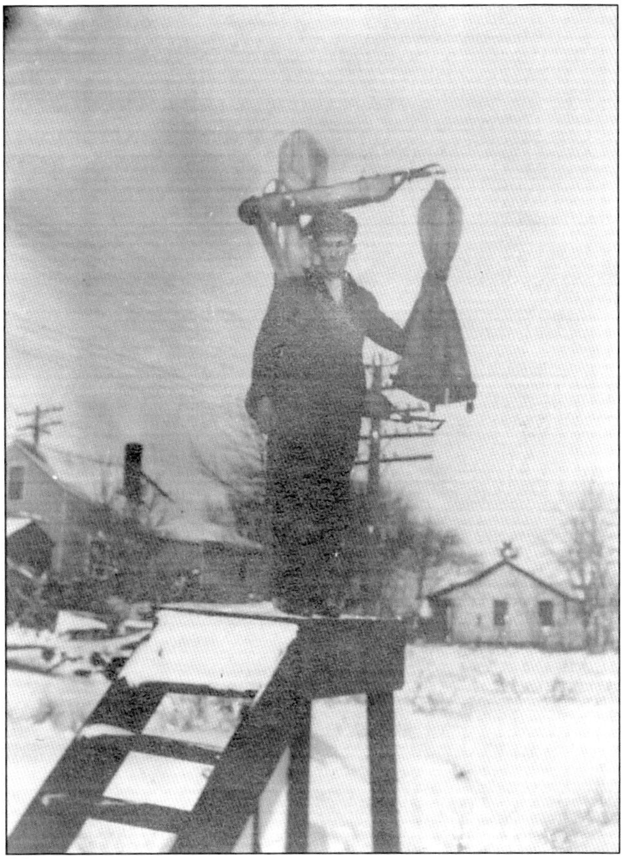

Bill Helenhouse guards the Wolf Road railroad crossing around 1940. On duty during daylight hours, Helenhouse and his partner at the Mokena Street crossing kept traffic at a safe distance with the arrival and departure of each train. This job was made obsolete in 1944, after the installation of electric gates at these two crossings.

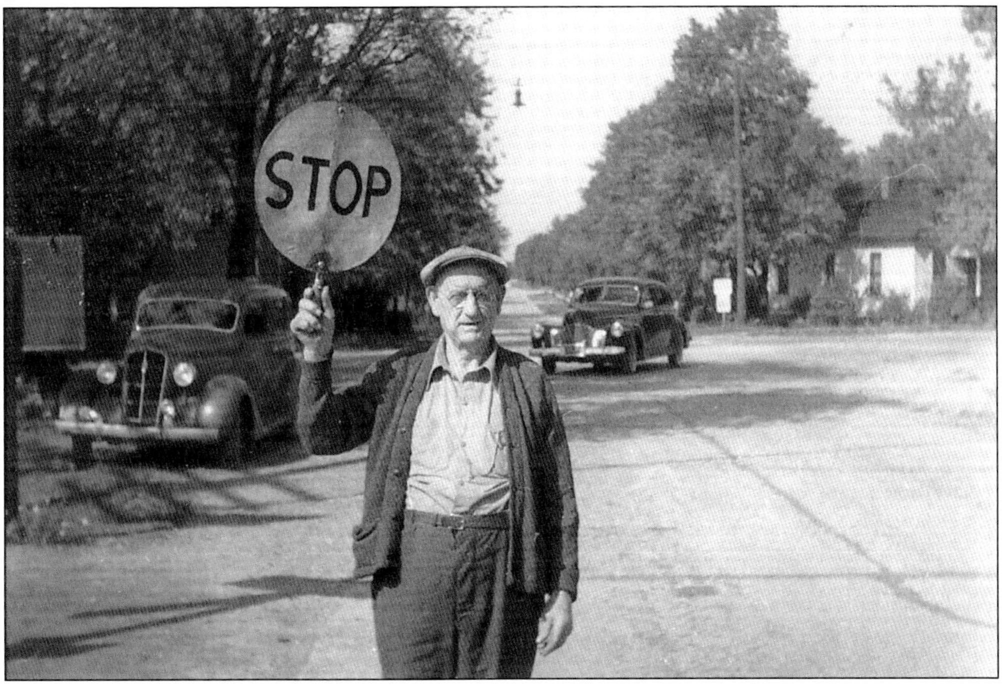

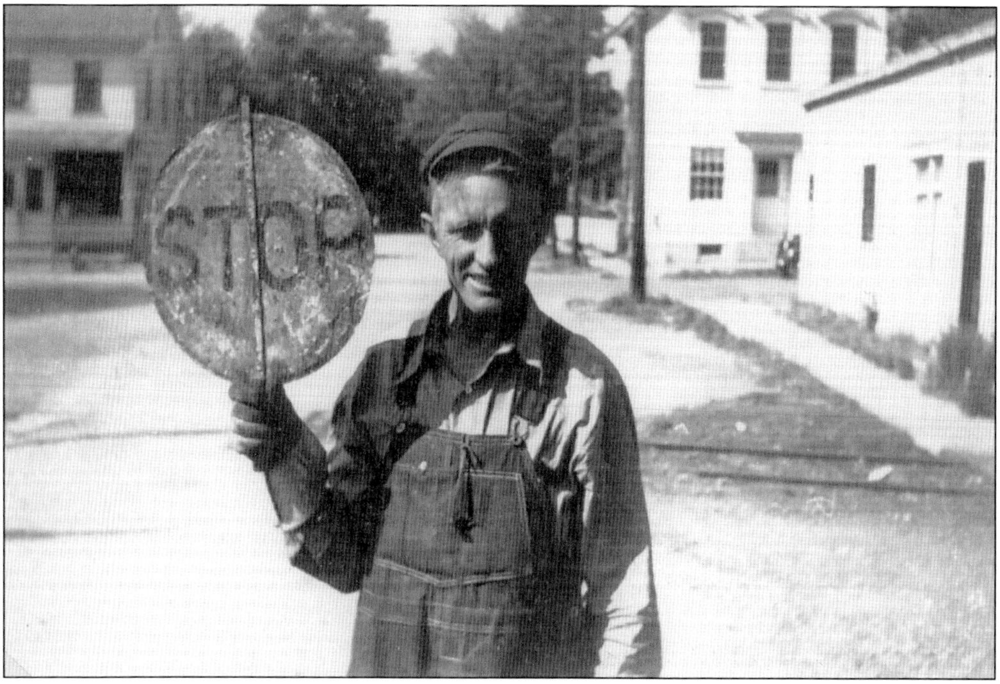

Harry "Slim" Schoen is shown in his usual spot, at the Mokena Street railroad crossing, around 1940. Having succeeded Paul Rinke Sr. as crossing guard in 1931, Schoen was previously in the employ of the Rock Island Railroad as a laborer, a common job for many other residents of Mokena.

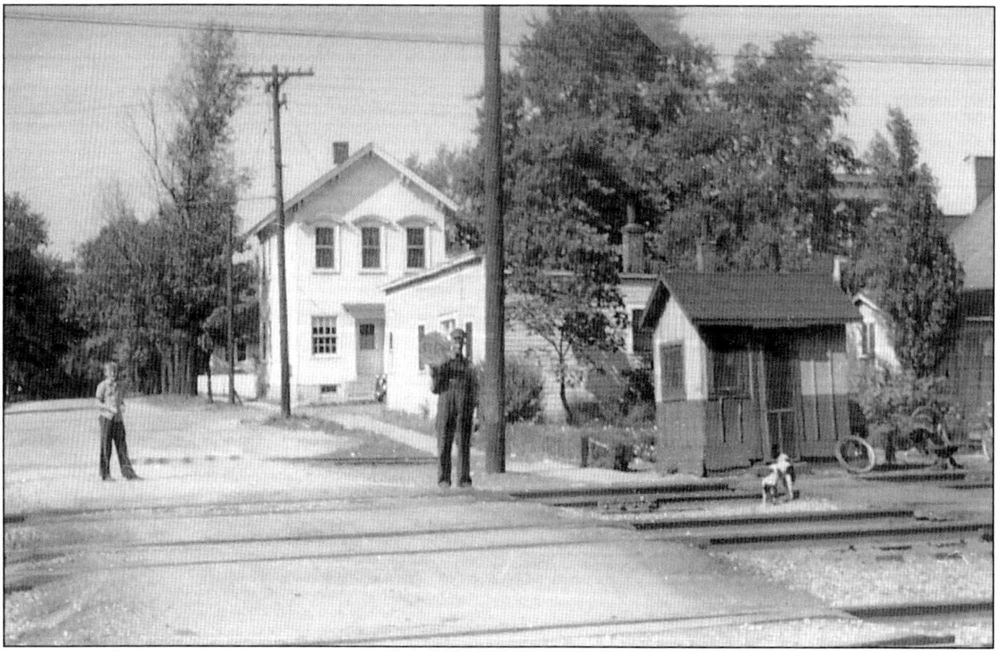

Harry "Slim" Schoen can be seen at the center of the Mokena Street crossing around 1940. To the right is a small shack, erected around 1900 after a fatal accident at this crossing, which served as a place of rest for the flagman, as he was sometimes known. Early flagmen in this era were Patrick Brennan, Thomas Kiniry, and Ferdinand Tonn.

Six

ONE WELL TRAVELED

Wolf Road, which meshes well into Mokena's suburban landscape, is for all appearances yet another heavily used local thoroughfare. Amongst the thousands of vehicles that pass over its surface every day, one would probably never discern its illustrious past. The road has existed in some form or another for hundreds of years; an early name derived from the Mahingan and Potawatomie tongues can be roughly transliterated as "Theak-a-Kee, Ty-Yan-ac-Kee," meaning "the trail of the wolf through the wonderful land."

Accounts have survived the years of the trail's early usage by natives, who had to traverse its narrow path single-file through wooded areas. Sections of the route were used by Jesuit missionaries and fur traders in the long-forgotten days before Illinois's statehood, and again, much later, by the area's first permanent settlers of European descent. Although Wolf Road is an important artery, the road suffered the same problem that all others did in decades past—unreliability in adverse weather. Heavy rains turned it into a muddy quagmire and wintry snows rendered it impassible.

With the advent of the automobile in the first decades of the 20th century, the paving of Wolf Road began. November 1930 saw the triumphant completion of the hard road through Mokena and southward to Hickory Creek. Due to the tireless boosting of William Semmler, editor of the *Mokena News-Bulletin*, the village got a major shot in the arm with its first paved street.

A significant stumbling block was posed by farmer Clarence Cleveland, who prevented the completion of the project through the Mokena region. The owner of a farm at the present-day corner of Wolf Road and Route 30, Cleveland steadfastly opposed construction through his timberland, a site that had great natural significance. After years of conflict between Cleveland and Will County, a settlement was reached and the road was slightly rerouted at Cleveland's property, resulting in the completion of paving from Hickory Creek to Route 30 in 1936. With hundreds of years of history, Wolf Road is more than just a street—it is a symbol of the spirit that built Mokena.

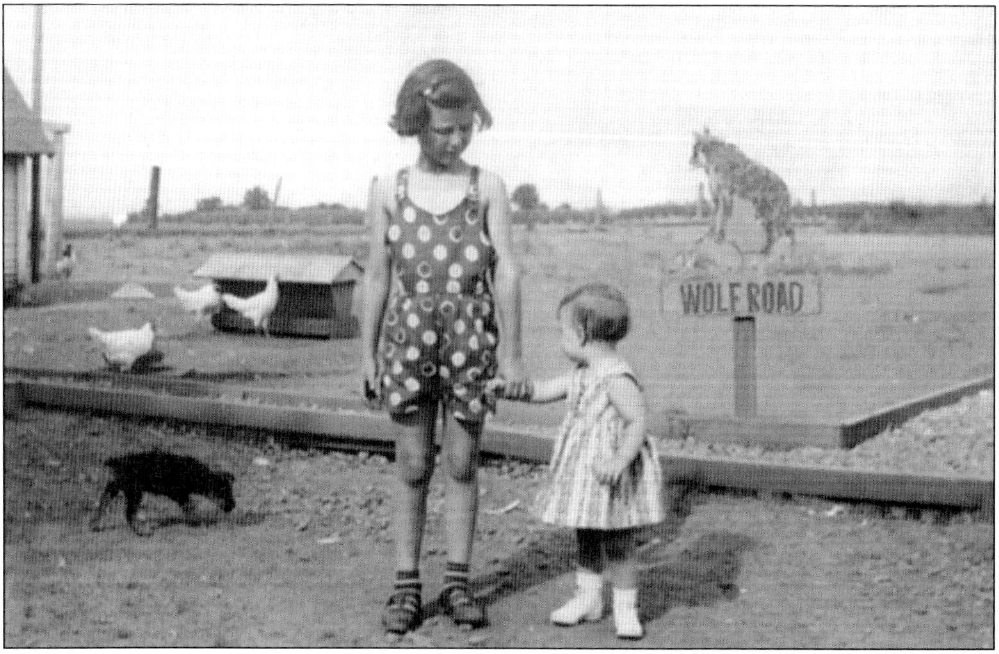

This c. 1939 image shows an everyday scene at the Bueschel Chicken Farm, formerly located on Wolf Road at the site of today's Granite Street. Donna Bueschel is at left, holding the hand of Beverly Raddatz. The Buschels acquired this property from J.V. Hall, who kept a small tavern on this property at the southeast corner of the present-day Wolf Road and Granite Street. Note the unique Wolf Road signage in the background.

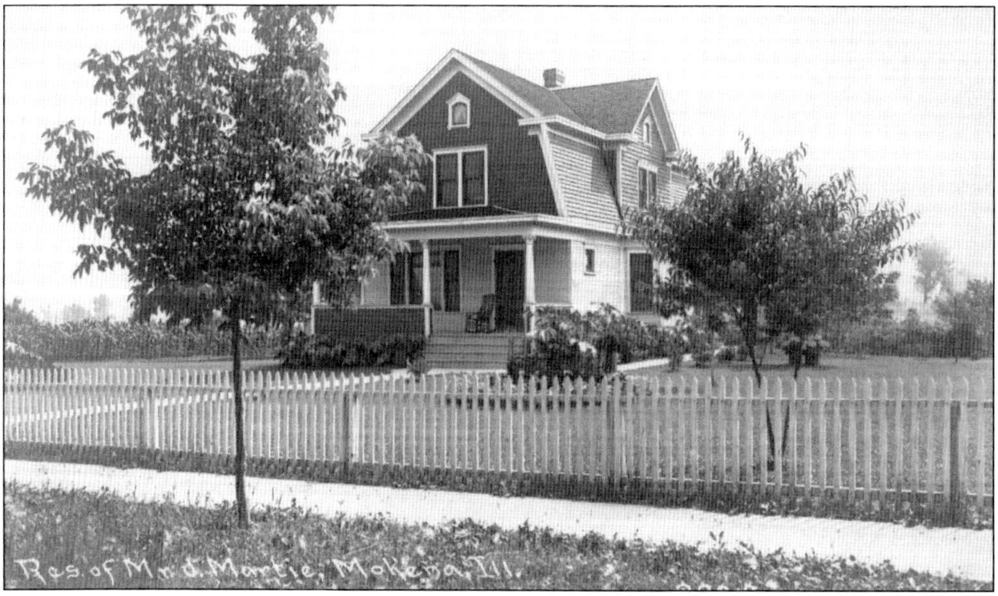

Easily recognizable as the present-day 19443 Wolf Road, the stately residence of John Martie Sr. was originally considered to be located well outside of Mokena. Pictured here around 1920, the home was built by Martie's brother Ben in the early 20th century. Originally a farmer farther north on Wolf Road, the Swiss-born John Martie immigrated to this region as a child in the 1850s. (Photograph courtesy of Richard Quinn.)

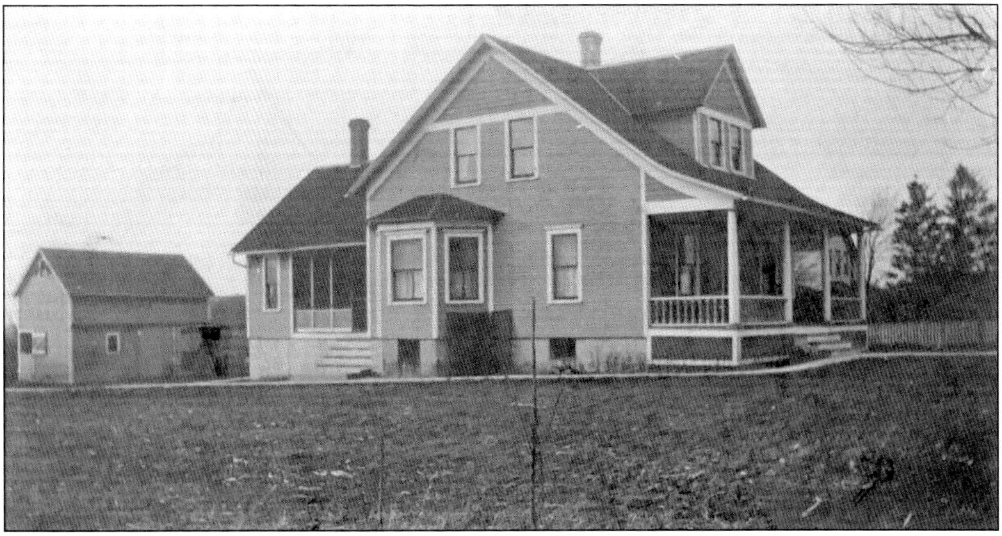

The home of Nicholas Lauffer, which still appears much the same at the present-day 19502 Wolf Road, is shown here around 1915. According to local legend, this home was the first in the Mokena area to contain a foundation of poured concrete. Lauffer's son-in-law, local garage owner Barney Hostert, moved into this property with his family in 1931. (Photograph courtesy of Richard Quinn.)

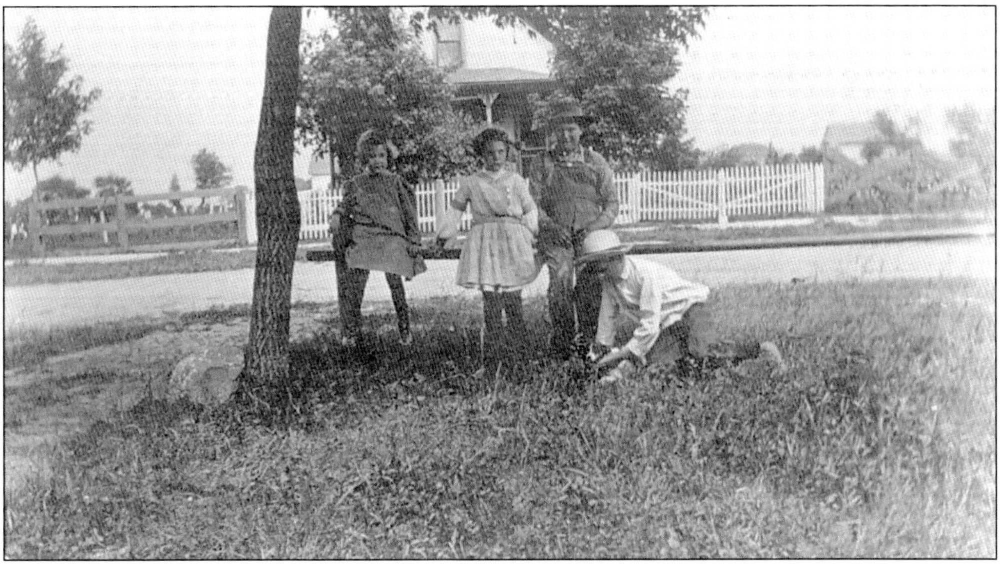

This 1912 view along Wolf Road shows siblings Florence and Harold Cooper, along with Ed and Julia Hirsch. Situated in the background at left is St. Mary's Cemetery, founded in 1865. The historic section of this burial ground contains dozens of grave markers dating from the 19th century, many of which contain German inscriptions.

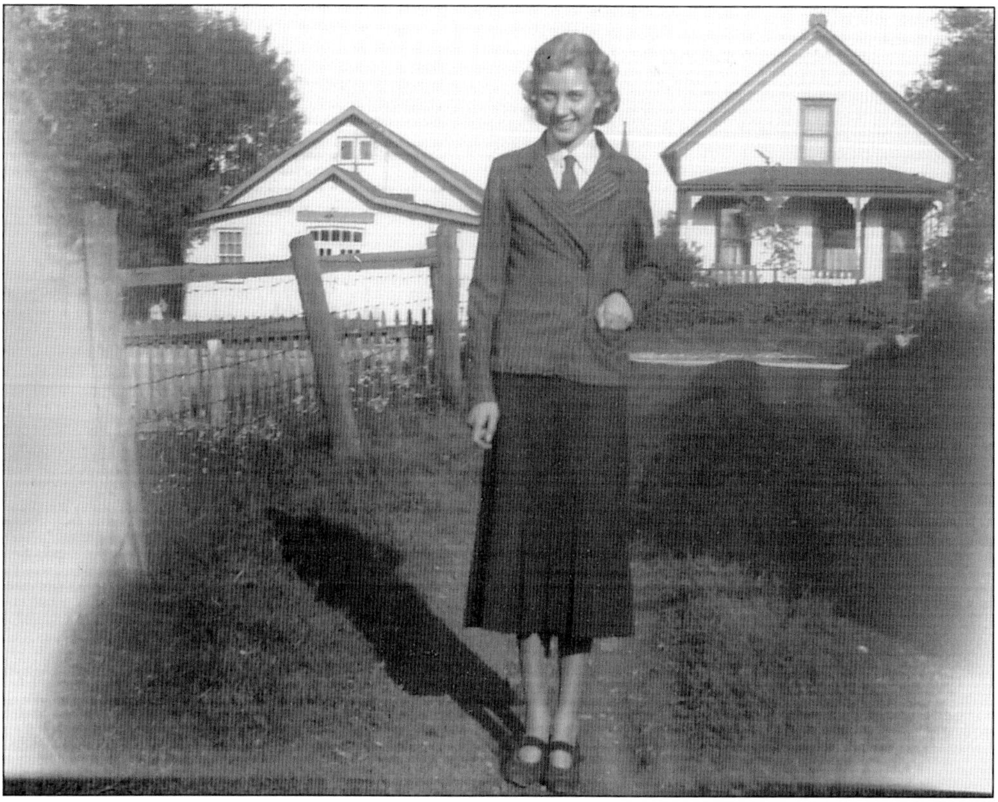

Cradle Mueller poses for a photograph just north of her friend Bernice Hostert's home around 1935. Viewed from the vantage point of the present-day intersection of 195th Street and Wolf Road, a fence on the Hirsch farm is seen at left in this image. Members of the Hostert family received milk in tin pails from this farm, complete with a level of cream at the top.

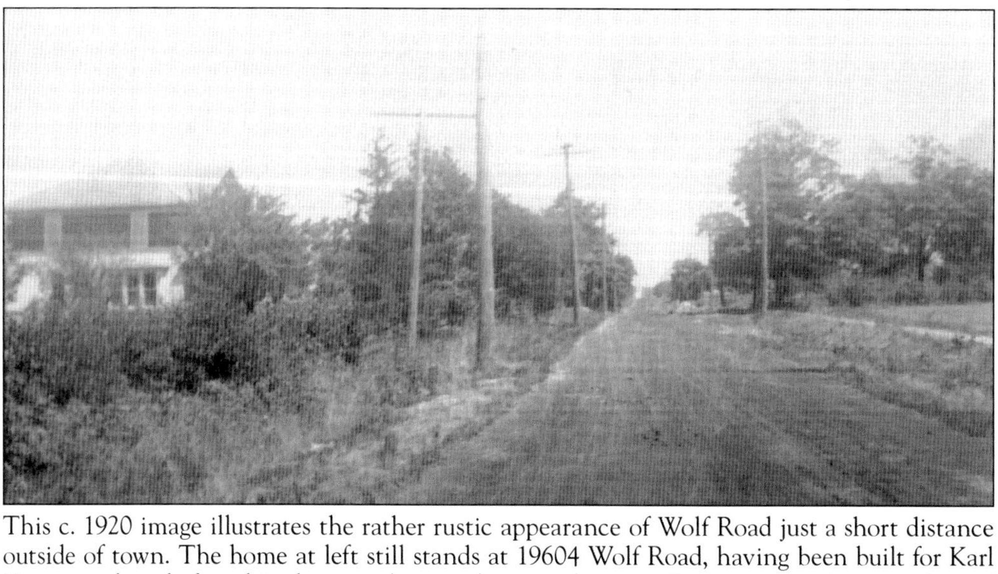

This c. 1920 image illustrates the rather rustic appearance of Wolf Road just a short distance outside of town. The home at left still stands at 19604 Wolf Road, having been built for Karl Krapp not long before this photograph was taken. At the time, Krapp was serving as cashier of the Mokena State Bank and had received the land through a family inheritance.

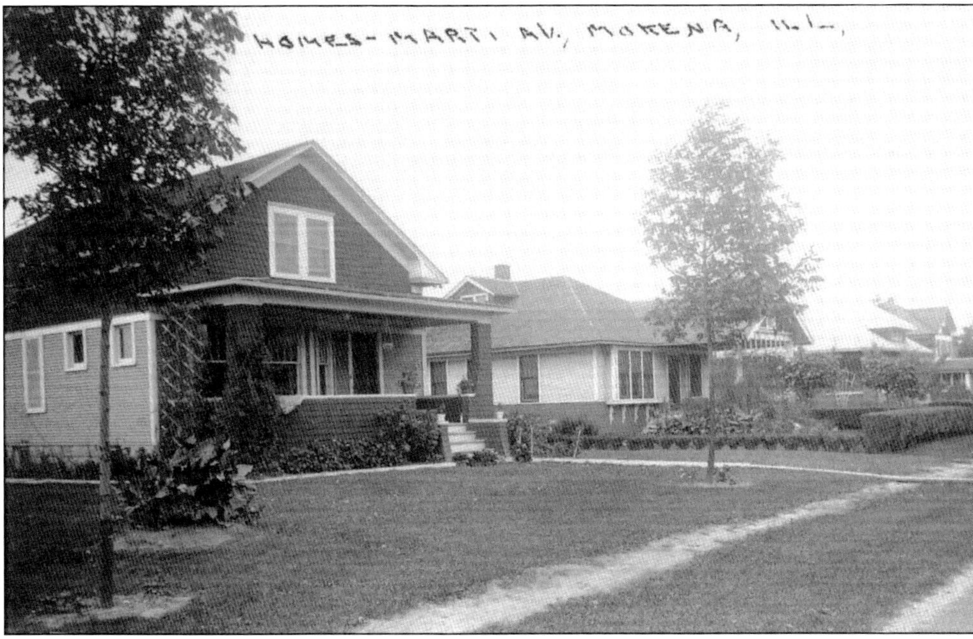

These comfortable homes, shown here around 1920, would have greeted a traveler as he headed north out of Mokena along Wolf Road. Still standing today, these residences reflect the World War I era in which they were constructed. Pictured from left to right are the homes of Gus Werner, Paul Rinke Jr., Josepha Fietterer, and Carl Krapp. (Photograph courtesy of Richard Quinn.)

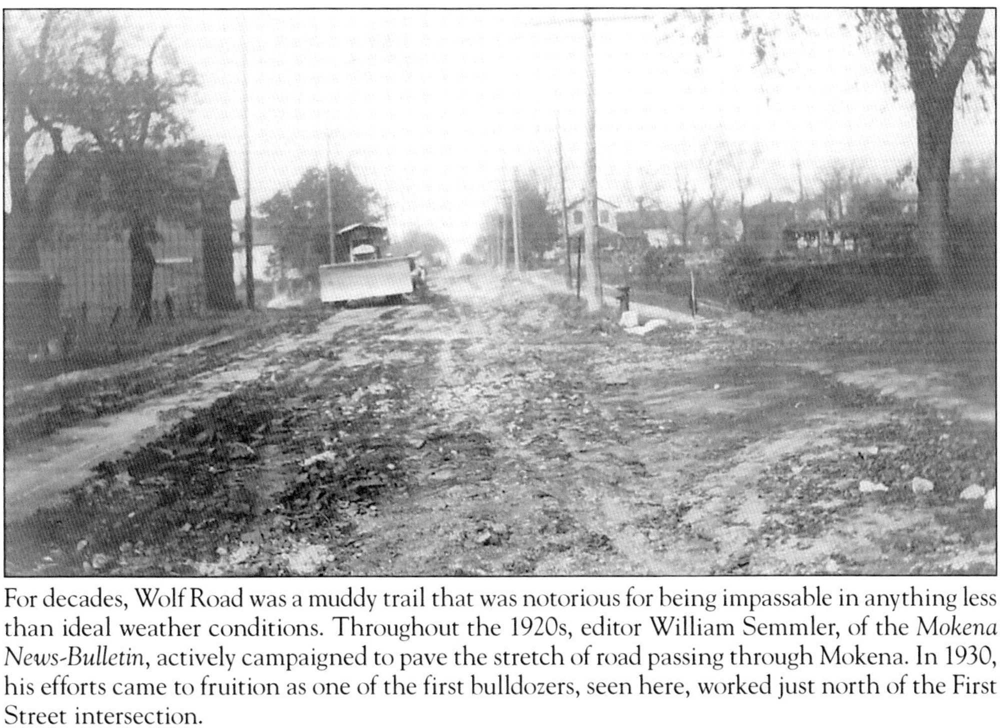

For decades, Wolf Road was a muddy trail that was notorious for being impassable in anything less than ideal weather conditions. Throughout the 1920s, editor William Semmler, of the *Mokena News-Bulletin*, actively campaigned to pave the stretch of road passing through Mokena. In 1930, his efforts came to fruition as one of the first bulldozers, seen here, worked just north of the First Street intersection.

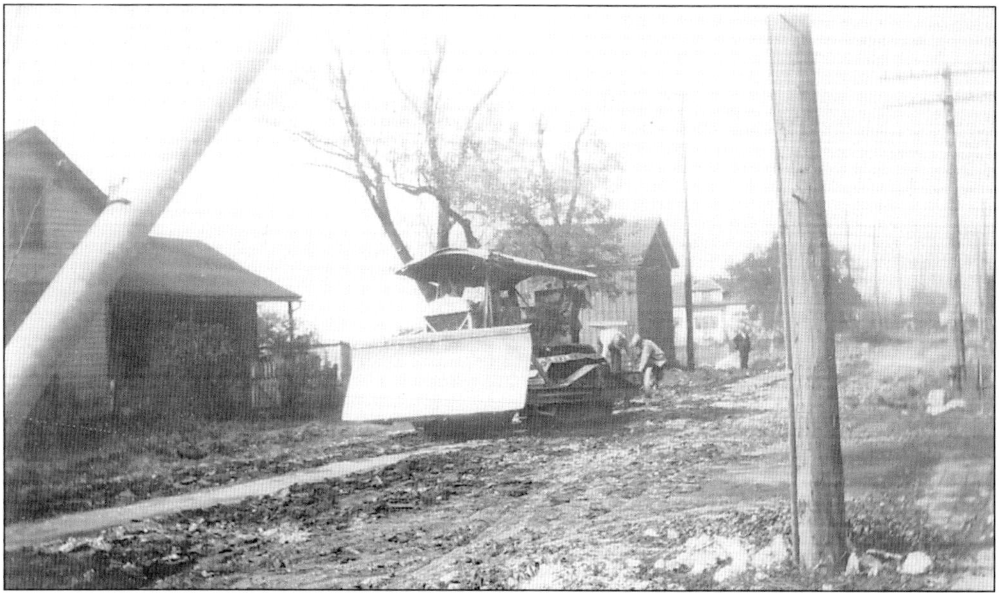

The first paving work begins on Wolf Road, seen here from the First Street intersection in 1930. The modernizing of the road through the Mokena area was not without its problems, however. Local farmer Clarence Cleveland vociferously protested a rerouting of Wolf Road through his woodland south of town. After much deliberating, a compromise was reached and the completion of paving to Lincoln Highway was completed in 1936.

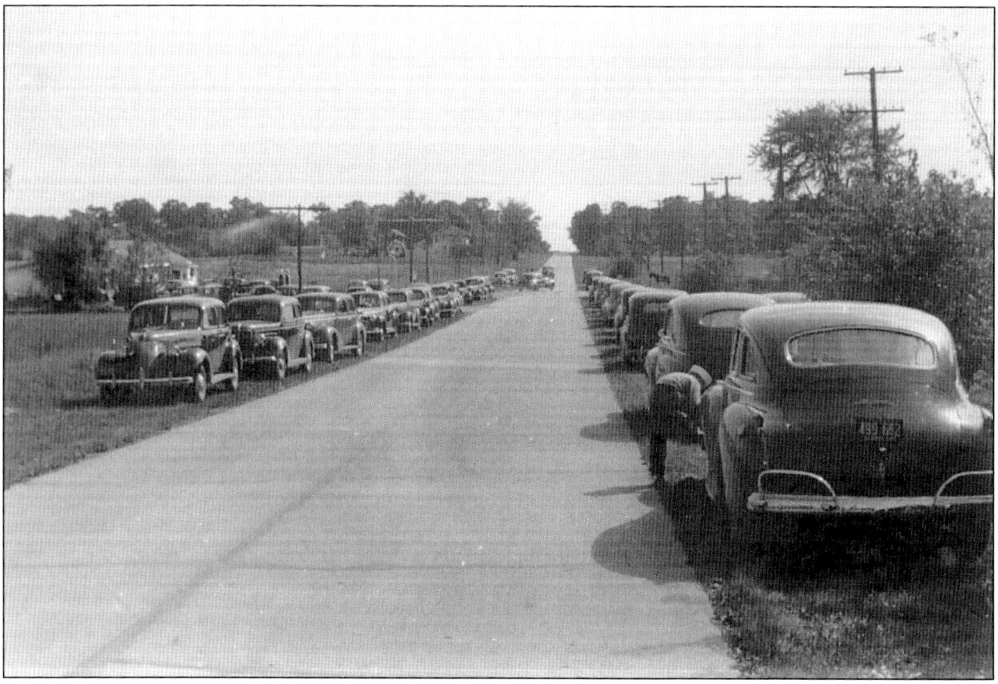

Facing south toward the intersection of Wolf and LaPorte Roads, this image depicts parking for the 1944 Fall Festival. Due to World War II, this event was held in lieu of the Mokena homecoming in a field at Robinson's Tavern to raise funds for the Mokena Women's Service Club so as to, in the words of the *Mokena News-Bulletin*, "help the Yanks on their way to Berlin."

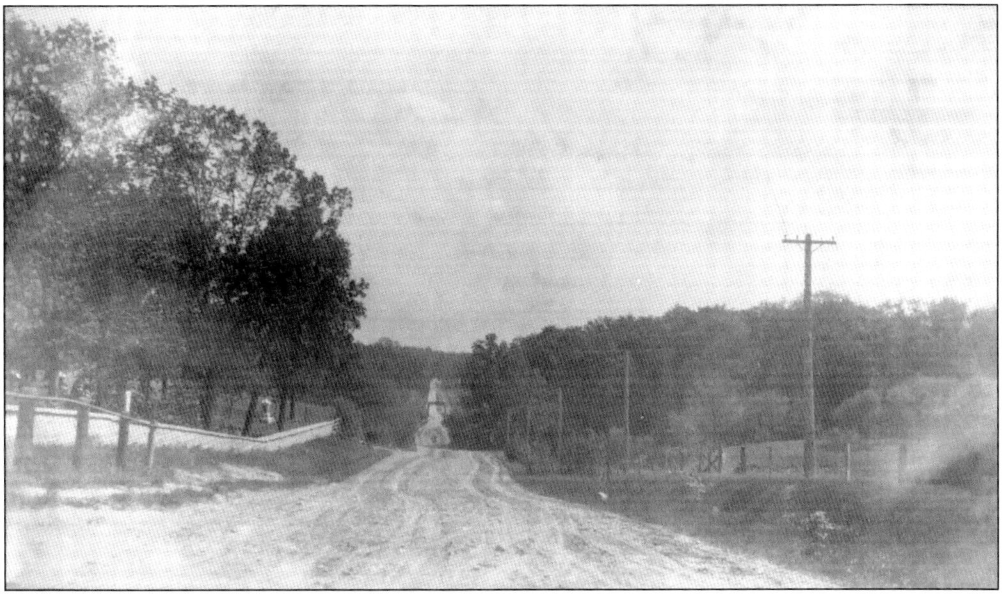

This photograph shows Wolf Road around 1915, looking south toward Hickory Creek. In early years, local residents referred to a section of this thoroughfare as "Martie Lane" because so many members of the Martie family kept farms along the road north of Mokena. St. John's Cemetery can be seen at left. (Photograph courtesy of Richard Quinn.)

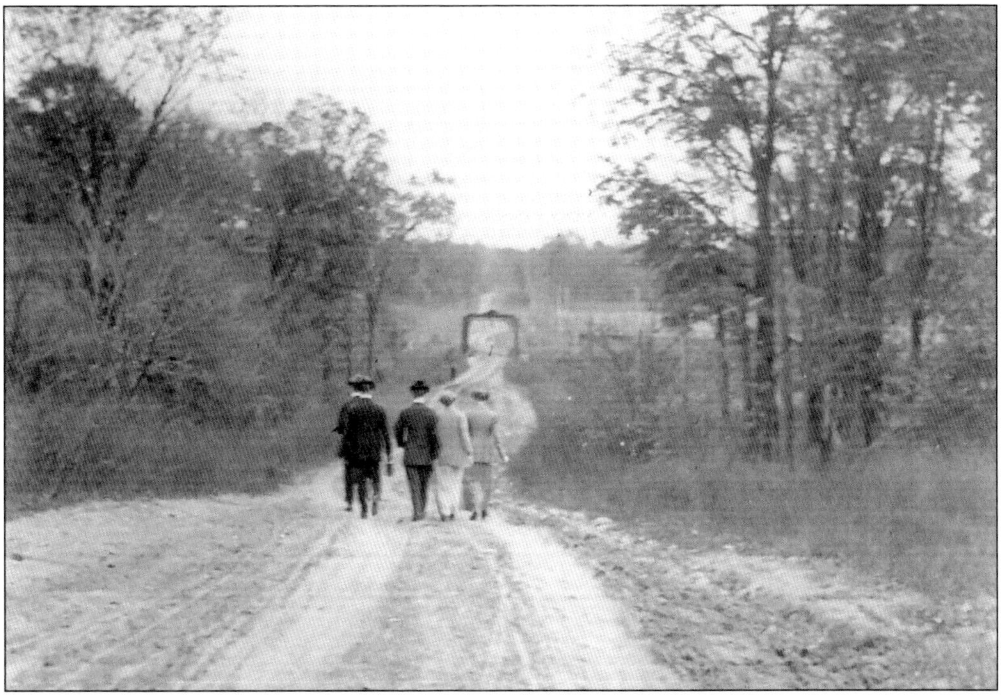

Merrymakers head south on a leisurely Sunday stroll down Wolf Road around 1920. Viewed from a point roughly equal with the present-day junction of 203rd Street and Wolf Road, one can easily discern the thin tracks of carriage wheels in the dirt of the road. Were these Mokenians headed to a picnic on the banks of Hickory Creek, or perhaps off to visit a friend on a nearby farm?

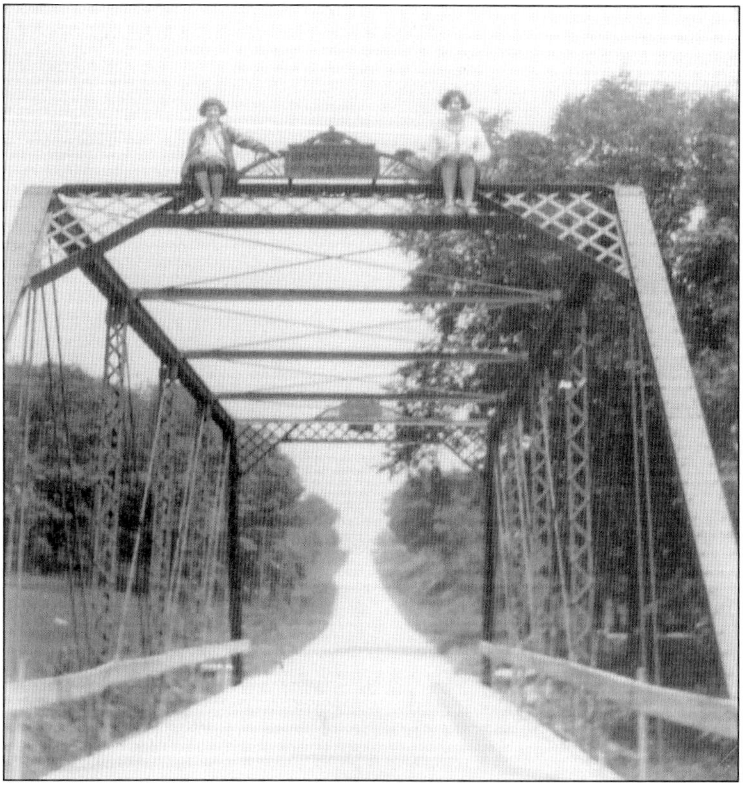

Built in an era before automobiles were imaginable on Wolf Road, this steel bridge over Hickory Creek was completed by Lane and Company in 1886. Here, Emma Yunker (left) sits atop the bridge, with her back toward Mokena, in 1924. Her friend is not identified. The meandering waters of Hickory Creek were and still are a popular spot for area fishermen.

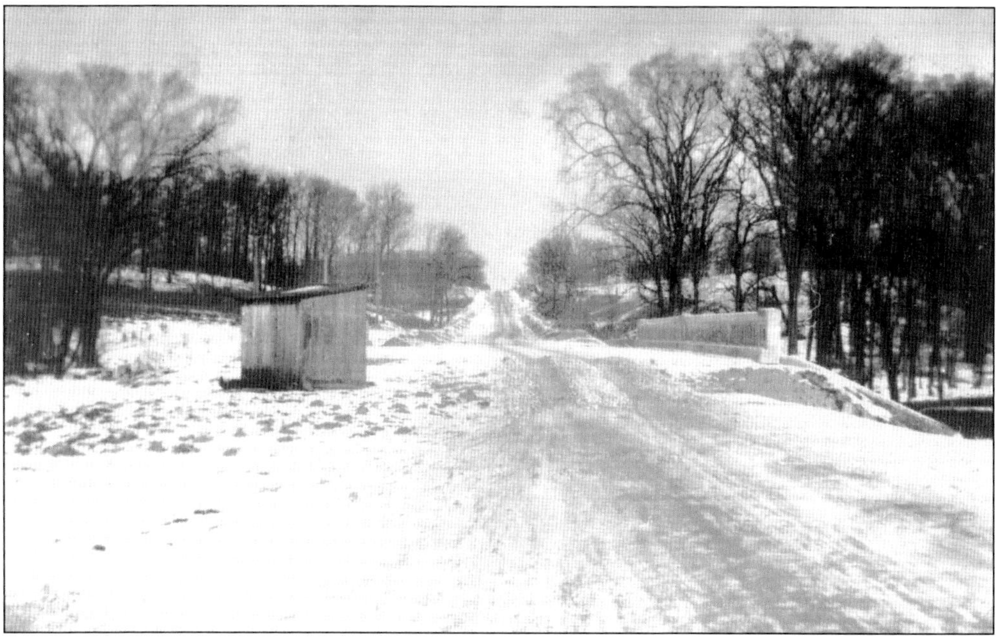

This c. 1930 image offers a serene winter view of Wolf Road, facing north from Hickory Creek. The new concrete bridge over the creek is visible at right, the old iron structure having been replaced earlier that year. The rise in the background, known amongst villagers as "Cemetery Hill," was a beloved winter spot for sled owners.

Seven

Amber Waves of Grain

Farmers formed America's foundation. Viewed through the lens of modern suburbia, it seems unlikely that the area around Mokena was a teeming center of agriculture for generations. This section of Will County was a farmer's paradise; the rich, fertile soil was plentiful, and the completion of the Chicago, Rock Island & Pacific Railroad in 1852 opened a gateway for the shipping of crops to city markets. A grain elevator in town was profitable for several lifetimes and, to epitomize Frankfort Township's status as a dairy region, the Bowman Dairy Company built a milk bottling plant in Mokena in 1907.

Although the farmer's life of old has been greatly idealized over the years, it was by no means an easy existence. To exemplify the toil of this existence, local farmer Martin Heim's health was ravaged so badly by strenuous work conditions that he abandoned the profession altogether. During a trip from Chicago in the days before the railroad, Diederich Brumund lost a valuable ox in a freak drowning accident. Weather was also a constant enemy; James Ducker once wrote off an entire season's crop to a severe hailstorm. Boys worked like men as soon as they were able, and schooling was only possible when the field and plow spared them.

This rather arduous life did have many upsides—fresh foodstuffs were generally always at hand; children had plenty of wide, open space in which to roam; and working together strengthened familial bonds. Goods from area farms were brought into Mokena to be traded with storekeepers, who would readily purchase locally produced milk and cheese. As early as the 1870s, cheese was made on the farm of J.G. Geuther, located at the northwest corner of the present-day 191st Street and Eighty-eighth Avenue intersection. Farmers and their rural lifestyles are fully woven into Mokena's historical background. Mokena owes its very existence to them and their generations of work.

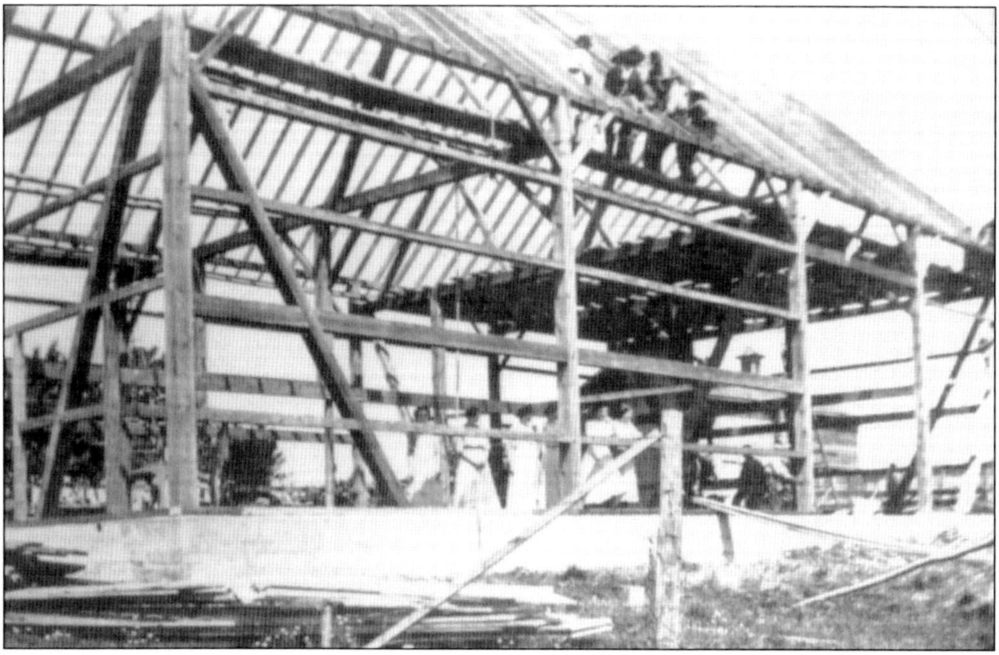

This image depicts the construction of a barn on the farm of Edward J. Maue in 1918. A well-respected dairy farmer, Maue was known for a feeding technique that led to high milk production in his cows. Maue and his older brother George owned large neighboring farms north of Mokena in the present-day vicinity of 183rd and 187th Streets.

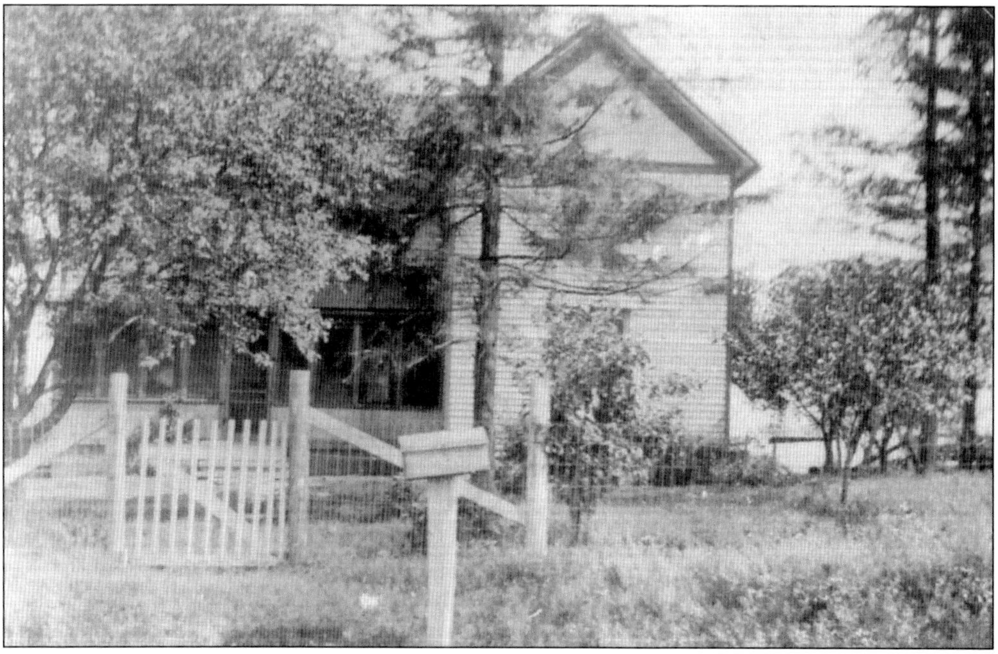

Formerly located on the north side of 191st Street at the intersection of Schoolhouse Road, the farm of Lawrence Kohl was a Mokena landmark until its demolition in the early 1990s. Having first arrived in the Mokena area in the latter part of the 1850s after fleeing Bohemia, members of the Kohl family still reside in the area to this day.

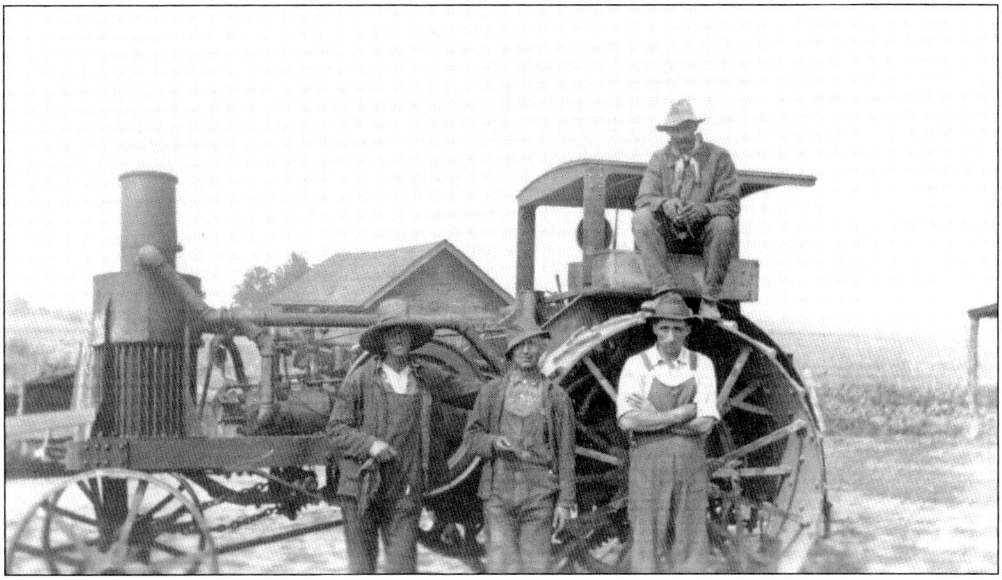

Farmworkers pause for a photographic opportunity on the Kohl farm around 1910. Pictured here are, from left to right, Lawrence Kohl, Bill Schweser, Elmer Benson, and Fred Yunker (atop the tractor). Working with others was a necessity for early Mokenians; if a farmer finished his duties early, he would often check with his neighbor to see if he needed help.

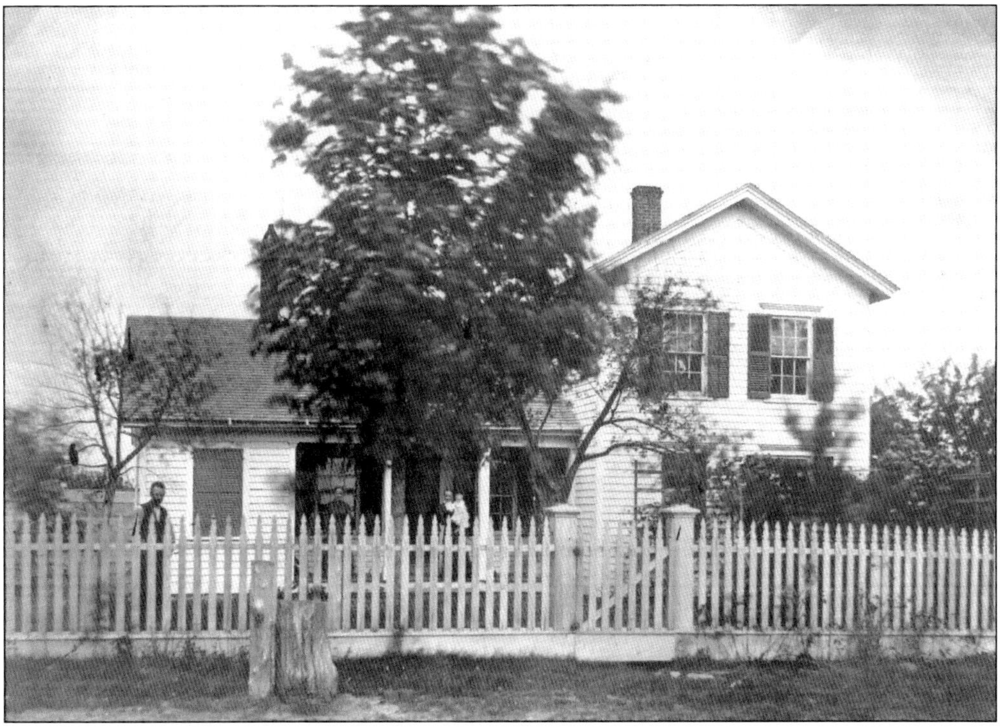

The farmhouse at 10600 191st Street is one of the oldest in the Mokena region. Likely built by German immigrant George Schweser around 1859, the farm remained in the hands of his descendants for over 100 years. Pictured here around 1905 are, from left to right, Lawrence Schweser, Mary (Storck) Schweser, and Ida (Schweser) Yunker (holding Ella Yunker).

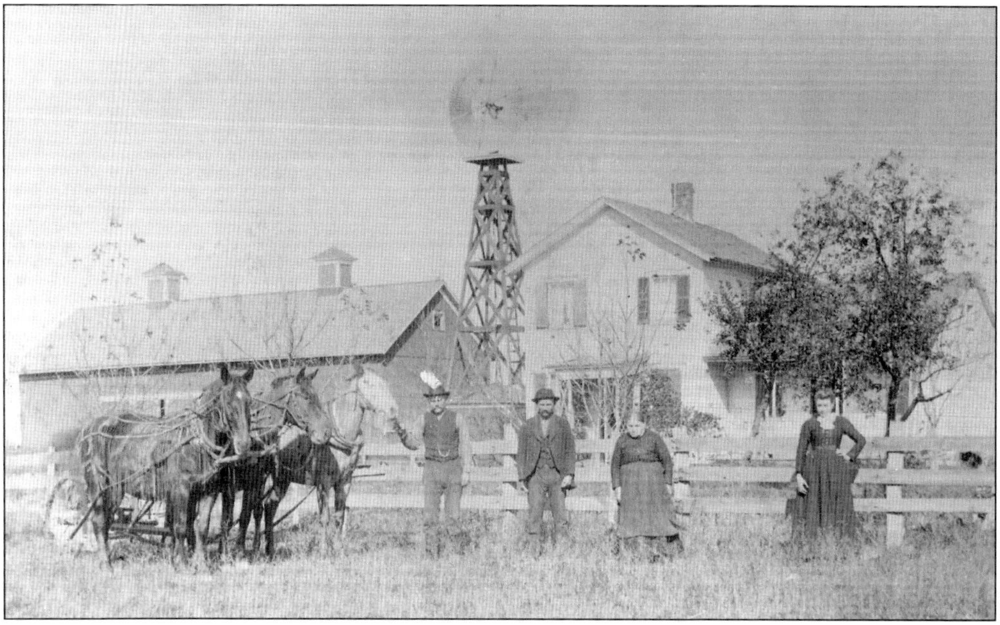

The Geuther farm, located near the northeast corner of LaGrange Road and 191st Street, is shown here around 1892. Posing in front of the farmhouse are, from left to right, Charles Geuther, Nicholas Geuther, Elisabeth (Baumgartner) Geuther, and Caroline Geuther. This family's patriarch, Johann G. Geuther, operated a cheese factory near Eighty-eighth Avenue in the 1870s and was killed by a Rock Island train outside Mokena in 1890.

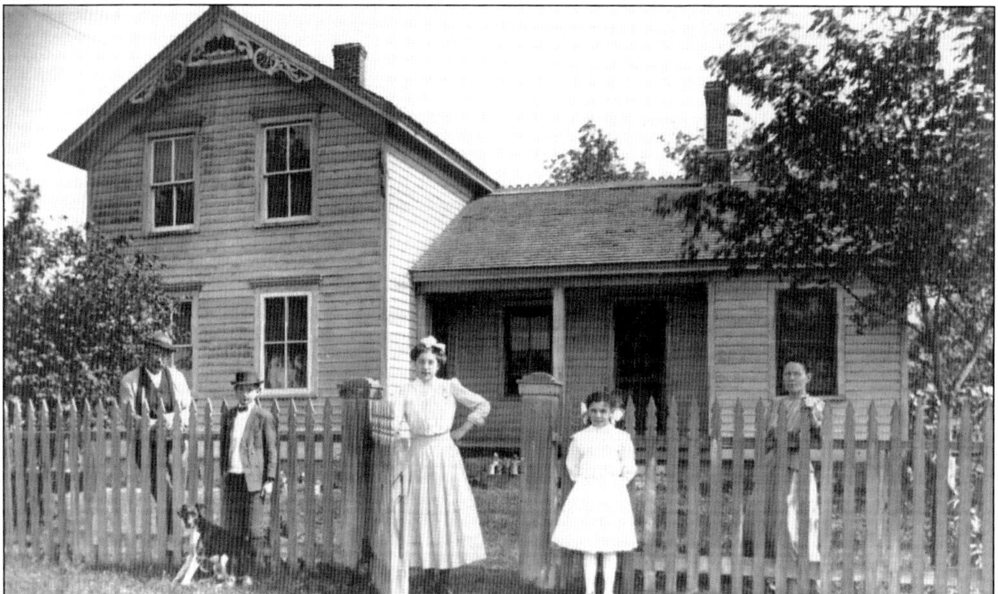

Descendants of one of the area's first German families, the family of dairyman Henry Schiek poses on their farm around 1910. Constructed approximately 1870 by Philipp Schiek, this farmhouse was a local landmark for generations, having formerly stood at 19200 Wolf Road. Pictured here from left to right are Henry Schiek, Dewey the dog, Lester Schiek, Alma Schiek, Mabel Schiek, and Carrie (Nonnemacher) Schiek.

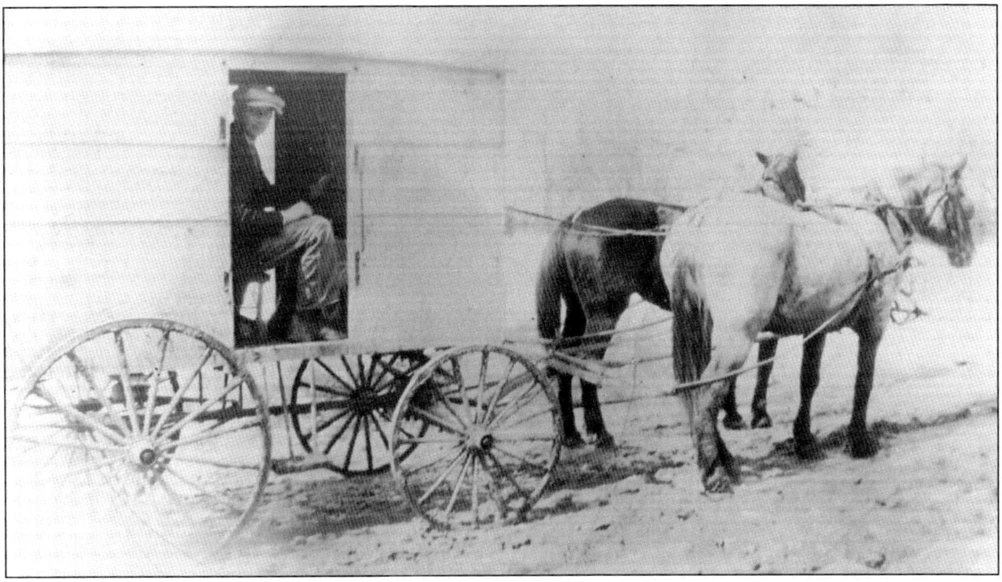

Nicknamed the "congenial milkman" by one of his contemporaries, Lester Schiek worked in the Mokena dairy business for the majority of his life. The Schieks had six area customers upon the inception of their business in 1902. Lester Schiek, seen here in the back of his father's delivery wagon around 1920, took over the delivery route in 1928, and was supplying 95 percent of Mokena residents with milk by 1950.

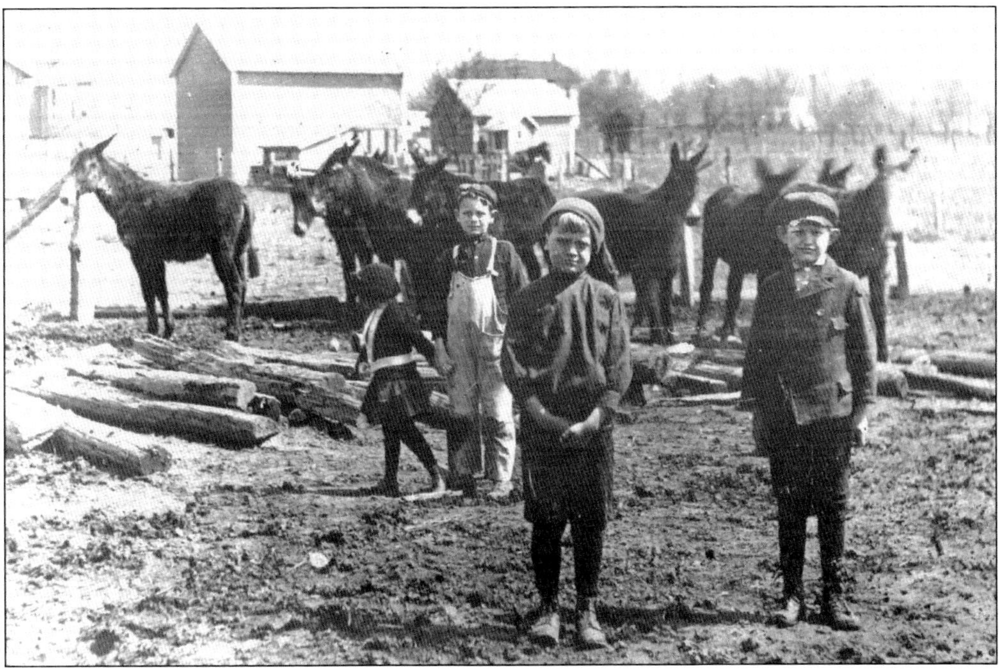

This farm, purchased by Bavarian immigrant Carl Hirsch in 1859, sat for decades at the present-day northwest corner of Wolf Road and 195th Street. Brothers Charles and Julius Hirsch, two well-known livestock dealers, took over the farm in the early 20th century. The children of Julius and Anna (Baer) Hirsch are seen here around 1910. They are, from left to right, Julia Hirsch, Carl Hirsch, and Ed Hirsch. John Reikal is at far right.

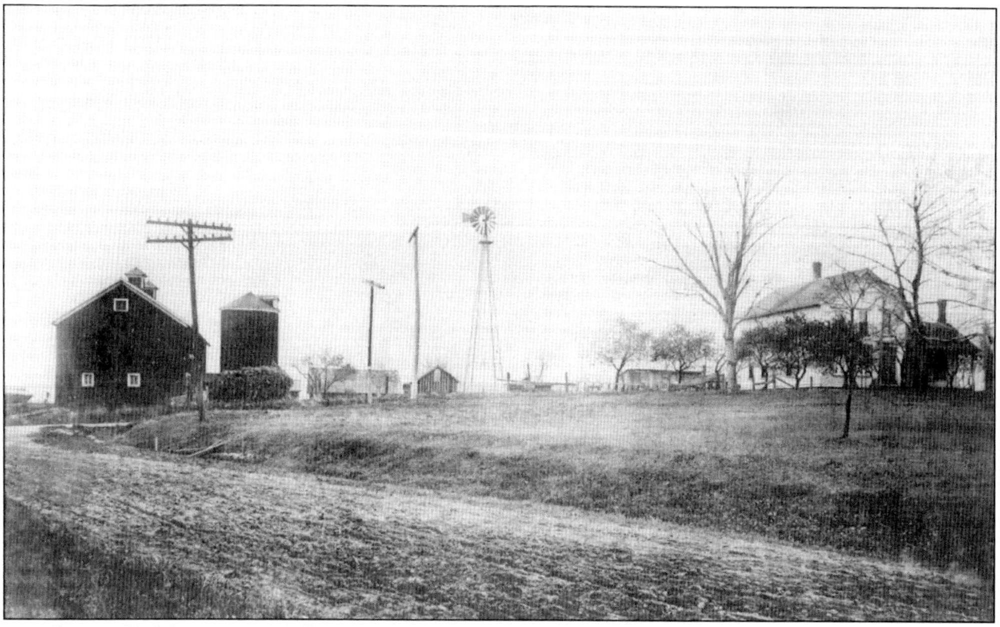

Fondly recalled by many residents as the Charles Erickson farm, this site, at the intersection of Front Street and Schoolhouse Road, belonged to George Schweser as early as 1873. A tangible link to Mokena's rich agricultural heritage, the historic home still remains, as does the large dairy barn, built around 1900. (Photograph courtesy of Richard Quinn.)

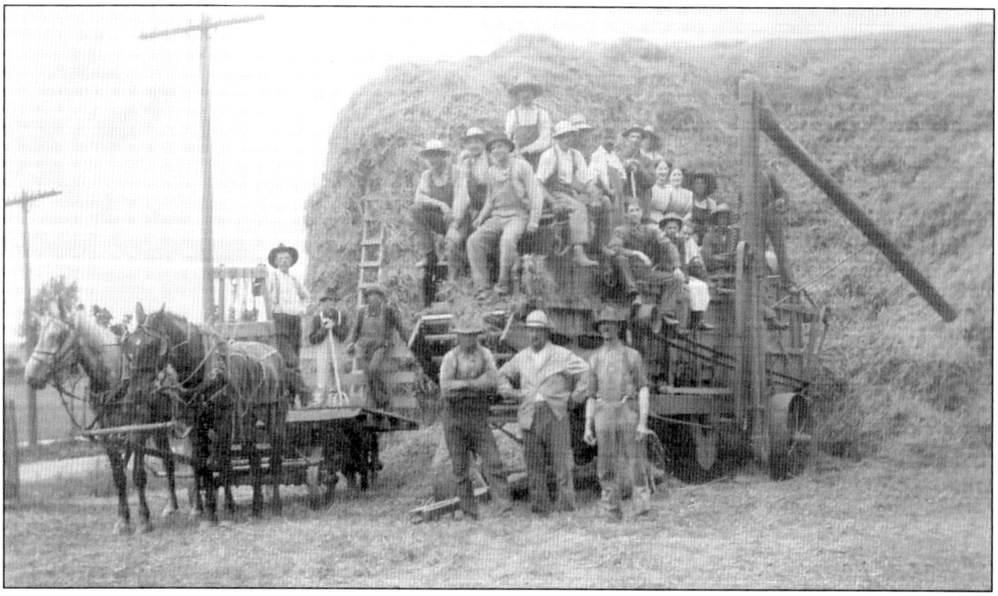

Although the Mokenians of today might consider this sight rather unusual, the results of mowing hay would have been a common sight for the area's forefathers. After mowing the hay, a process in which grass is cut and used for fodder, farm workers and a few spectators pose with the results of their hard work around 1910 on the Schoolhouse Road farm of John Erickson.

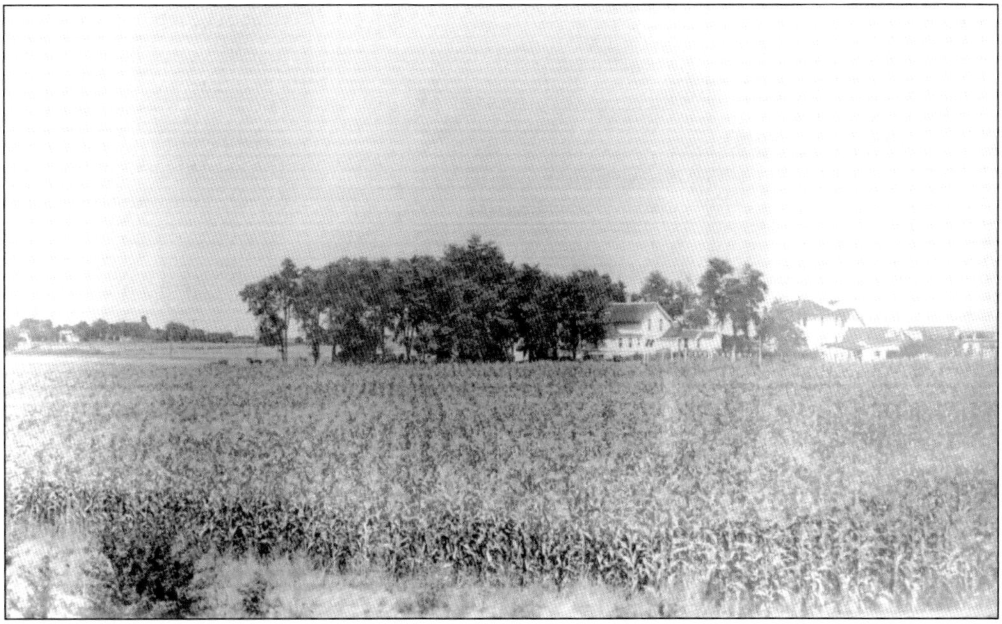

Looking roughly northeast from LaPorte Road and Center Street, this image from about 1910 shows the farm of Kate Knox. At the end of the 19th century, chemists analyzed water from a well at this site and purported its strength as a healing agent of, among other ailments, rheumatism. By 1910, the Mokena Mineral Spring Company had been founded and 4,000 gallons of local water were being shipped to Chicago each week.

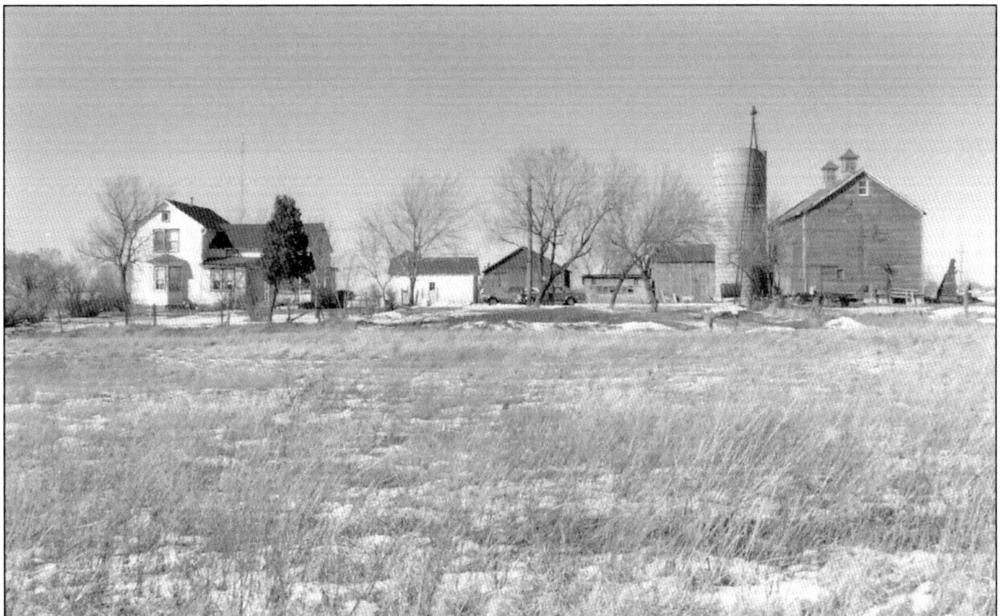

This farm, formerly located at the northwest corner of LaPorte and LaGrange Roads, was a local landmark for generations. The farm, purchased from the Dickmann family by Nicholas Marti Jr. in 1882, was eventually handed down to Marti's son Immanuel. After passing into the ownership of Henry Langland around 1950, the farm was torn down in the 1980s.

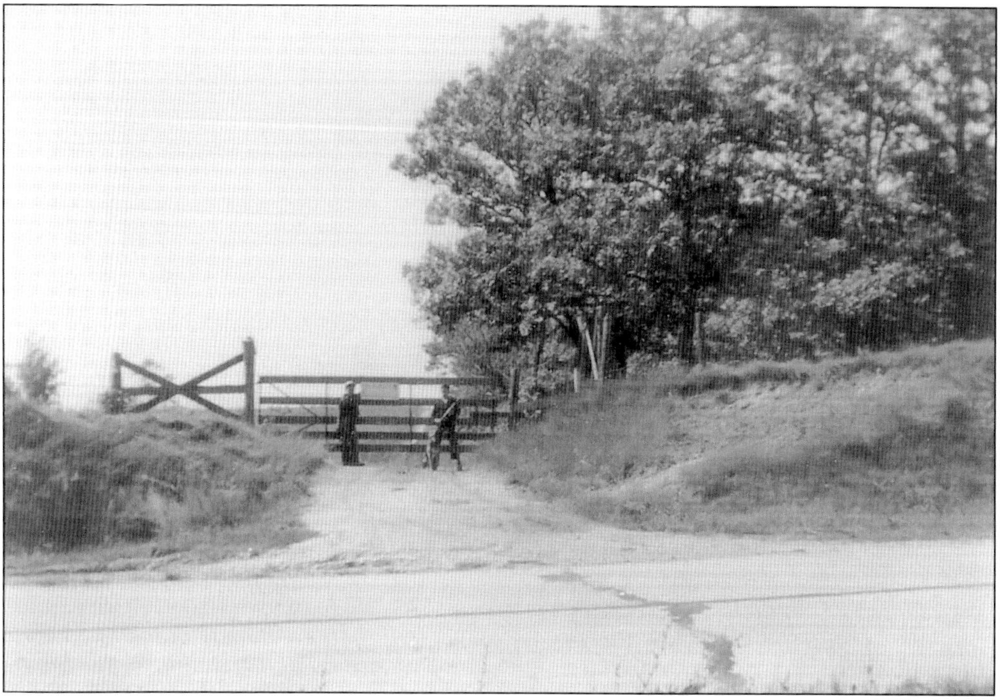

The Wolf Road entrance to the Kluth sisters' country home is seen here. A modest farm, which the Kluths acquired from Martin Sandrock in the pre–World War II era, stood at the end of this winding rural lane that was later named after them.

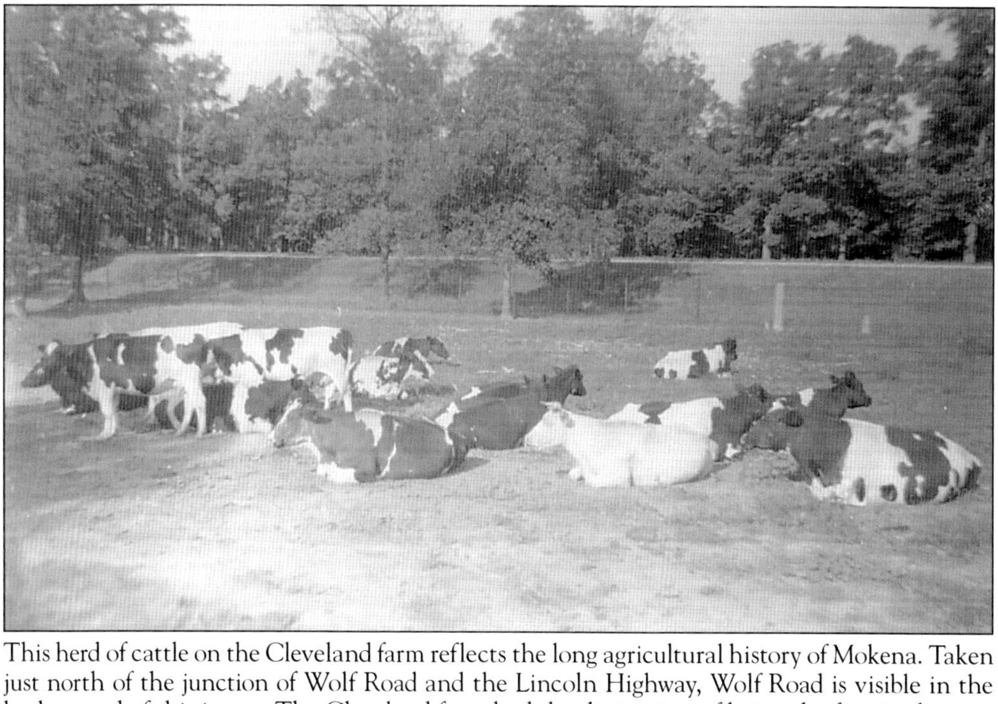

This herd of cattle on the Cleveland farm reflects the long agricultural history of Mokena. Taken just north of the junction of Wolf Road and the Lincoln Highway, Wolf Road is visible in the background of this image. The Cleveland farm had the distinction of being the first in the area to feature a silo made of concrete blocks.

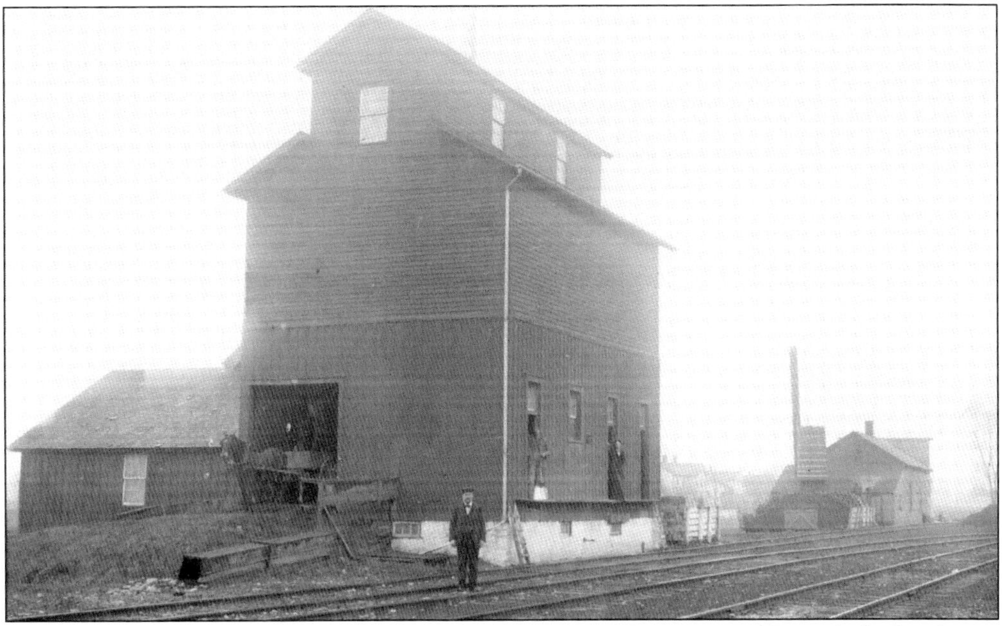

The grain elevator east of 19709 Mokena Street is perhaps the most visible symbol of Mokena's agricultural background. Still standing today, this structure was built in 1884 after the previous elevator was destroyed in a mysterious fire. Shown here around 1900, the elevator was then owned by local businessman John A. Hatch. From this site, Hatch dealt in grain, feed, coal, and tile. (Photograph courtesy of Richard Quinn.)

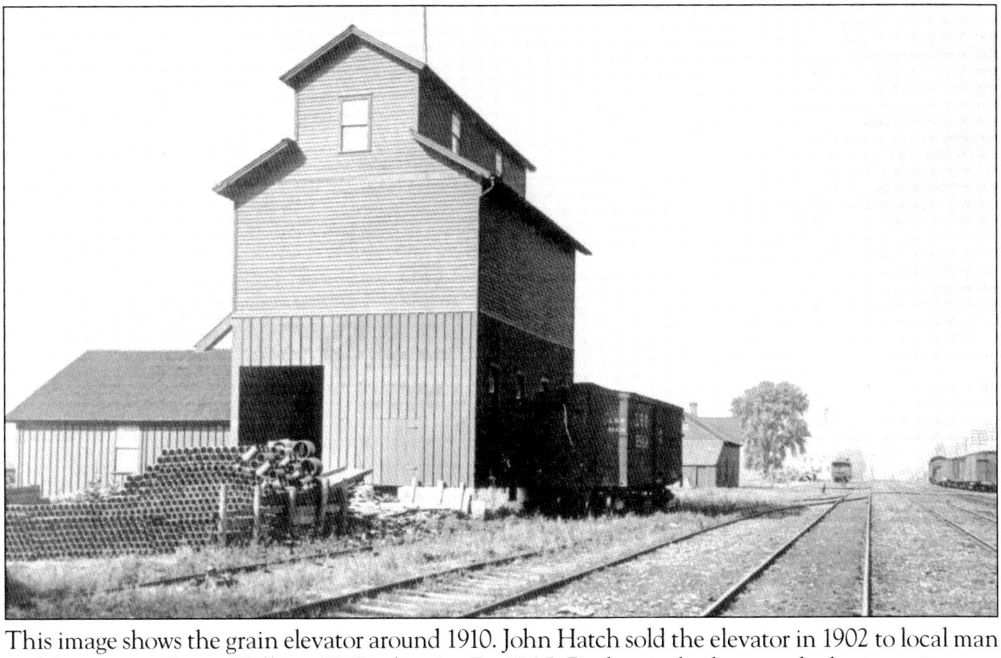

This image shows the grain elevator around 1910. John Hatch sold the elevator in 1902 to local man and former employee William H. Bechstein. By 1905, Bechstein had pursued a business interest in Seneca, Illinois, and transferred ownership of the building to the Liess brothers, of Mokena. Within two years, Bechstein came back to town and reacquired the feed and coal business. Two of Bechstein's employees in this era were Oscar Klose and Charles Knapp.

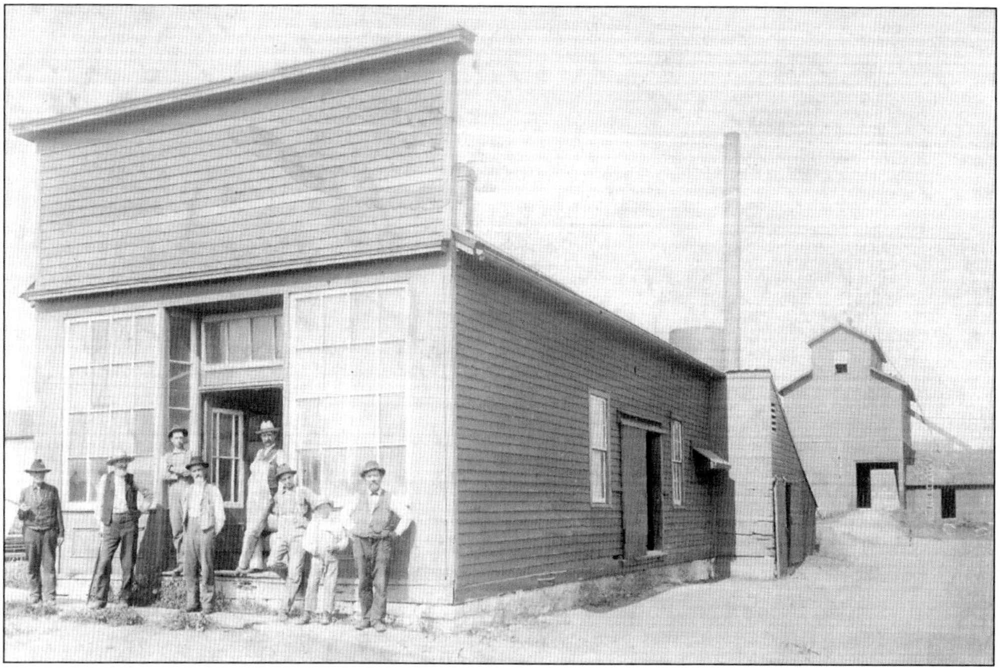

Pictured here around 1910 is the feed house of W.H. Bechstein at the Mokena grain elevator. The elevator's business transactions were conducted in this building, which formerly stood at the location of today's 19709 Mokena Street. At one point, large millstones were housed in the feed house. Visible here from left to right are unidentified, ? Mattes, Henry Leonhardt, John Liess, Will Bechstein, unidentified, Ralph Hacker, and Carl Hacker Sr.

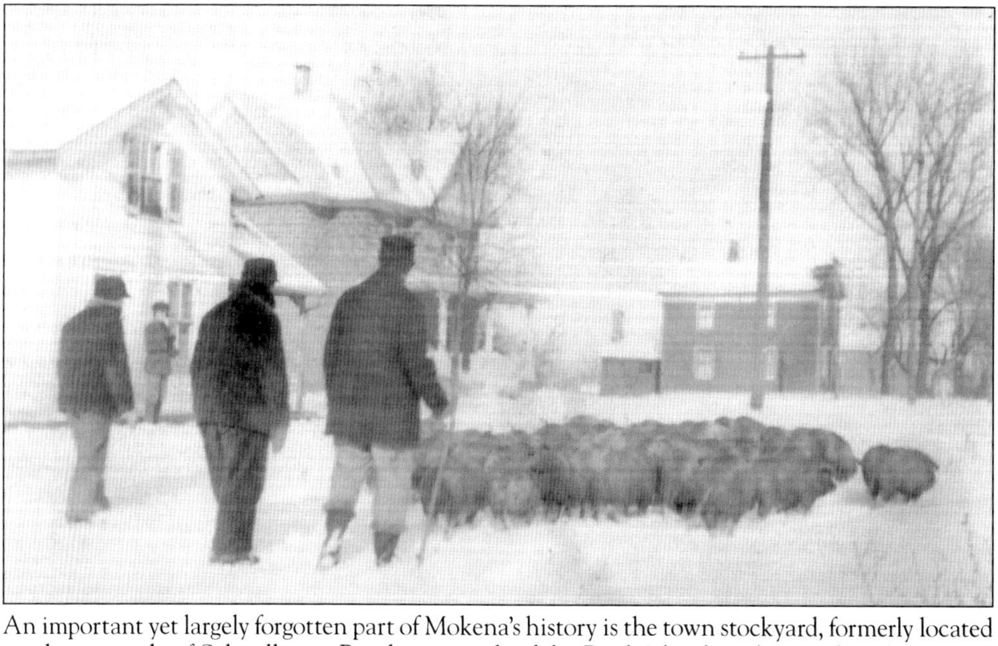

An important yet largely forgotten part of Mokena's history is the town stockyard, formerly located on the west side of Schoolhouse Road, just south of the Rock Island tracks. As this photograph of First Street from around 1920 shows, it was once a common sight to see livestock being driven through town en route to the yards. Joe Hirsch is pictured at right.

Eight

For the Fun of It

Leisure activities are the string that binds a community together and the times that vast friendships are born and relationships are solidified. Although village residents of yesteryear lived and loved in a vastly different world, they knew the surrounding countryside was a natural playground for generations of Mokena youth. The waters of Hickory Creek provided ample fish for anglers, lush forests were rife with game for hunting and trapping, and the southward-sloping hill on Wolf Road, at St. John's Cemetery, was popular for winter sledding.

One of the earliest known recreational organizations in Mokena was the local Turnverein, led by John Liess. Tracing its history to 1877, this German-style gymnastic squad competed against those of neighboring communities and was headquartered in a hall on the southwest corner of Front Street and Wolf Road before the building was lost in a fire. Mokena's churches were also social focal points; among other community groups, St. John's church had their own *Jugendverein*, or youth society, as early as the 1890s.

Perhaps the most beloved festival in Mokena was the local homecoming celebration. Started in 1938 by the Mokena Civic Association, this autumn gala was akin to a quaint, several-days-long party along Front Street. What began as a yearly tradition ended around 1956 when an apparent tornado struck the festival site, causing its hosts to permanently shut down the event for insurance reasons. Several later imitations lacked the congenial atmosphere of the original, thus permanently consigning the Mokena Homecoming to history.

Sports have been locally beloved as well, with baseball being an early favorite. Around 1900, a baseball diamond was located on the George Marti farm at the present-day 19004 Wolf Road. About 10 years later, the diamond was moved to the Elmer Benson farm, east of town. A rivalry between the Mokena and Frankfort baseball teams drew thousands of spectators from across the region, and a farmer's barbed wire fence strung across left field was the source of many rips in players' uniforms. Although Mokena's forerunners may have led different lives, they also understood the importance of fun.

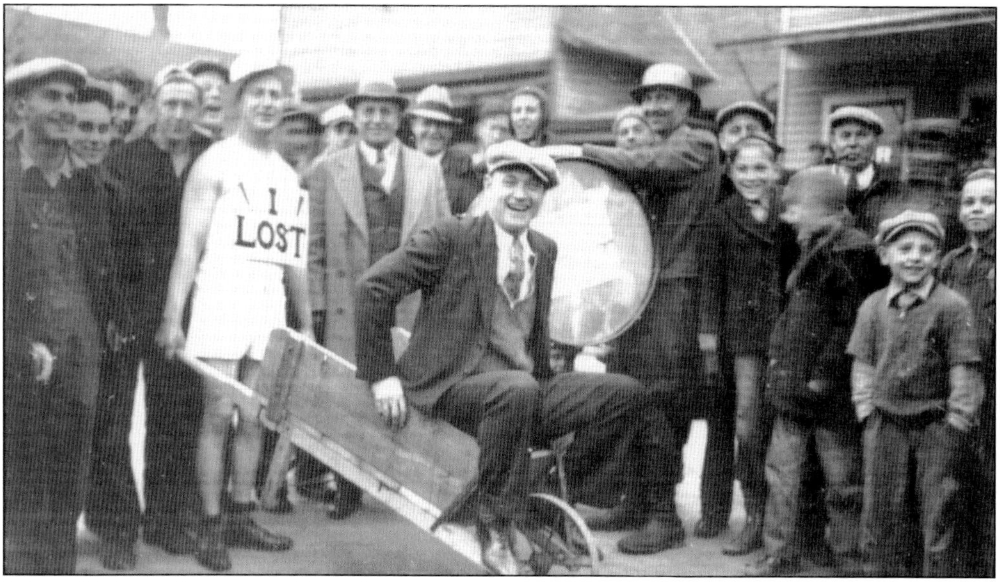

Life in Mokena during the Great Depression was not easy, but residents still found time to be lighthearted. In this image from April 1935, George Bennett hitches a ride from Albert Hentsch after winning an election bet. The bet stated that the loser, clad only in his underwear, would have to push the winner down Front Street from Morry's Tavern to the city hall and back.

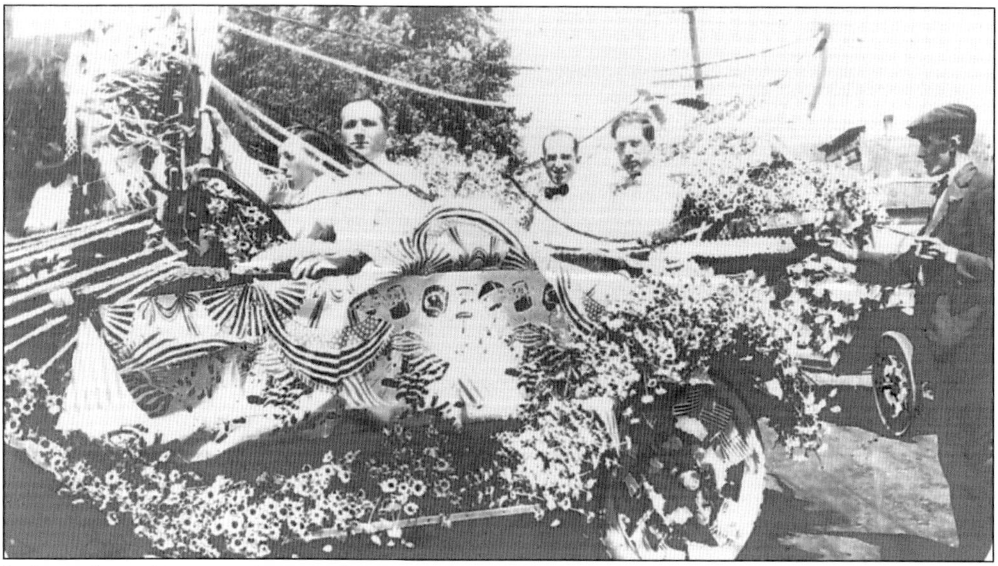

Independence Day parades are a long-standing tradition in Mokena. In what is likely the oldest known photograph of a local Fourth of July celebration, local merchants Christie and Elmer Sippel and brothers Ona and Ozias McGovney pose inside a patriotically decorated auto on Front Street on the nation's 140th anniversary, in 1916. An unidentified Mokenian applies the finishing touches to the car at right.

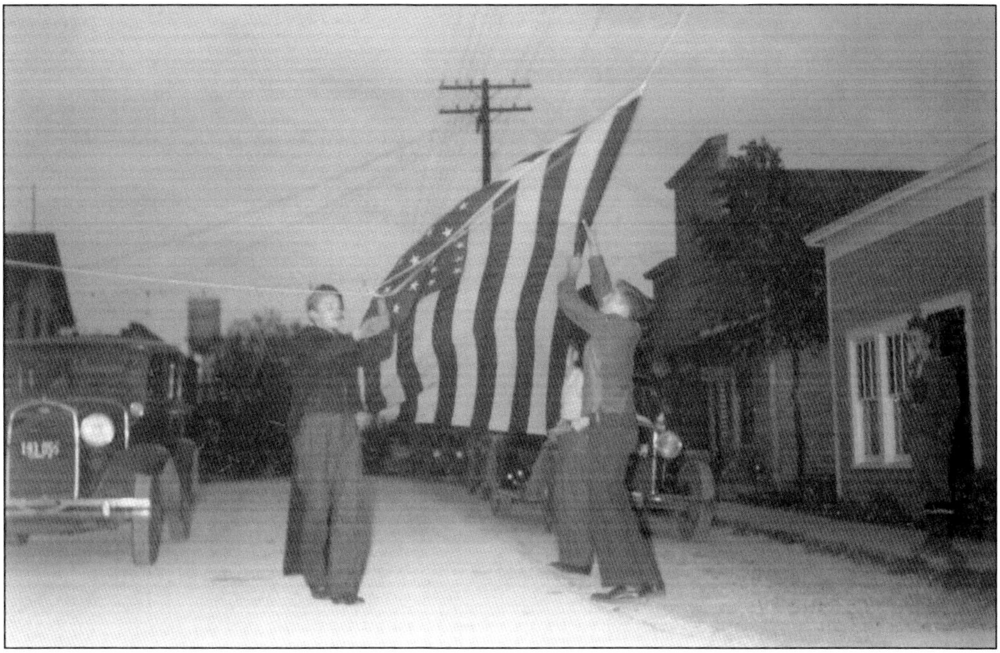

After a day of celebrating, local boys lower the Stars and Stripes at the intersection of Front and Mokena Streets during Mokena's first homecoming celebration, held on October 21 and 22 in 1938. Initiated by the Mokena Civic Association, the homecoming was an annual village festival that featured agricultural exhibits, lively music and dancing, and home-style food. The structure shown second from right is the present-day 11037 Front Street.

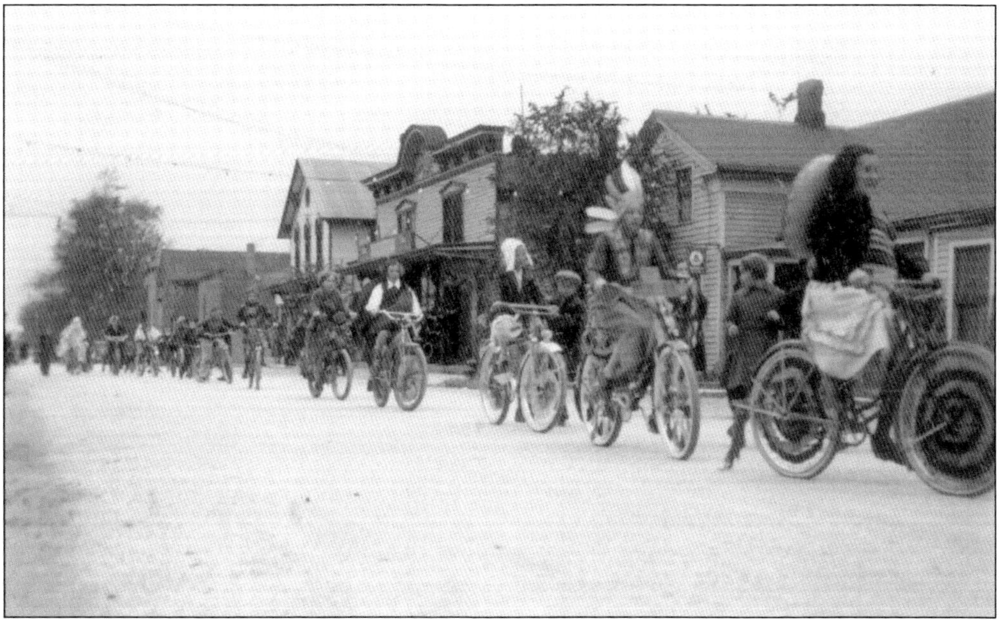

The Saturday of Mokena's first homecoming fete, in October 1938, was reserved for a bicycle parade of village youngsters down Front Street. The inaugural homecoming highlighted a special open-air dance platform on the grounds of the Rock Island depot that was reserved for jitterbugging. The present-day 11116 Front Street is visible in the background.

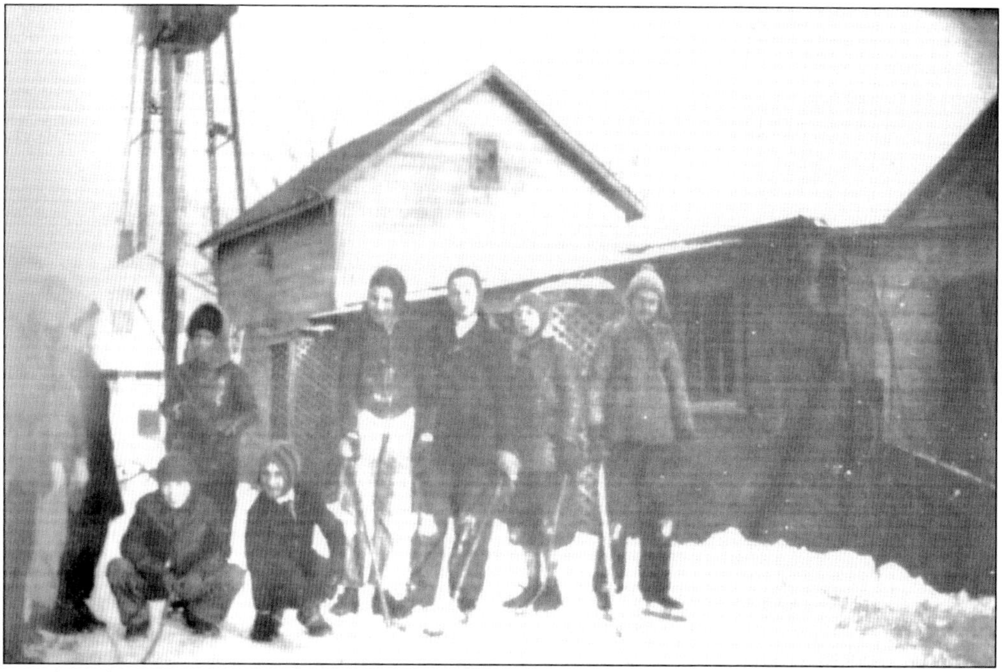

Harsh Midwestern winters provided Mokenians with ample free-time activities. A group of young ice skaters are seen here around 1938 in the vicinity of Front Street, with the village water tower in background at left. Judging by the sticks that several youth are holding, it appears that an impromptu hockey match was taking place.

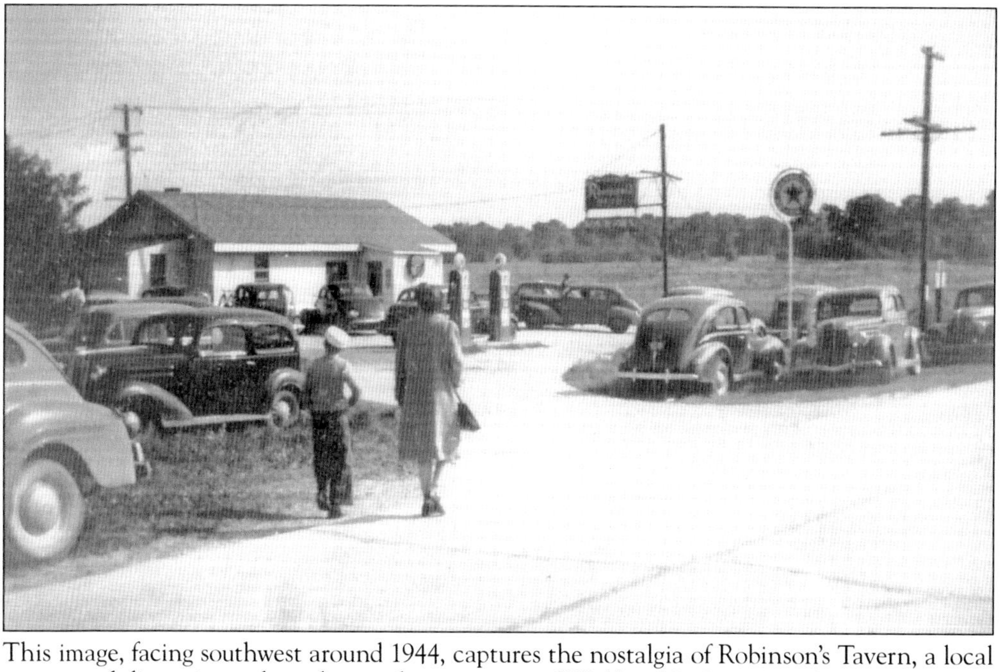

This image, facing southwest around 1944, captures the nostalgia of Robinson's Tavern, a local tavern and diner situated on the northeast corner of Wolf and LaPorte Roads. A well-known baseball field was dedicated behind the tavern in July 1940, having the distinction of being the only diamond for miles around with floodlights for night games.

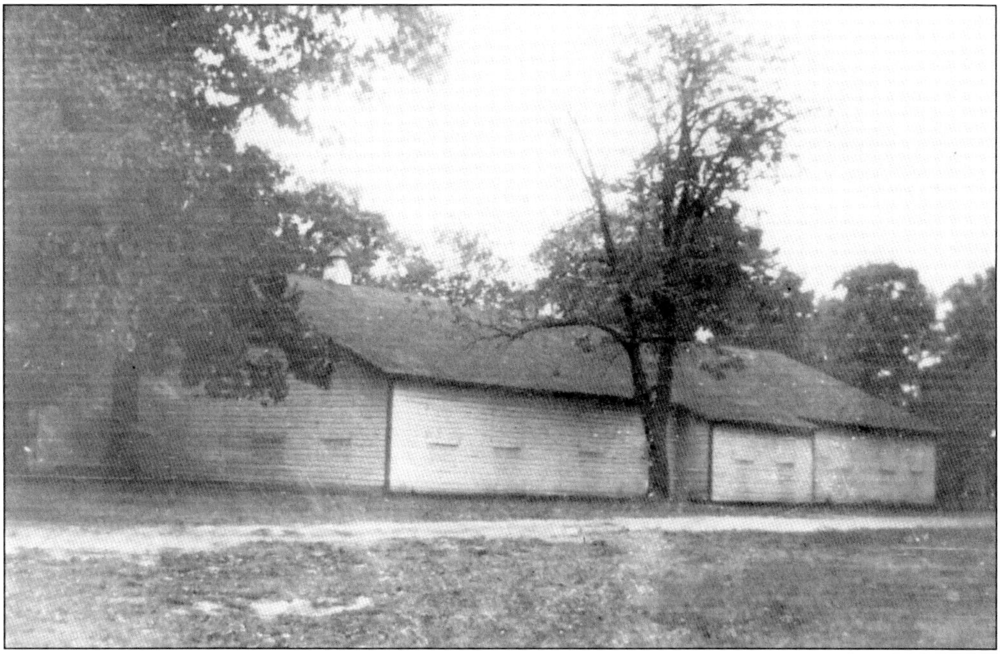

With dancing having long been a popular local pastime, the Mokena Men's Club leased several acres south of the village to erect this dance pavilion in 1907. This pavilion, which stood on the west side of Wolf Road at the present-day site of Woodland Circle, often hosted the popular traveling bands of Sammy Berk and Harry Sweet. Upon opening, admission was 50¢ for men and free for women.

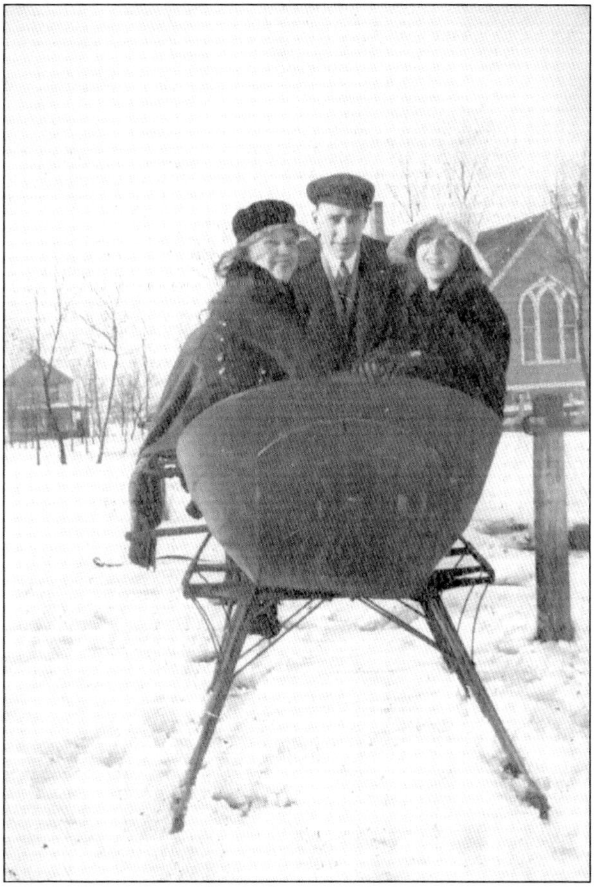

In this c. 1922 image, a young couple, Roy Kropp (center) and Elfriede Kreis (right), enjoy a sleigh ride through wintry Mokena with Roy's mother, Selma (Schaub) Krapp. The present-day 11110 Third Street is recognizable in the background at left, and the former Immanuel Lutheran church is at right. (Photograph courtesy of David Kropp.)

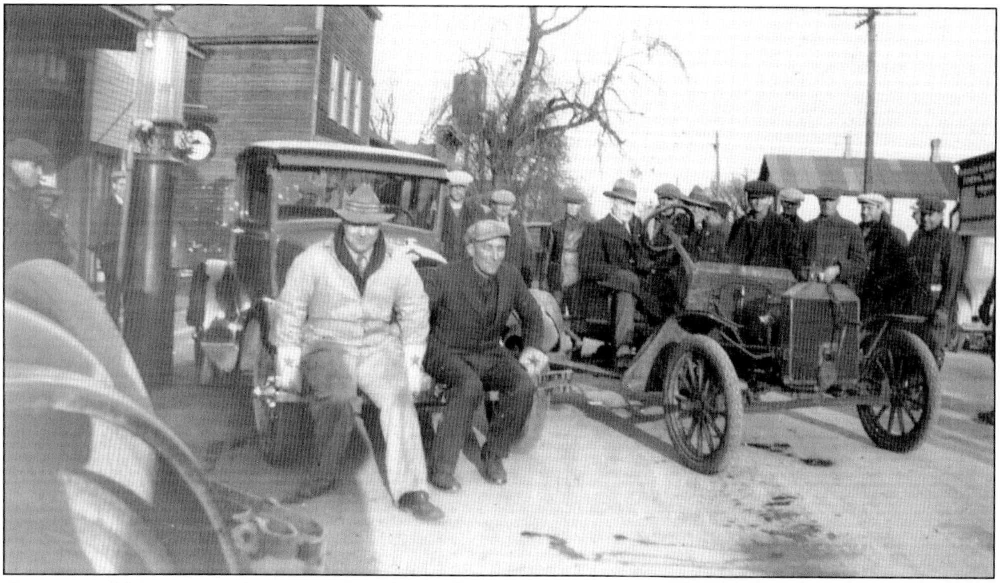

An unusual leisure activity enjoyed in the Mokena area was a type of polo played using automobiles. The stripped-down Model T Ford at right was used in such a game, held on a playing field located off 187th Street, near Marley. This c. 1925 image depicts a game crowd at the Cooper and Hostert Ford Agency on Front Street. (Photograph courtesy of Richard Quinn.)

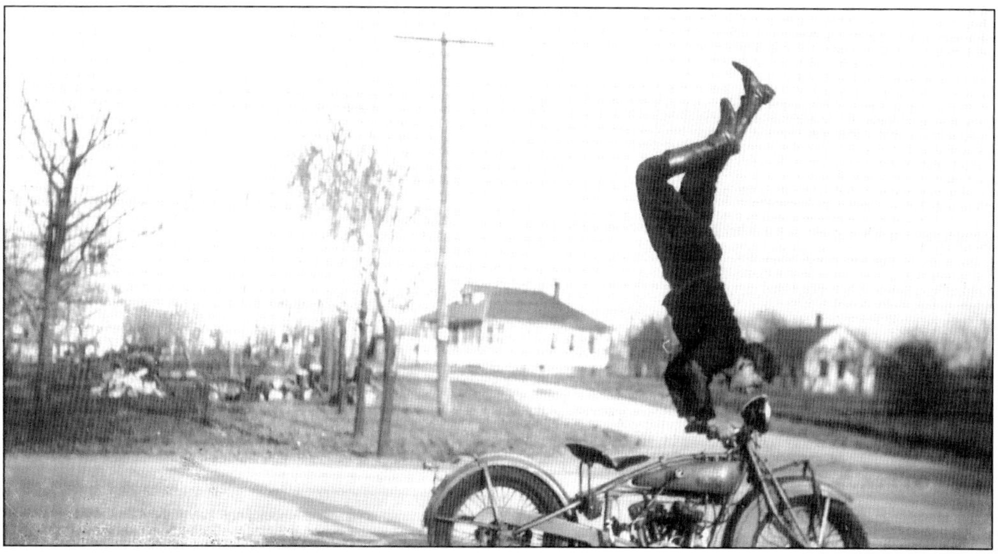

Seen here around 1933, hometown daredevil George Walsh strikes an intrepid pose on his motorcycle. Looking east from the intersection of Wolf Road and Denny Avenue, at this time, this area was considered the southern edge of Mokena. Walsh, a motorcycle buff, converted a barn on his Third Street property into a spot for local repairs.

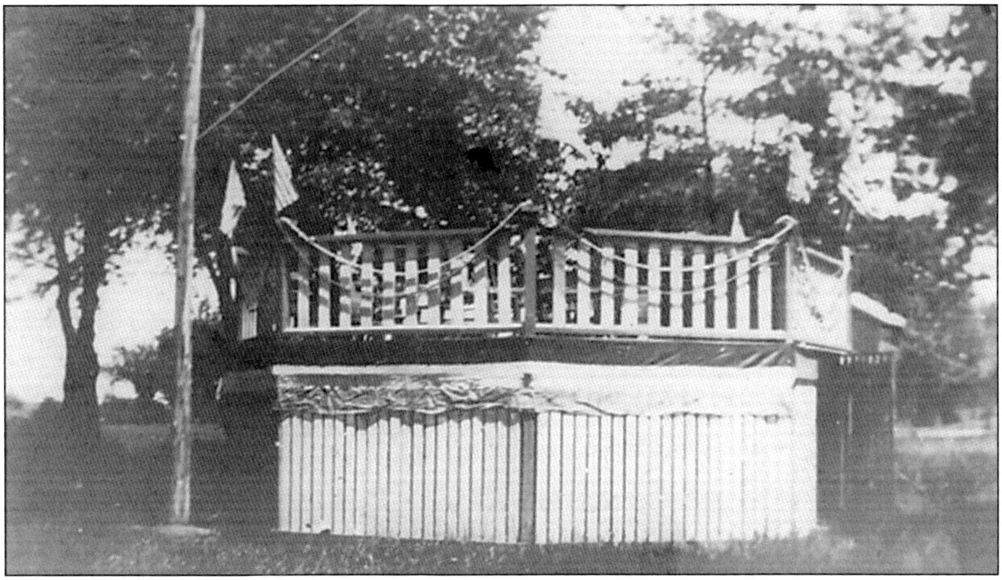

This bandstand, located near the southwest corner of Third and Union Streets, was built entirely by volunteer effort. The Frank Mall Lumber Company donated building materials, Phillip Hacker and Herman Schweser assisted in construction, and good Samaritans provided light poles and benches. Seen here around the time of its completion in 1920, local musicians hosted open-air performances on the bandstand. (Photograph courtesy of David Kropp.)

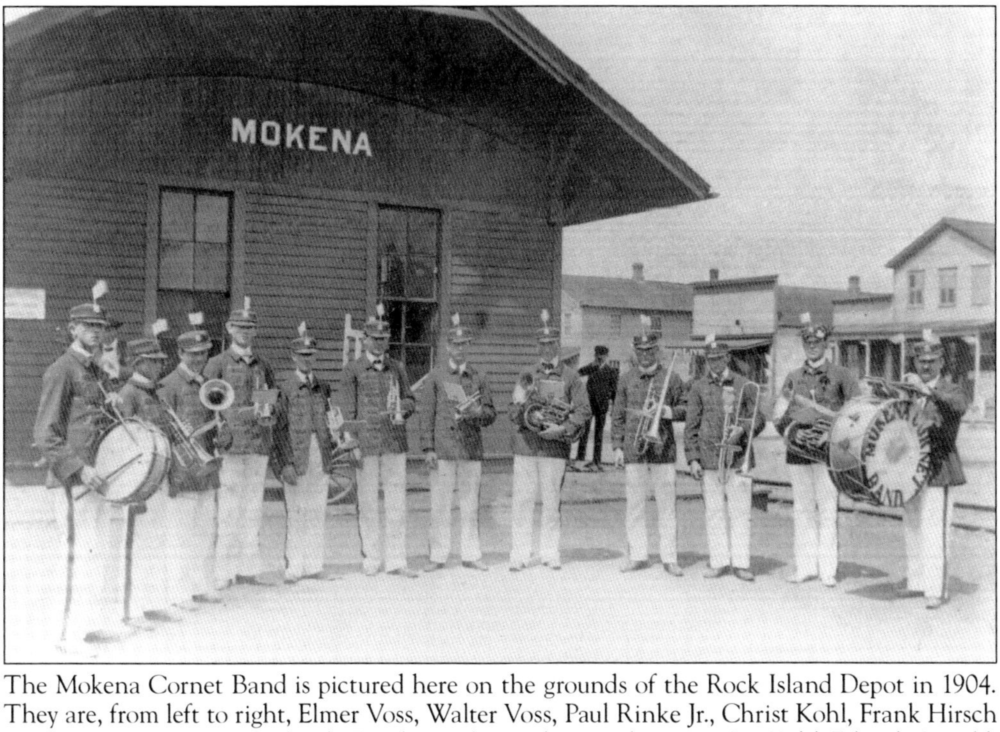

The Mokena Cornet Band is pictured here on the grounds of the Rock Island Depot in 1904. They are, from left to right, Elmer Voss, Walter Voss, Paul Rinke Jr., Christ Kohl, Frank Hirsch Jr., Ben Mager, Henry Leonhardt, Frank Knudson, Christ Hohenstein, Joe Kohl, Erhardt Oswald, and Henry Stellwagen. The band was a popular draw at local festivities and was known for their crimson uniform coats.

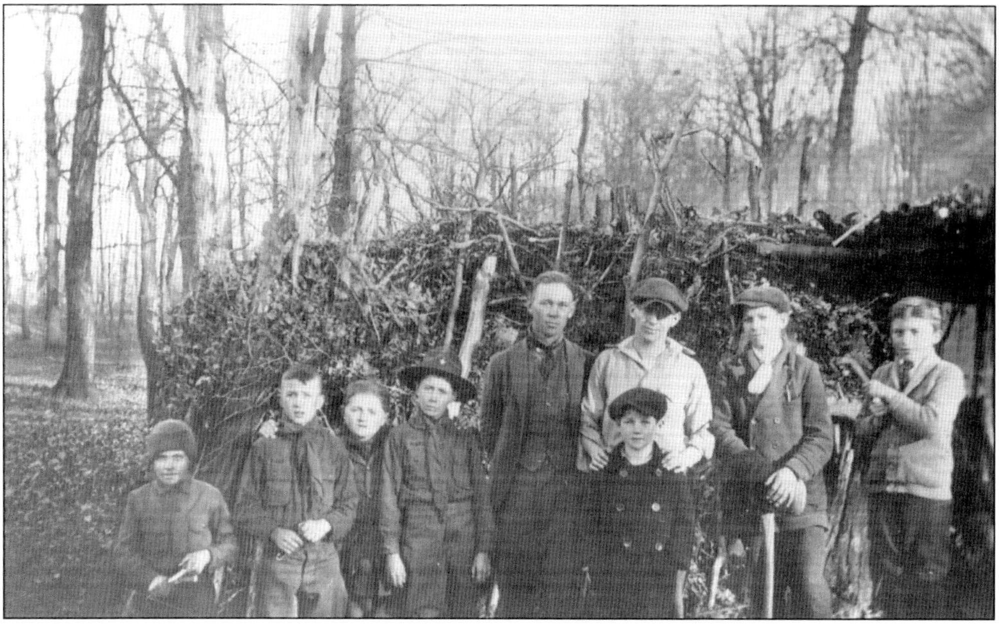

Boy Scout Troop 40, established in 1938, has been a part of Mokena for decades. Seen here on April 10, 1921, an earlier troop of Mokena Scouts pose with a shelter they built near Wolf Road and Hickory Creek. Pictured here are, from left to right, Alfred Heiman, Harley Gillette, Chuck Liess, Marvin Lockwood, Helmer Johnson, Scoutmaster Acy Woods (with his hands on the shoulders of Roy Clark), Clark, George Aschenbrenner, and Louis Schenkel.

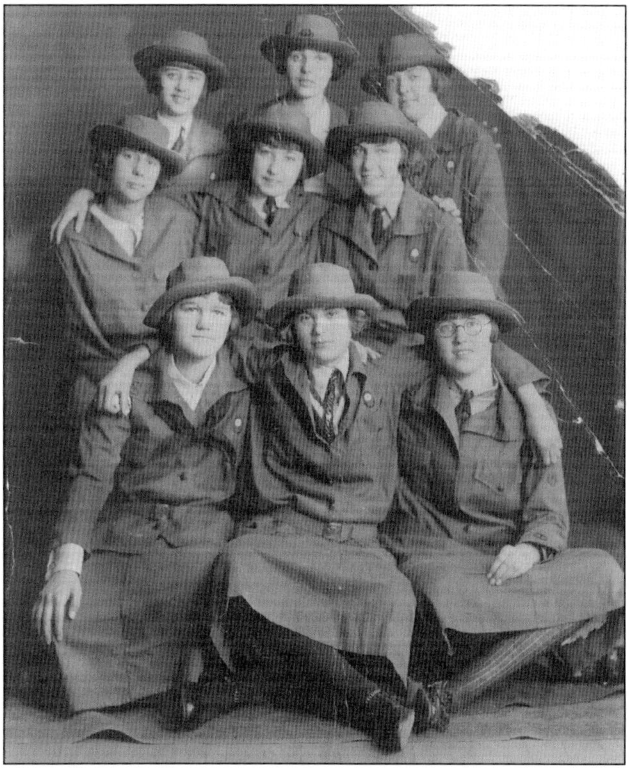

Long committed to community activities in Mokena, local Girl Scouts are seen in this group photograph taken around 1925. They are, from left to right, as follows: (first row) Fern Liess, Helen Nielsen, and Ethel Sorenson; (second row) Marie Mauger, Evelyn Hacker, and Edna ?; (third row) Dolly Hensel, Luetta Darling, and Elizabeth Lynk.

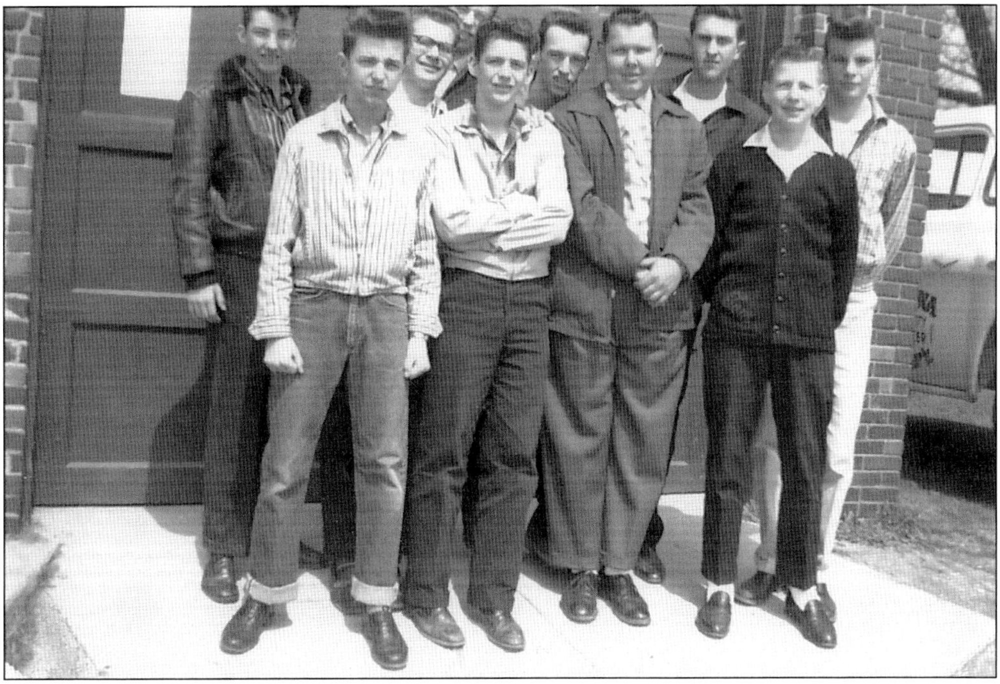

Boy Scout Troop 40 is pictured at the Mokena Village Hall in 1957. Shown here are, from left to right, (first row) Ron Ford, Jim Miller, adult leader Howie Thacker, and Dan Williams; (second row) Cliff Cheatwood, Lowel Noodwang, Ray Lorenz, Tom Miller, Robert Munch, and Jim Haislet. Munch was Mokena's first Eagle Scout, blazing an honorable path that has since been followed by many Mokenians.

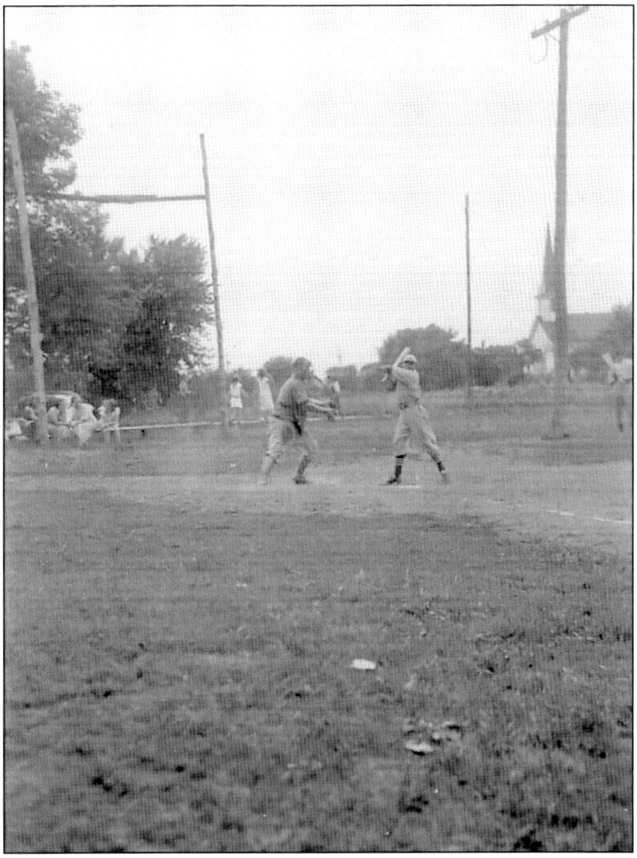

Fitting the moniker "America's Pastime," baseball has been a favorite sport of Mokenians for over 100 years. Following the establishment of the first local team around 1900, many different locations in and around the village served as playing areas. A baseball diamond once located on the present-day site of 11028 Third Street is seen here in the mid-1930s.

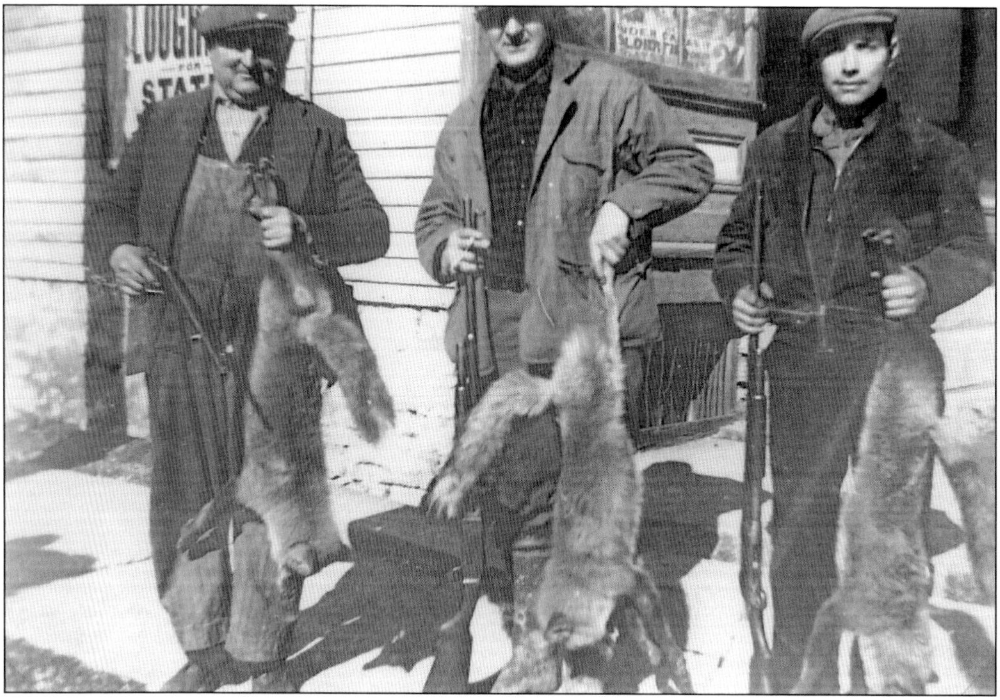

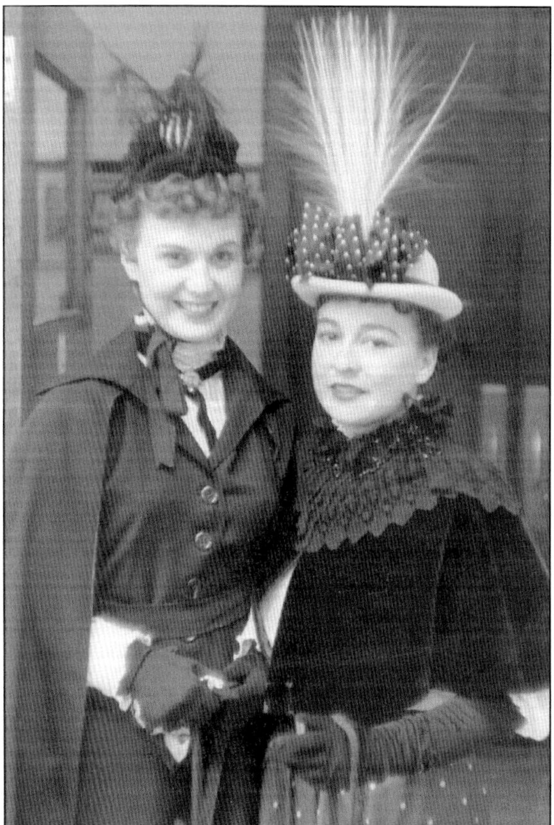

The formerly rural nature of Mokena allowed many residents to enjoy hunting in their free time. A foxhunt is commemorated in this February 1937 image of local hunters Herman Schweser, Fred Cappel, and Alfred Heiman displaying their game. Of interest is Schweser's .410 shotgun, handheld in the manner of a pistol.

Village citizens, being as cultured as their city counterparts, enjoyed the theatrical piece *Curse of the Aching Heart*, staged by the Mokena Village Players, in April 1955. Lead performer Shirley Guendling stands at left, with Shirley Jones on the right. Guendling later became a beloved local author of children's literature, with her work appearing in the publications *High Five* and *Ladybug.*

Nine

Not Without Thy Wondrous Story

Much of Mokena's history remains a rich patchwork of loose ends, extra pieces, and spare details. More often than not, it is difficult to pigeonhole certain aspects of this chronicle into specific areas. This chapter represents the miscellaneous stories that simply do not fit anywhere else. Throughout Mokena's history, numerous events have attached themselves to the village's narrative, making it truly unique. From the deadly 1864 saloon riot that drew the attention of Chicago newspapers to the daring yet foiled 1882 safe-blowing at the Mokena Exchange Bank, not to mention the oil fever that gripped the region in the 1920s, every event has made a collective mark on the community.

Although this volume is brimming with historic images, it should not be forgotten that several generations of Mokena's past were never documented by photographs. Imagery of the village made prior to 1900 is exceedingly rare, almost nonexistent. Of the small handful known to exist, all of those photographs are included in this book. The past appearance of entire sections of the village is left to the imagination because they eluded the photographic lens. To date, no pictures have surfaced of Allen Denny, the captivating founder of Mokena. His visage remains lost to time.

To understand the story of Mokena, one must appreciate all the events of the past, not only stopping at major milestones and oft-cited happenings. Each piece of the puzzle makes up the big picture built upon the foundation that Mokena's forefathers laid over 150 years ago. Although it might be difficult to fathom, each and every Mokenian is a piece of this puzzle, coming together to form the Mokena of tomorrow.

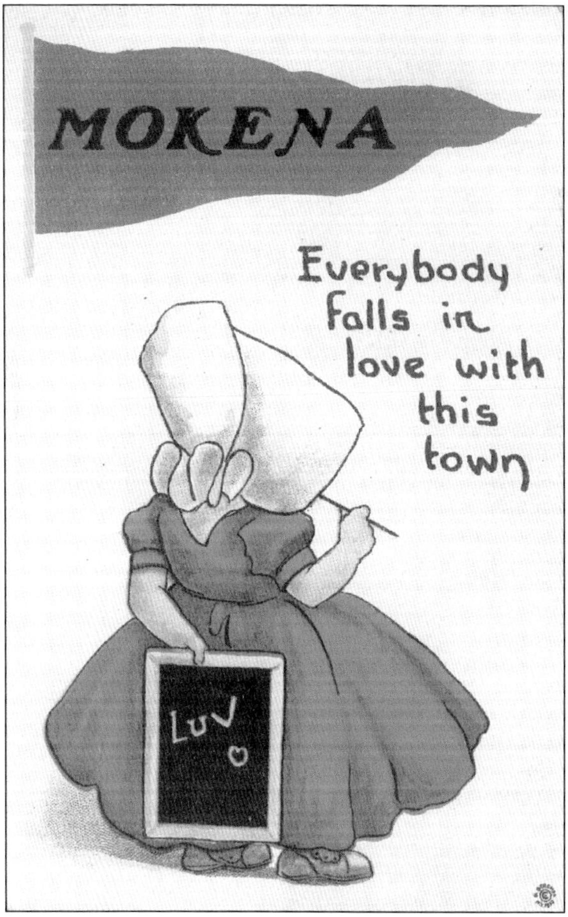

This local postcard with sentimental flair dates from around 1920. Many Americans kept postcards depicting views of their hometowns, popular collector's items in the first few decades of the 20th century, and included them in their family photo albums. In the period shortly before and after World War I, several dozen postcard images were made in Mokena.

Mokena's Front Street is shown here, looking west from the top of the first village water tower. This c. 1938 image shows the arrival of a coal-driven freight train on the Rock Island Railroad. Since the trains emitted huge plumes of smoke, it was once commonplace for buildings along Front Street to be covered in thick black soot. The grain elevator of Albert and Fred Cappel is visible left of center.

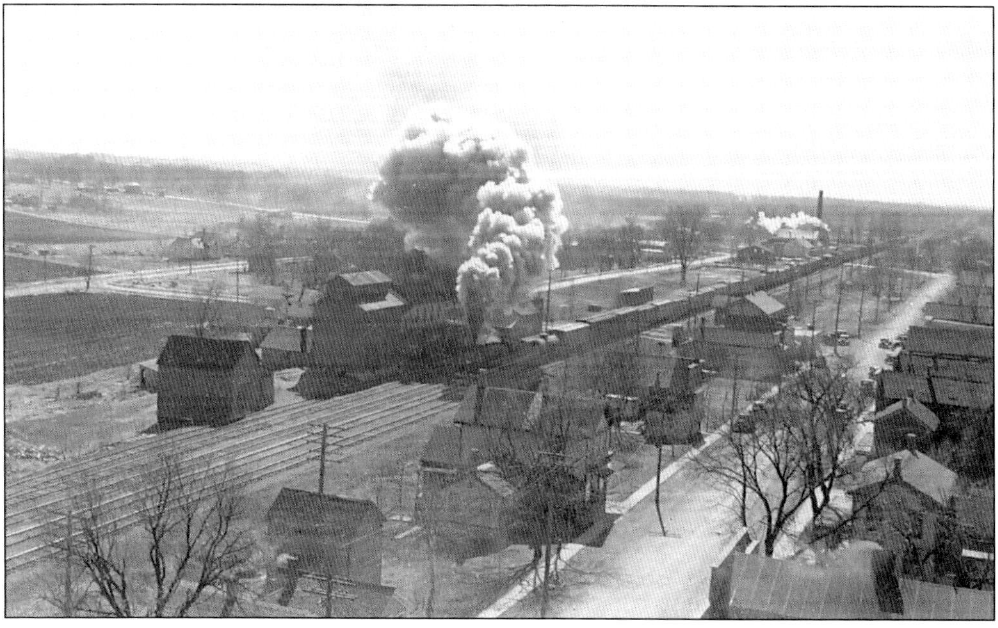

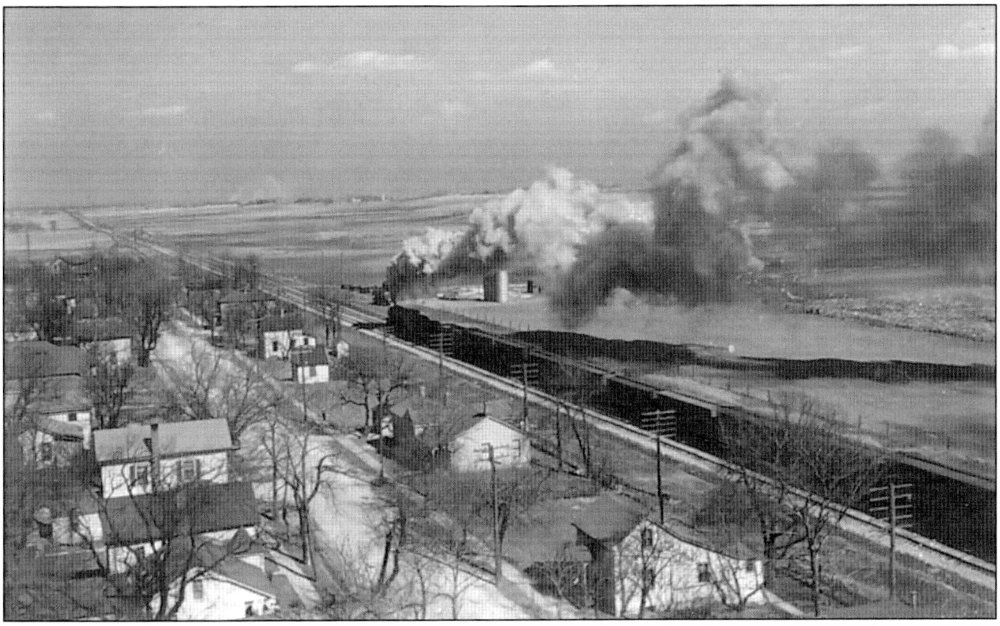

Facing east from high atop the original Mokena water tower, a freight train is seen here passing through the village. Several of the east Front Street homes visible here have been demolished since this photograph was taken around 1938. The oil tanks of the Mokena Oil Company are visible under the spiral of smoke at center.

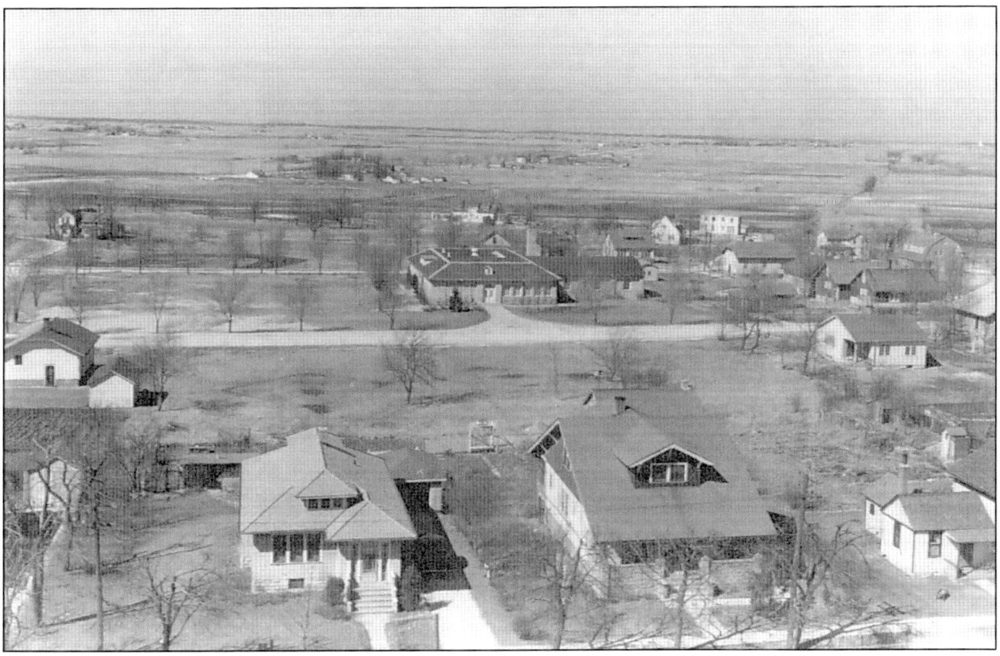

Here, Mokena is shown as it appeared around 1938 from the northern face of the town water tower. The two homes in the foreground, still remaining at 10944 First Street (left) and 10942 First Street (right), are perfect examples of post–World War I architecture in the region. The wide expanse of farmland outside Mokena illustrates villagers' close proximity to agricultural life in this period.

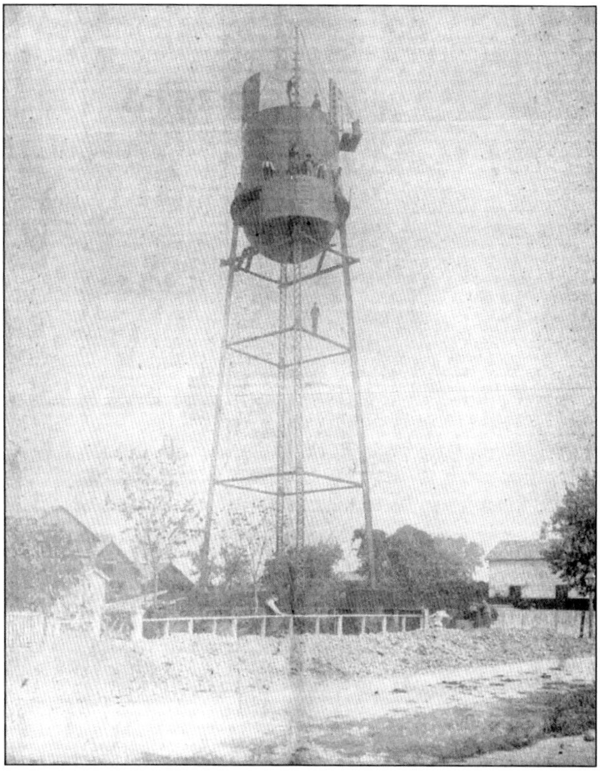

Flames ravaged Mokena businesses and homes time and time again throughout the 19th century. In 1898, Mayor Christian Bechstein and the village board ordered the construction of this 60,000-gallon water tower on Front Street to create a permanent source of fire protection. Julius Oswald, Frank Liess, Jake Zahn, and Joe Kohl are among the local men standing in the tower's midsection. The village jail and firehouse are obscured by trees at left.

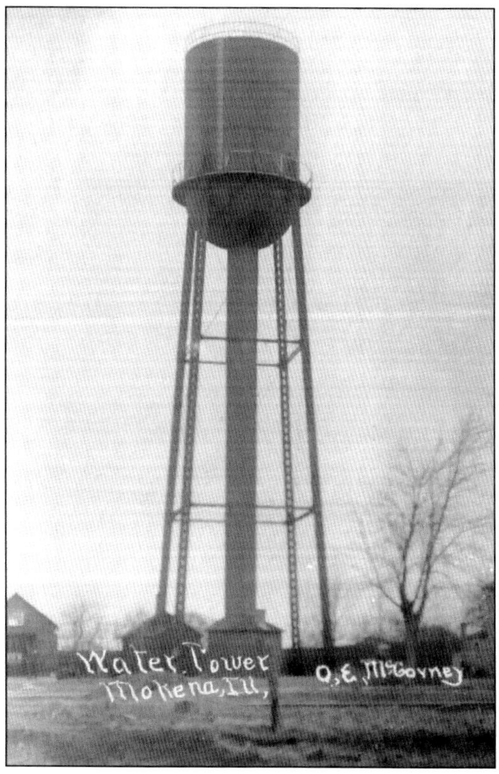

After it was constructed by the Chicago Bridge and Iron Company in 1898, local residents were first allowed to connect private lines to the water tower in 1900. This historic landmark, which stood just north of the present-day 10940 Front Street, was torn down in 1984. In the earliest years of its existence, a windmill located a short distance east of this location pumped water into the large tank.

Prior to the construction of this brick structure in 1916, Mokena had no official city hall. This building, which contained meeting space for the village board, jail cells, and space for the village fire engine, remains at 10940 Front Street. To make way for this edifice, an original wooden jailhouse was placed on log rollers and relocated across fields to a new location south of LaPorte Road, where it was converted into a residence.

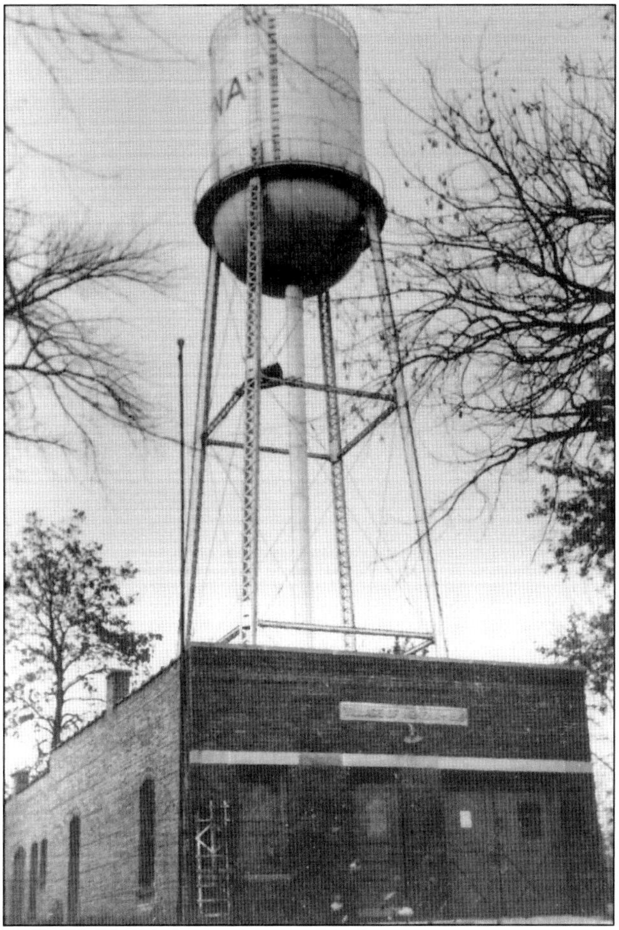

To combat the treacherously muddy roads of the 19th century, Mokenians were known to spread cinders over trouble spots and, in some cases, to build flagstone walkways at intersections. This 1935 image depicts the first proper paving of Front Street, although a 1923 foray into paving the business section with a substance called "Tuftread" left the village in debt, and the hard surface was worn away a year later.

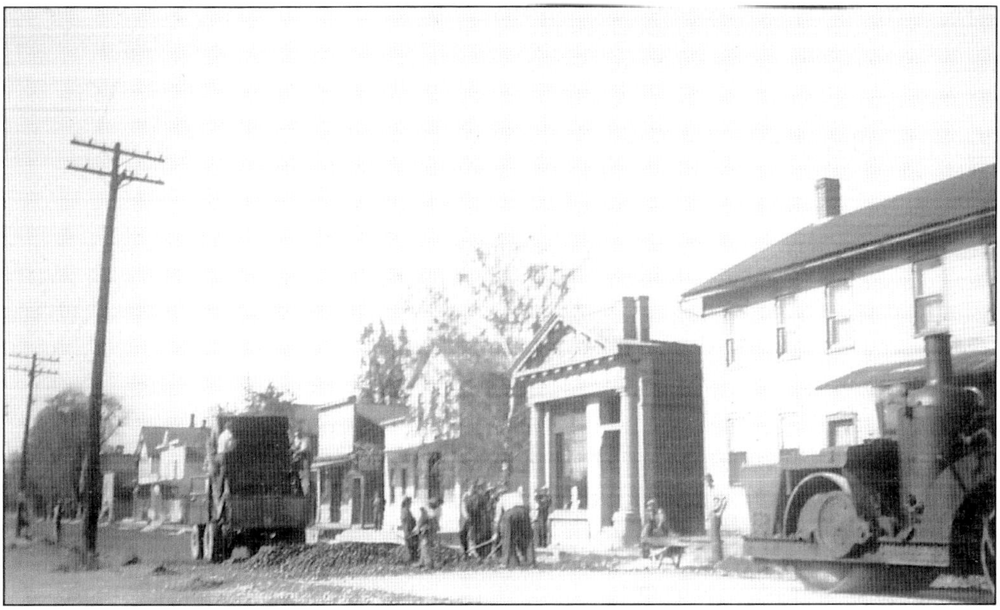

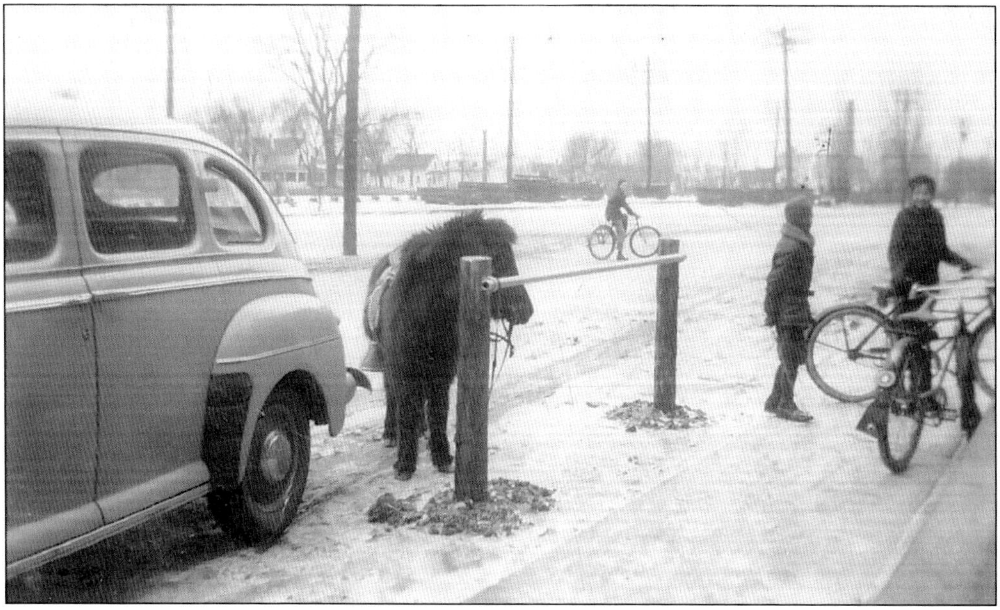

Following America's entry into World War II in December 1941, everyday life in Mokena went through a great change. Because of the fear of gas rationing, Morry Larson installed this hitching post in front of his Front Street tavern in January 1942. By the war's end, 125 local men and women had served in the armed forces—of this group, Lt. Oliver Lauffer and Lt. Berle Needham were killed in action.

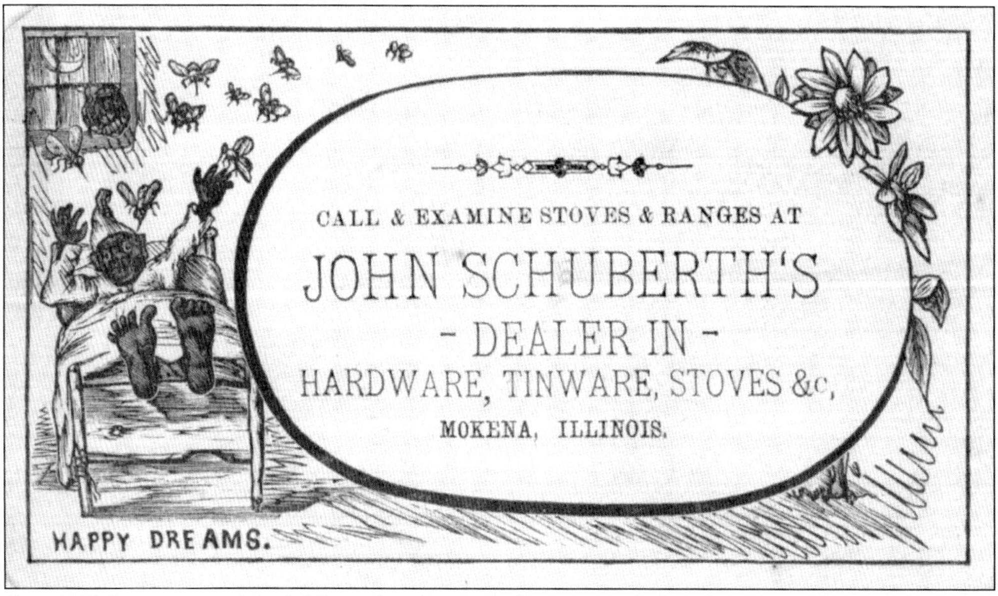

A c. 1885 business card for Mokena hardware dealer John Schuberth is shown here. Schuberth, along with his parents and siblings, left their native Bavaria and settled in the future Frankfort Township in 1847; Schuberth established a shop on the present-day site of 11014 Front Street in 1862. Active in local affairs, Schuberth held the office of township supervisor and collector during a period in the 1870s. (Photograph courtesy of Carol Norton.)

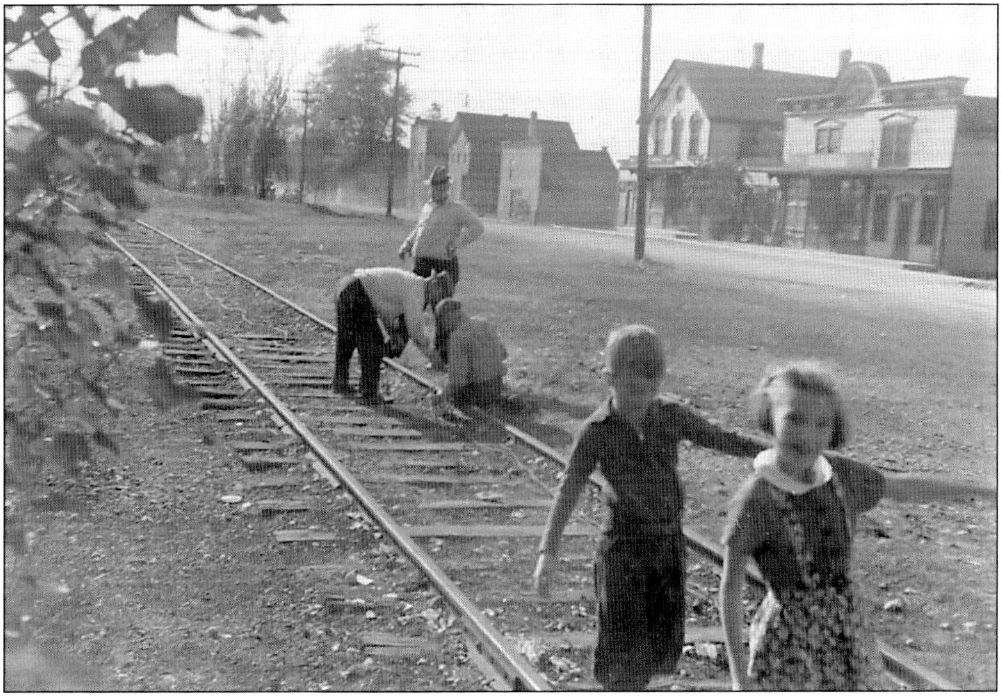

The open stretch on the south side of Front Street, from Wolf Road to Mokena Street, was used for railroad purposes for most of Mokena's past. Depicted here around 1935, the Wannemacher Grocery Store and Hensel's Pharmacy can be seen in the background at right; the Wannemacher building still stands at 11116 Front Street.

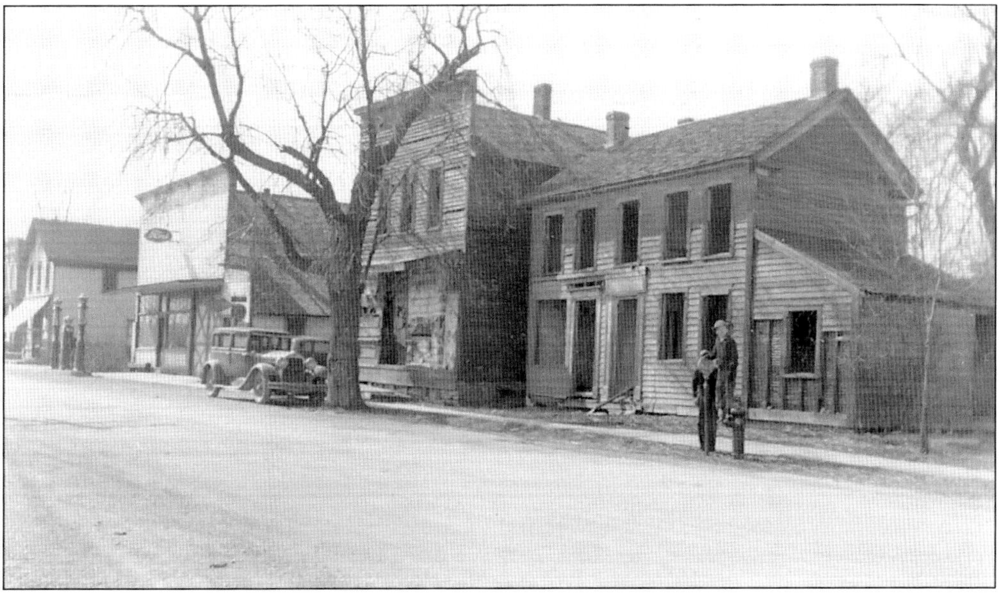

These two dilapidated Front Street buildings were, for decades, a source of major vexation to the village. Owned by the Stellwagen family and alternately known as "The Shacks" or "The Haunted Houses," certain residents were known to cross the street to avoid walking in front of them. Photographed around 1935, they stood immediately to the west of 11014 Front Street.

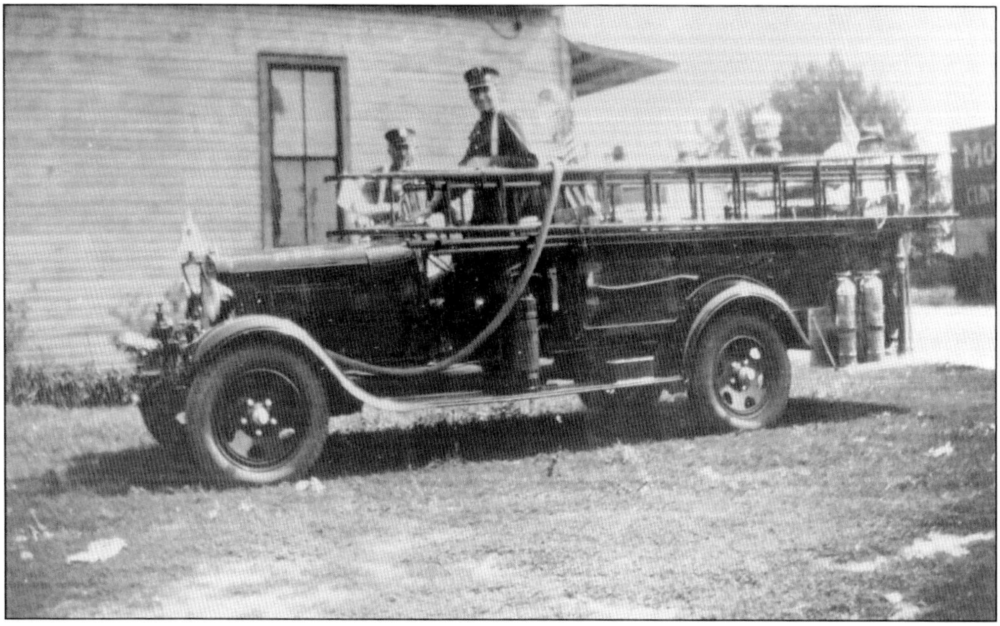

The first semblance of proper fire protection in Mokena dates to 1883, when local hardware merchant Julius Mavis was appointed fire marshal. The Mokena Volunteer Fire Department was established in 1917, at which time a wooden hose cart was still pulled by hand. Chief Herman Schweser (left) and Barney Hostert are seen here in September 1933 with Mokena's first automotive fire engine, donated that year by Elmer Sippel.

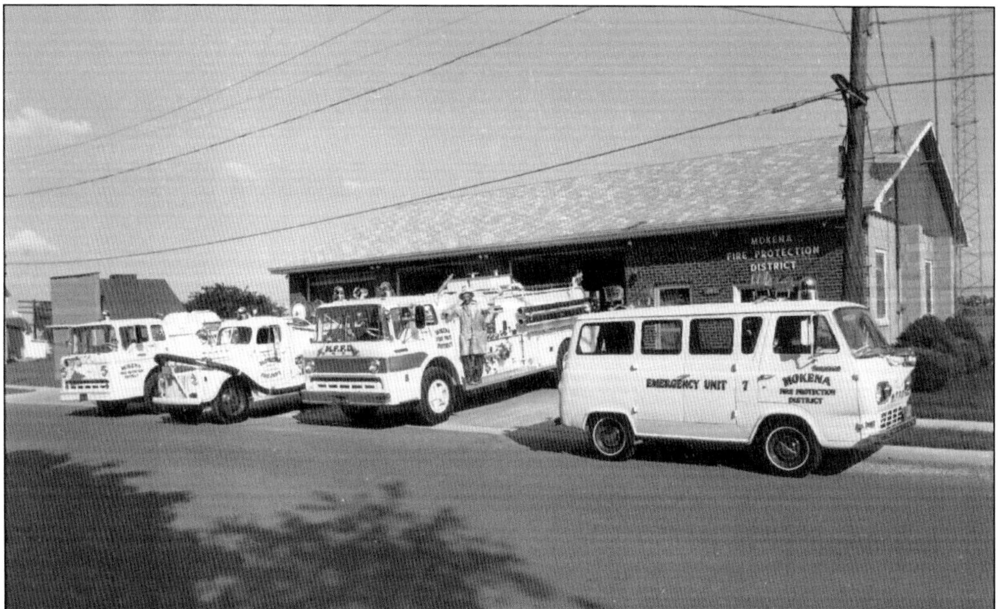

The Mokena Fire Department erected this station, built using funds raised entirely by local residents, in 1960. This image was taken in 1970, three years before the firehouse was enlarged with an addition to the west. In 1995, the building was refurbished and ownership was transferred to the Mokena Police Department. The building still stands at 10907 Front Street.

Mokena's first telephone exchange was finished in 1898 by the Northwest Company, allowing a wonder of modern technology to connect village residents with the outside world. A switchboard was later installed in the Rinke home on Front Street, where sisters Elizabeth and Mary Rinke were operators. Posing here with a smile around 1915 is Elizabeth Rinke. (Photograph courtesy of Richard Quinn.)

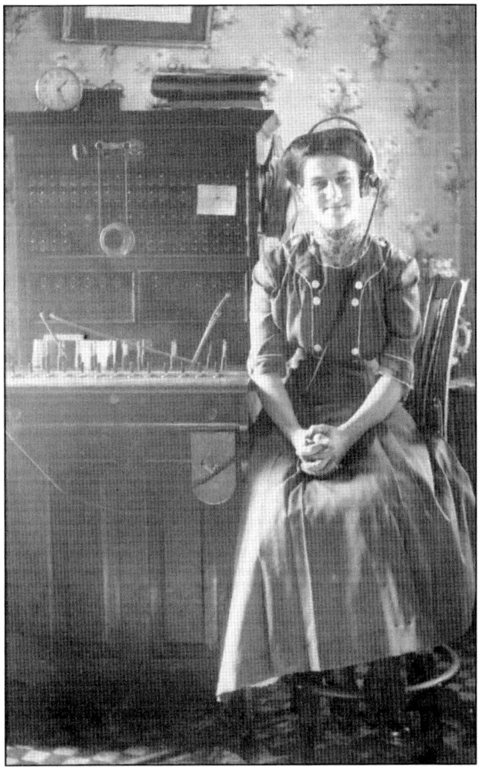

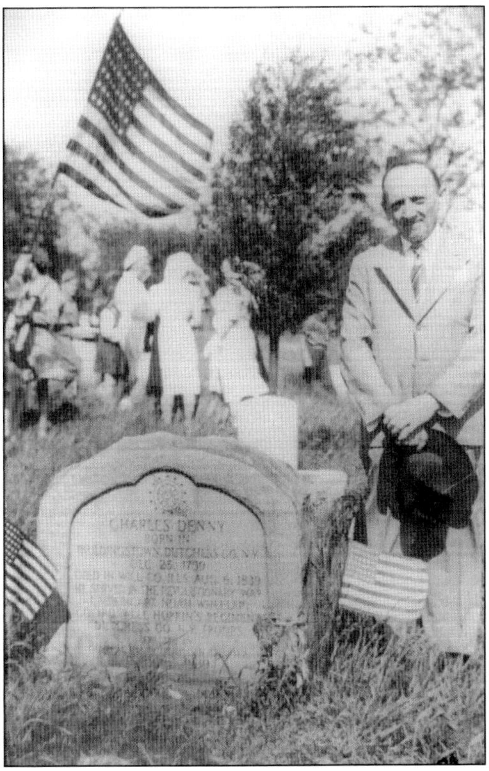

In 1917, while he was a reporter for the *Joliet Herald-News*, local man William Semmler first discovered the grave of Revolutionary War veteran Charles Denny in the tangled overgrowth of the old Denny Cemetery on Wolf Road. Pictured here around 1940, when he was the editor of the *Mokena News-Bulletin*, Semmler facilitated the 1939 dedication of a granite boulder over Denny's grave by the Daughters of the American Revolution.

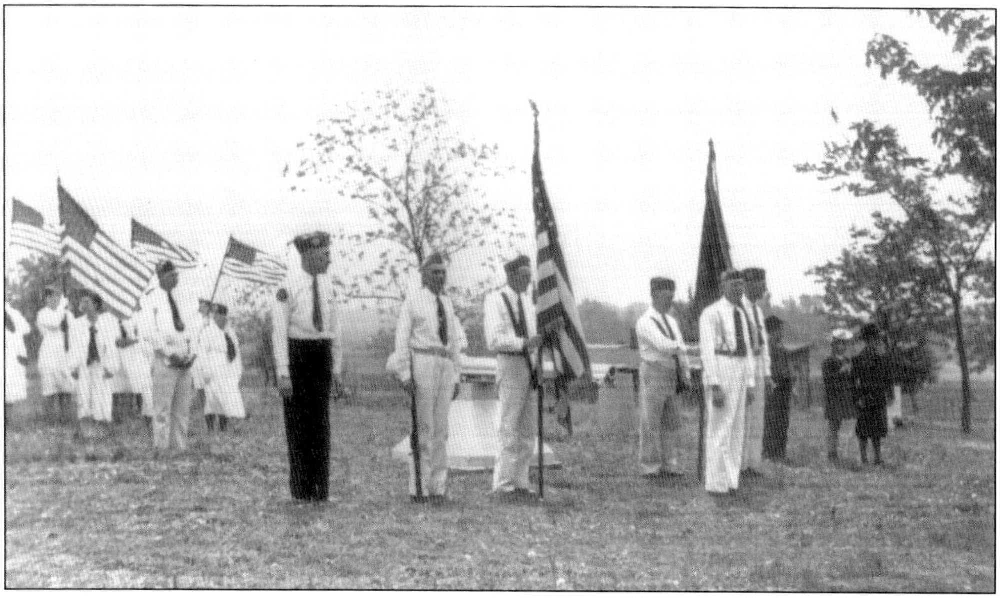

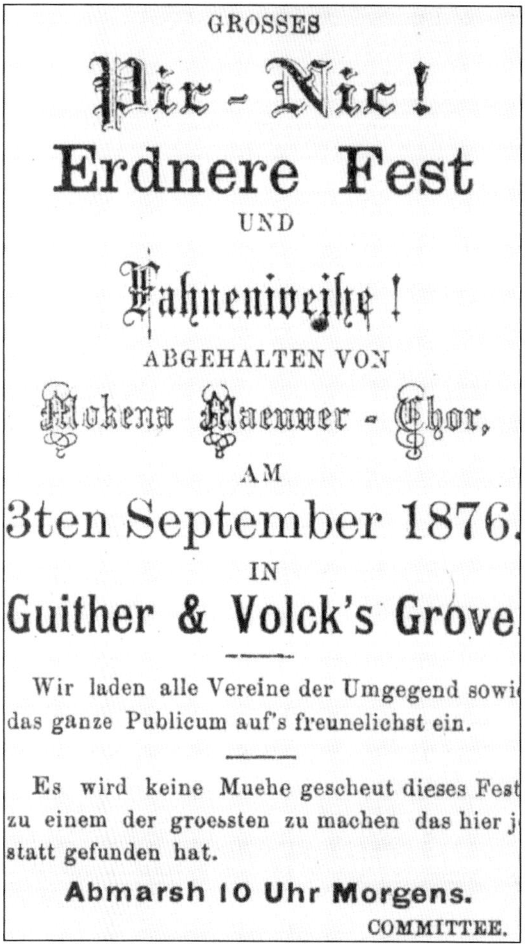

Undoubtedly one of Mokena's most historic locations, Pioneer Memorial Cemetery on Wolf Road has been host to many patriotic commemorations over the years. The cemetery, originally known as Denny Cemetery after the family who founded it, had its first known burials in 1839 and appears to have been in regular use until the end of the Civil War in 1865. A Memorial Day celebration is pictured here around 1940.

The legacy of Mokena's early settlers is plainly represented in this German-language advertisement, printed in the August 15, 1876, issue of the *Mokena Advertiser*. Inviting "all social clubs and the entire public of the region" to a grand picnic held by the Mokena Men's Choir at Guither and Volck's Grove, the dedication of a banner was to be a main event.

Wilbur Hatch, born in Mokena in 1902 to John Ozias Hatch and Clara Jackson, was musically talented from an early age. Pictured here in 1939 with his wife, Peg, Hatch became the conductor of the Desi Arnaz Orchestra on the television show *I Love Lucy*. Before his death at Studio City, California, in 1969, Hatch was a music consultant for *Mission: Impossible* and *Star Trek*, among other programs. (Photograph courtesy of Carol Norton.)

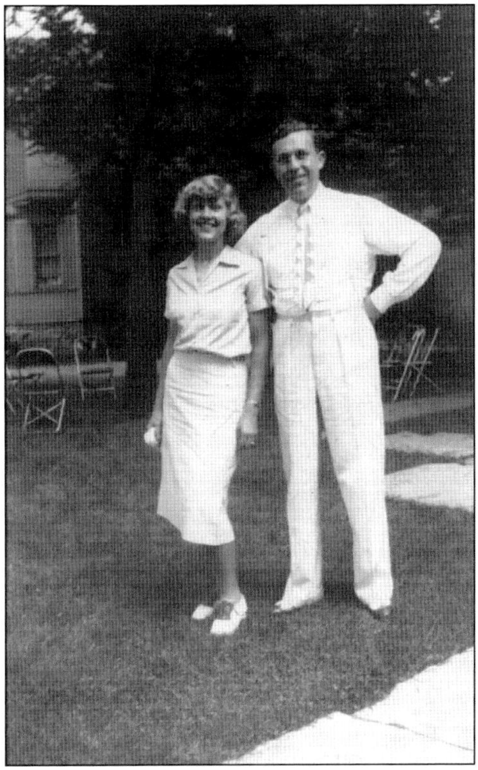

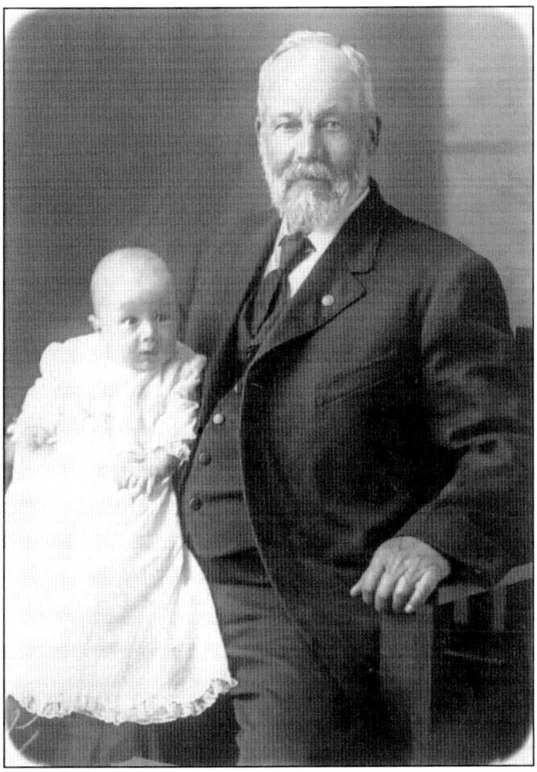

A beloved neighbor and friend, John A. Hatch is seen here around 1909 with his granddaughter Ora Pittaway. Hatch was born in Frankfort Township in 1842 and became a battle-tested veteran of the Union army, later describing the Civil War as "horrible, bloody work." Hatch, Mokena's first village clerk, was also a grain merchant and the owner of a popular general store. (Photograph courtesy of Carol Norton.)

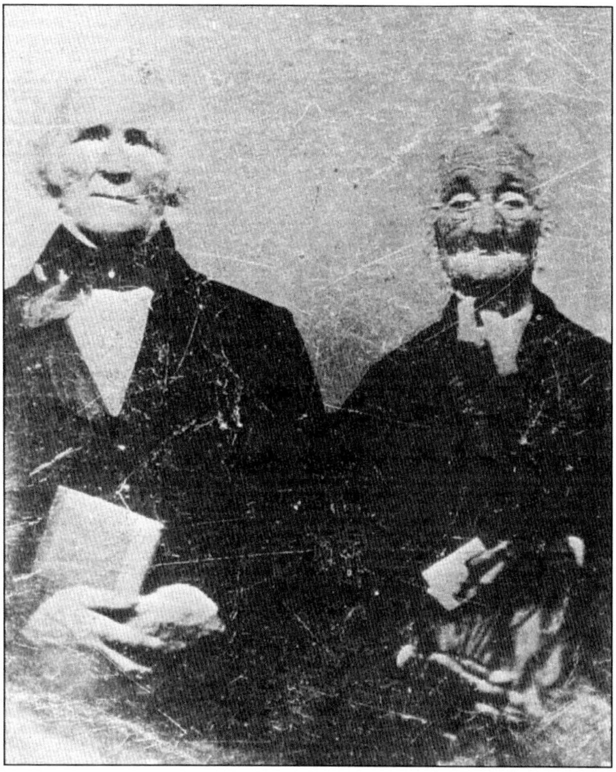

In the earliest known photograph of any Mokenians, pioneers John and Betsey Atkins are seen here around 1860. Having trekked by wagon from Vermont to the sparsely settled Hickory Creek Settlement in 1834, the pious Atkins was a veteran of the War of 1812 and came into possession of a large tract of land near today's LaPorte Road before passing away in 1864.

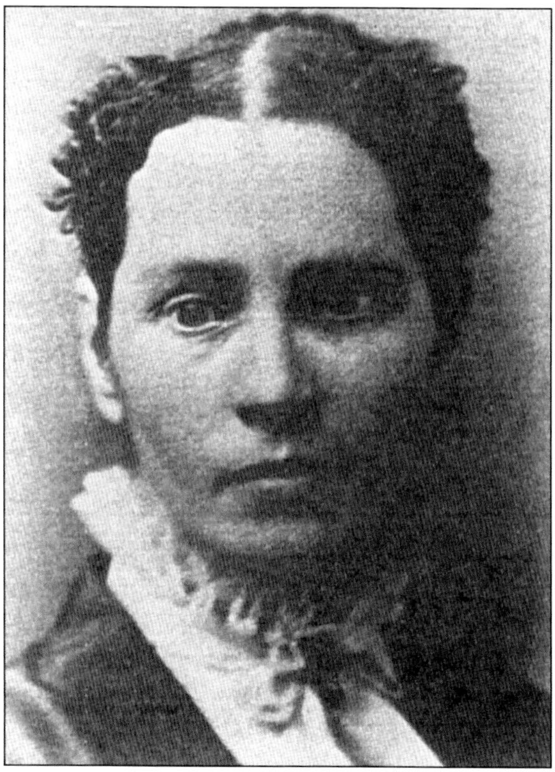

Julia Atkins, the granddaughter of pioneer John Atkins, was born around 1834 and knew the Mokena region from its first settlement by white Americans. Atkins handwrote the first and only known edition of the *Mokena Star* in November 1852, declaring that Mokena would soon "become one of the largest cities on the main Rock Island route." With her creation, Atkins had the honor of composing the village's first newspaper.

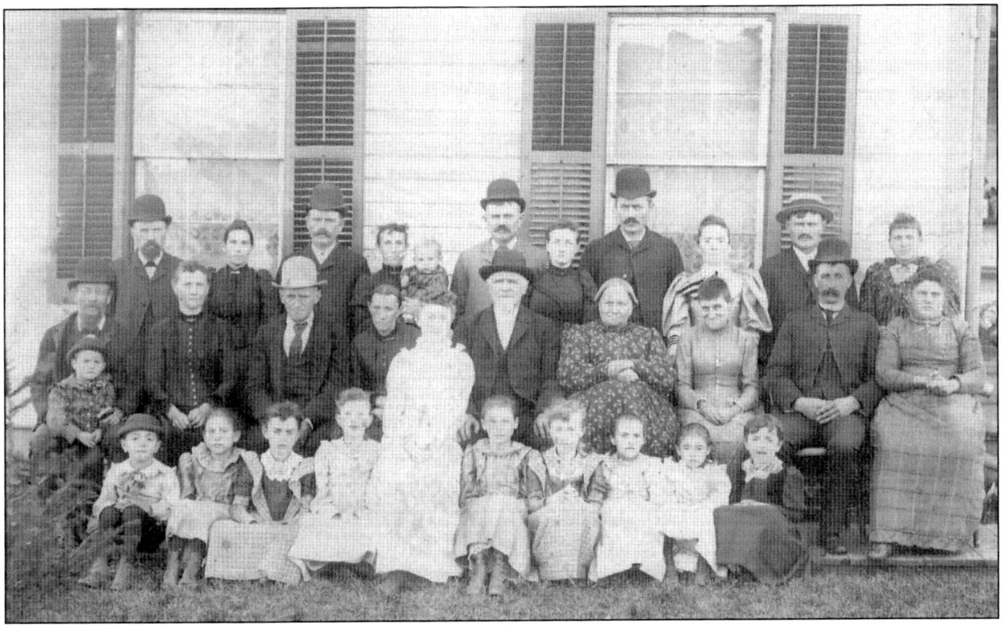

Several families of Swiss origin played a significant role in the growth of Mokena. A native of Rapperswil, Switzerland, Nicholas Marti came to Frankfort Township as an immigrant farmer in 1851 at the age of 27. After marrying Maria Baumgartner a year later, their union was blessed with seven children. In this 1895 image, Nicholas and Maria Marti are surrounded by their children, grandchildren, and extended family.

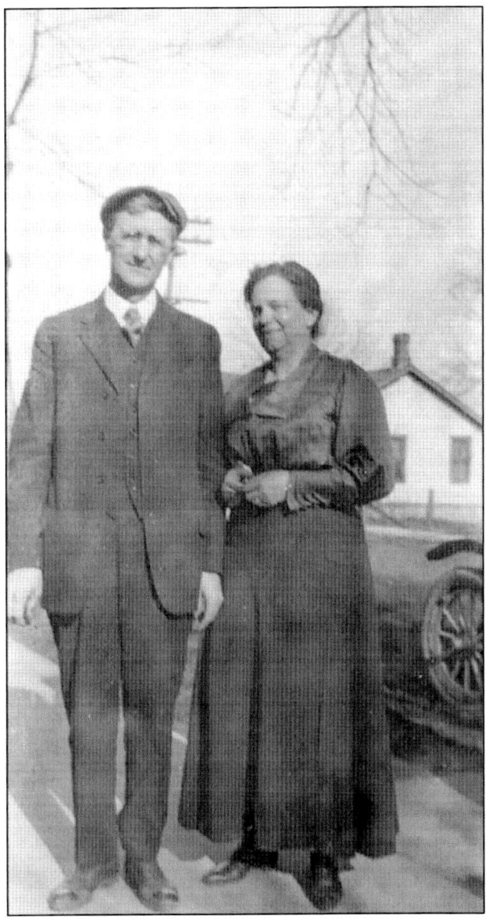

Emil and Selma (Schaub) Krapp, adored residents of Mokena, are seen here near their Front Street residence in 1918. Born in 1870, Emil Krapp was a cattle buyer by trade and spent his entire life in the village. Active in church affairs and quite musically talented, Selma Krapp was the organist at St. John's church for years. (Photograph courtesy of David Kropp.)

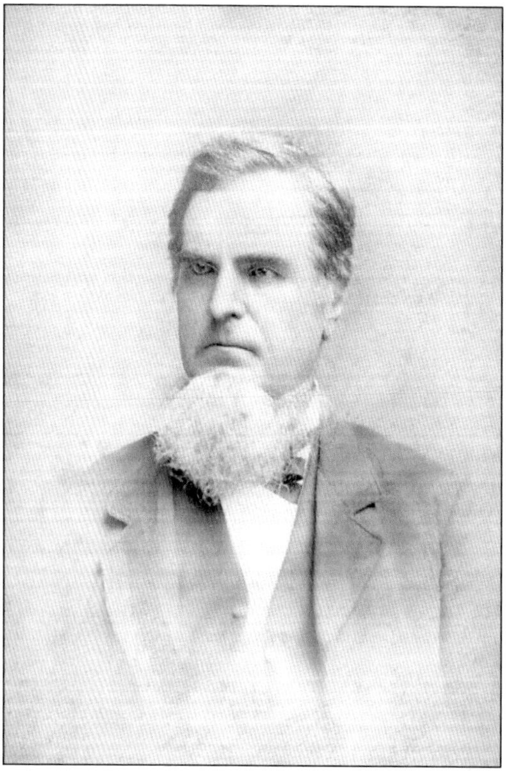

Ozias McGovney arrived with his parents at the age of seven as part of the first white American family that settled in the future Frankfort Township in 1831. A well-known justice of the peace, McGovney was appointed the first mayor of Mokena and held office from 1880 to 1884. McGovney was the first of several generations of his family to hold public office in the village. (Photograph courtesy of Carol Norton.)

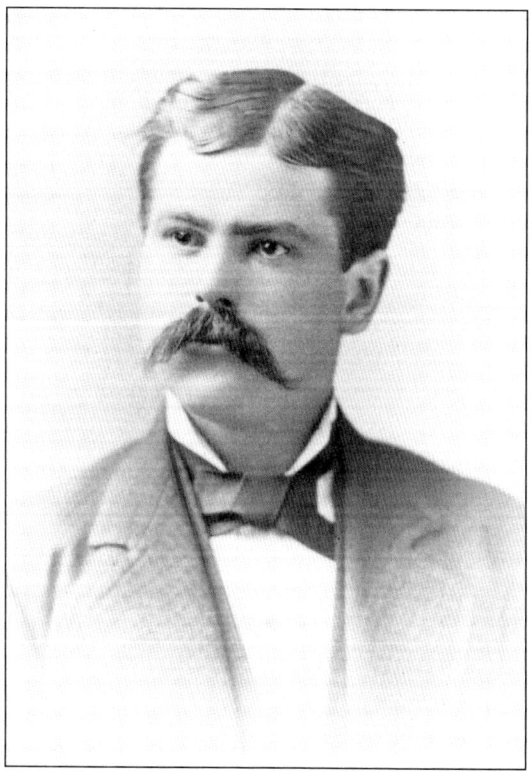

Born in 1855, Ozias Erwin McGovney was the son of Mokena's first mayor and, while a young man, operated a general store in town with his father. Later working as the proprietor of a store in Manhattan, Illinois, he was elected the first mayor of that city in 1886. After relocating to Mokena in 1887, McGovney served as mayor from 1890 to 1894 as well as holding the office of postmaster.

Ona Elsworth McGovney served as mayor of Mokena from 1903 to 1915, the third generation in his family to hold the office. Originally a Will County schoolteacher, McGovney came to hold most of the village's offices before his untimely death, at age 59, in 1938. McGovney's daughter Elmira served as village treasurer and is remembered as the first woman in Mokena to hold an elected office.

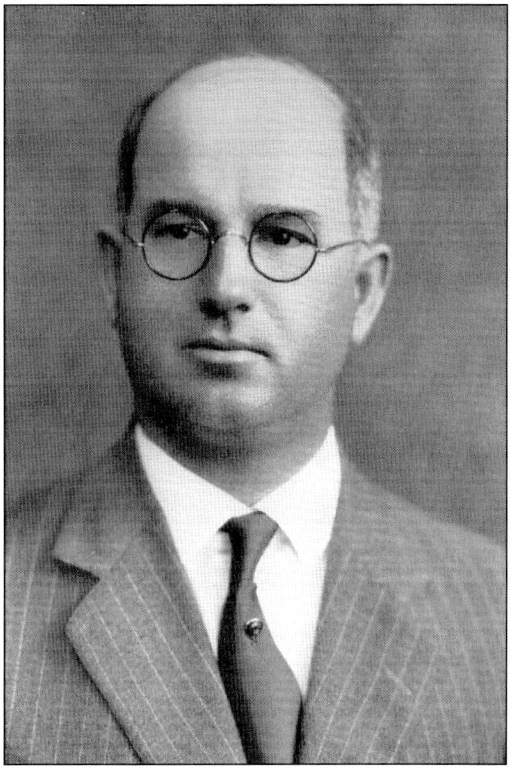

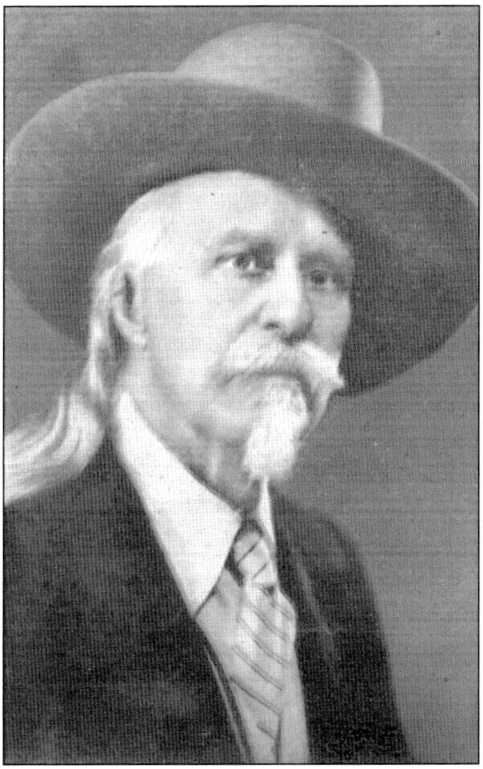

One of Mokena's most unique personages was Col. Don C. Hall, seen here around 1940. Hall arrived in Mokena in 1923 with his wife, Clara, and the Halls were known for their Shakespearian theatrics and their feats of traveling, having hitchhiked across America. Although his "colonel" was purely an honorary title, Hall, a former member of the Wisconsin legislature, was also known throughout the area as the spitting image of Buffalo Bill Cody.

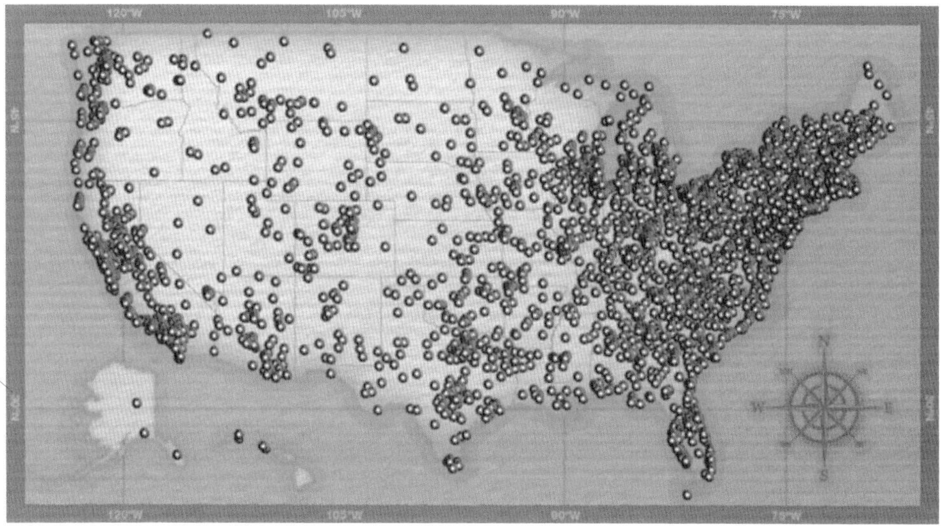

Consistent with our mission to preserve history on a local level, this book was printed in South Carolina on American-made paper and manufactured entirely in the United States. Products carrying the accredited Forest Stewardship Council (FSC) label are printed on 100 percent FSC-certified paper.

MADE IN THE USA